JEAN
HYPPOLITE

LOGIC
AND
EXISTENCE

SUNY Series in Contemporary Continental Philosophy
Dennis J. Schmidt, editor

TRANSLATED BY
LEONARD LAWLOR AND AMIT SEN

JEAN
HYPPOLITE

LOGIC
AND
EXISTENCE

STATE UNIVERSITY OF NEW YORK PRESS

Originally published in France under the title *Logique et existence* by Presses Universitaires de France, Paris. © 1953 Presses Universitaires de France

Published by
State University of New York Press, Albany

For information, address the State University of New York Press, State University Plaza, Albany, NY 12246

Production design by David Ford
Marketing by Fran Keneston

Library of Congress Cataloging-in-Publication Data

Hyppolite, Jean.
      [Logique et existence. English]
      Logic and existence / Jean Hyppolite ; translated by Leonard Lawlor and Amit Sen.
         p. cm. — (SUNY series in contemporary continental philosophy)
      Includes bibliographical references and index.
      ISBN 0-7914-3231-9 (alk. paper). — ISBN 0-7914-3232-7 (pbk. : alk. paper)
      1. Hegel, Georg Wilhelm Friedrich, 1770–1831—Contributions in doctrine of logic.   2. Hegel, Georg Wilhelm Friedrich, 1770–1831—Contributions in notion of phenomenology.   3. Logic.   4. Hegel, Georg Wilhelm Friedrich, 1770–1831. Wissenschaft der Logik.   5. Phenomenology.   6. Hegel, Georg Wilhelm Friedrich, 1770–1831. Phänomenologie des Geistes.   I. Title.
II. Series.
B2949.L8H913   1996
193—dc20   96-13009
                                                                              CIP

10   9   8   7   6   5   4   3   2   1

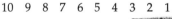

CONTENTS

Part 2. Speculative Thought and Reflection

Part 3. The Categories of the Absolute

Hyppolite is the one who has established for us all of the problems which are ours. . . . Logic and Existence . . . is one of the great works of our time.
—Michel Foucault[1]

LEONARD
LAWLOR

TRANSLATOR'S PREFACE

Originally published in France in 1952, *Logique et existence* illuminates what Hyppolite himself calls Hegelianism's "most obscure dialectical synthesis" (*see below*, p. 188): the relation between the phenomenology and the logic.[2] As he says, "how does the passage from the Phenomenology to absolute Knowledge work? This question is the Hegelian question *par excellence*, and the very purpose of this work lies in the

---

1. From a eulogy presented by Foucault, at a commemorative program for Jean Hyppolite, 19 January 1969 at the École Normale Supérieure, and published in the *Revue de Métaphysique et de Morale* 2 (1969), 131–36.

2. In his earlier *Genesis and Structure of Hegel's "Phenomenology of Spirit,"* Hyppolite already recognized that the most difficult, perhaps insoluble,

attempt to pose this question by confronting Hegel's diverse attitudes concerning it" (*see below*, p. 27). Hegel solves this almost insoluble problem by means of a notion of correspondence (*see below*, p. 35). Correspondence means, according to Hyppolite, that the phenomenology and the logic mutually presuppose one another (*see below*, p. 26). Hyppolite says, "Experience and the Logos are not opposed. The discourse of experience and the discourse of being, the *a posteriori* and the *a priori*, correspond to one another and mutually require one another. There would be no possible experience without the presupposition of absolute knowledge, but the path of experience points ahead to absolute knowledge" (*see below*, p. 36). The logic presupposes the phenomenology insofar as it is only across (*à travers*) the history of humanity that the logos appears (*see below*, pp. 177, 179), and the phenomenology presupposes the logic insofar as it is only the concept that "explains" (*see below*, p. 36) or "supports" (*see below*, p. 66) experience. Mutual correspondence therefore implies, for Hyppolite, that man is "the house (*la demeure*) of the Universal, of the Logos of Being" (*see below*, p. 187). But mutual correspondence does not imply that man is equivalent to universal self-consciousness in Hegel (*see below*, p. 179); experience cannot be reduced to the concept, and the concept cannot be reduced to experience.

Hyppolite's non-reductionistic interpretation of the relation between the phenomenology and the logic effectively ended the simple anthropological interpretation of Hegel popularized by Kojève before World War II. Because of Hyppolite, no reading of Hegel would be able to push man up to the immodest position of being the Absolute, the end of history, the source of nothingness. Like Husserl's transcendental reduction, speculative thought, according to Hyppolite, "will be a reduction of the human condition. The Logic's dialectical discourse will be the very discourse of Being, the *Phenomenology* having shown the possibility of bracketing man as natural Dasein" (*see below*, p. 42). Hyppolite's inter-

---

problem of Hegelianism lies in the relation between *The Phenomenology* and the *Science of Logic.* See Jean Hyppolite, *Genèse et structure de la Phénoménologie de l'esprit de Hegel*, 2 vols. (Paris: Aubier, 1946–47), 59, 67, 558, 565–67, 575; English translation by Samuel Cherniak and John Heckman (Evanston: Northwestern University Press, 1934), 56, 65, 578, 586–88, 596. For more on the development of Hyppolite's interpretation of Hegel, see also Jean Hyppolite, "La 'phénoménologie' de Hegel et la pensée Française contemporaine," in *Figures de la pensée philosophique* (Paris: Presses Universitaires de France, 1971), 241. See also Mikel Dufrenne's review of *Genèse et structure*, "À Propos de la thèse de Jean Hyppolite," in *Fontaine* 11 (1947: 461–70; Gaston Fessard, "Deux Interpretes de la Phénomenologie de Hegel," in *Études* 255 (1947): 368–73.

pretation of the relation therefore fueled the fire of French anti-human-ism, which Heidegger's "Letter on Humanism" had already ignited. In short, *Logic and Existence* opened the way for the theme that would dom-inate French thought after Sartre's *Being and Nothingness*; the concept of difference found in the philosophies of Deleuze, Derrida, and Foucault would not exist without the publication of *Logic and Existence*. Correspondence implies not only that the phenomenology and the logic mutually presuppose one another but also that there is a difference between them.[3]

Hyppolite recognizes the similarity of Nietzsche's thought to that of Hegel (*see below*, pp. 57, 59). The proclamation that God is dead means that there is no second intelligible world behind the first phenom-enal world; there is no transcendent "beyond." As Hyppolite says, "Hegelian logic recognizes neither the thing-in-itself nor the intelligible world. The Absolute is not thought anywhere else than in the phenome-nal world. Absolute thought thinks itself in our thought. In our thought, being presents itself as thought and as sense. And Hegel's dialectical logic, like the logic of philosophy, is the expression of this doctrine of complete immanence." (*see below*, pp. 58–59). Although it completes immanence (*see below*, p. 176), Hegel's speculative logic maintains the distinction between essence and appearance (*see below*, pp. 59–60). Rather than being one of externality—one thing next to and outside of another—this distinction is one of internality (*see below*, pp. 100, 118). Internal or essential difference is the production of a double which is not an ontic double, which is not another thing. Internal difference then is being's own self-difference; being differentiates itself (by twisting itself, by folding itself over, by reflecting itself) in order to think itself, accord-ing to Hyppolite (*see below*, pp. 61, 75, 76, 106). Being becomes its own other; it becomes both subject and object; it contradicts itself.

The nature of Hegelian self-contradiction can be seen clearly in two ways: in the passage from the finite to the infinite and in the dialec-tic of diversity. If we conceived the difference between the finite and the infinite as external, this would amount to placing the finite on one side and the infinite on the other. The finite and the infinite would be like two

---

3. The phenomenology and the logic differ, according to Hyppolite, in regard to the element in which their respective dialectics take place: the phe-nomenology in the element of experience; the logic in the element of the con-cept. Only once in *Genesis and Structure* Hyppolite does say that "[Absolute knowledge] is expressed by language, which is authentically the prefiguration of the logos of the *Logic*" (595 [574]), although Hyppolite indicates the fact that language prefigures the logos in his discussion of sense-certainty. If anything, this insight into the role of language in Hegel inspires all of *Logic and Existence*.

things set side by side. The result of this side by side position would be that the infinite itself would be limited and would no longer be infinite; having the finite as its boundary, the infinite would in fact be finite. Therefore, in order for the infinite to be truly infinite, it is necessary to make the finite internal to the infinite. Likewise, in order for the finite to be truly finite, it must contain the infinite within itself: without the infinite as its limit, the finite would be everywhere; it would be infinite. As Hyppolite says, "What is at issue is not to put on one side unity, infinity, universality, and on the other multiplicity, the finite, the particular. But, in order to do that, we have to twist thought, we have to force it to look contradiction square in the face and to turn it into a means of surmounting the differences onto which the understanding holds. The infinite is not beyond the finite, because then it itself would be finite; it would have the finite outside of itself as its limit. Similarly, the finite negates itself; it becomes its other" (see below, p. 97). In other words, both the infinite and the finite must contradict themselves and contain their others within themselves. Similarly, in the dialectic of diversity, Hegel finds negation. A thing that is big in relation to one thing is small in relation to another; each thing is what it is and is not what it is not. In the Sophist, Plato had tried to transform this negation into alterity; thereby he sought to avoid contradiction (see below, pp. 112–13). "In contrast," according to Hyppolite, "Hegelian dialectic will push (poussera) this alterity up to (jusqu'à) contradiction. Negation belongs to things and to distinct determinations insofar as they are distinct. But that means that their apparent positivity turns out to be a real negativity. This negativity will condense the opposition in negation; negation will be the vital force of the dialectic of the real as well as that of logical dialectic" (see below, p. 113). For Hyppolite's Hegel, "opposition is inevitable not because there is only a multiplicity of things, of finite modes, or of monads, but because each is in relation with the others, or rather with all the others, so that its distinction is its distinction from all the rest. The complete distinction of a thing reconnects it to the whole Universe, that reduces differences to essential and internal difference, the difference between a thing or a determination and its other. This duality is the speculative duality, the fundamental double" (see below, p. 115). Determining a thing's difference from all the rest implies that the thing's most basic quality is discovered. In other words, opposition is inevitable because all quantitative differences are turned into qualitative differences. The advantage of qualities, for Hegel, is that they cannot be defined in isolation from one another; each quality makes an internal reference to its opposite. This internal reference—contradiction—allows Hegel to infinitize or totalize being.

It is precisely this drive to totalization, this pushing of difference up to contradiction, that Derrida and Deleuze reject. In fact, according to

Deleuze, Hyppolite's emphasis of Hegel's drive to contradiction ultimately justifies the humanistic reading of Hegel.[4] Nevertheless, due to Hyppolite, both Deleuze and Derrida recognize the importance of Hegel's transformation of difference into essential difference. For instance, there would be no notion of contaminating différance without Hyppolite's analysis of essential difference in *Logic and Existence*; in a note to his 1964 "Violence and Metaphysics," Derrida says that "Pure difference is not absolutely different (from nondifference). Hegel's critique of the concept of pure difference is for us here, doubtless, the most uncircumventable theme. Hegel thought absolute difference, and showed that it can be pure only by being impure."[5] He also says however in the 1972 collection of interviews, *Positions*, "I have attempted to distinguish différance . . . from Hegelian difference, and have done so precisely at the point at which Hegel, in the greater *Logic*, determines difference as contradiction only in order to resolve it, to interiorize it, to lift it up . . . into the self-presence of an onto-theological or onto-teleological synthesis."[6] Similarly, for Deleuze, the project of a philosophy of difference lies in formulating the notion of an internal, but non-conceptual difference. This new notion of difference must, for Deleuze, be non-conceptual because "it is in relation to the form of identity in the generic concept, that difference goes as far as opposition, that it is pushed as far as (*poussée jusqu'à*) contrariety."[7] As Deleuze says, "Our claim is not only that difference in itself is not 'already' contradiction, but that it cannot be reduced or be traced back to contradiction, since the latter is not more but less profound than difference."[8] Thus, for both Derrida and Deleuze, if one wants to construct a

---

4. See Appendix, 191–95 below.

5. Jacques Derrida, "Violence et métaphysique,"in *Ecriture et différence* (Paris: Seuil, 1967), 227n1; English translation by Alan Bass as "Violence and Metaphysics," in *Writing and Difference* (Chicago: University of Chicago Press, 1978), 320n91.

6. Jacques Derrida, *Positions* (Paris: Minuit, 1972), 59–60; English translation by Alan Bass as *Positions* (Chicago: University of Chicago Press, 1981), 44.

7. Gilles Deleuze, *Différence et répétition* (Paris: Presses Universitaires de France, 1968), 48; English translation by Paul Patton as *Difference and Repetition* (New York: Columbia University Press, 1994), 31. All citations to *Difference and Repetition* will contain the reference to the French page number in parentheses after the English page number. Cf. also appendix, 000; and *Difference and Repetition*, 44n10 (64n1), where Deleuze makes explicit reference to *Logic and Existence*.

8. Deleuze, *Difference and Repetition*, 51 (73).

genuine (that is, non-humanistic) notion of difference, contradiction must be pushed back down to diversity, back down to alterity.[9] Since Hyppolite defines the Hegelian concept as sense, the problem of the other in Hegel (which is still that of difference) is the problem of nonsense.[10] Following Hegel, Hyppolite continuously makes use of the ambiguity found in the word sens (*see below*, p. 24). Non-sense (or experience) is sense insofar as sense is understood as what is received through the senses, understood as what is directed towards (as what is not yet) meaning. As intuition, sense is the concept in itself; it is pre-expressive, but not non-expressive. As Hyppolite says, "One does not go from a silent intuition to an expression, from an inexpressible to an expressed, any more than from nonsense to sense. The progress of thought, its development, is the very progress of expression" (*see below*, pp. 21, cf. 12–13). For Hyppolite, thought never goes from nonsense to sense, but only from sense to sense, from expression to expression, from determination to determination. As he says,

> Here perhaps we get to the decisive point of Hegelianism, to this torsion of thought through which we are able to think conceptually the unthinkable, to what makes Hegel simultaneously the greatest irrationalist and the greatest rationalist who has existed. We cannot emerge from the Logos, but the

---

9. See Bruce Baugh, "Hegel in Modern French Philosophy," in *Laval theologique et philosophique* 49.3 (October 1993): 423–38, especially 437–38. While in many respects this article is excellent—it traces the influence of Jean Wahl's *La Malheur de la conscience dans la philosophie de Hegel* (Paris: Rieder, 1929)—it suffers from a lack of understanding Hyppolite, who, influenced by Wahl's study of unhappy consciousness, develops in *Logique et existence* an anti-humanist reading of Hegel. This anti-humanist reading, as I am trying to argue here, influences Deleuze, Foucault, and Derrida. Thus it is strange to see Baugh put Derrida in the tradition of French humanistic readings of Hegel. *See also* Michael S. Roth, *Knowing and History: Appropriations of Hegel in Twentieth Century France* (Ithaca: Cornell University Press, 1983), especially 69–80.

10. Clearly, the phrase, "sense and nonsense," refers to Merleau-Ponty. In *The Phenomenology of Perception* (1945), Merleau-Ponty had already exploited the ambiguity of the word *sens*. See Maurice Merleau-Ponty, *Phénoménologie de la perception* (Paris: Gallimard, 1945), 245–46, 251, 342, 358, 373–74, 492; English translation by Colin Smith as *The Phenomenology of Perception* (Atlantic Highlands, N.H.: Humanities Press, 1962), 212, 217, 296, 310, 323, 430. For the connection between Hyppolite and Merleau-Ponty, see Jean Hyppolite, "Sens et existence dans la philosophie de Maurice Merleau-Ponty," in *Figures de la pensée philosophique*, 2:731–58. Hyppolite also cites Merleau-Ponty on pages 24–25 of *Logic and Existence*.

Logos emerges from itself by remaining itself; since it is the indivisible self, the Absolute, it thinks the non-thought. It thinks sense in its relation to nonsense, to the opaque being of nature. It reflects this opacity into its contradiction. It raises thought, which would be only thought, over itself by obliging it to contradict itself; it turns this contradiction into the speculative means by which to reflect the Absolute itself. (*see below*, p. 102)

One cannot underestimate the importance of this comment. Hyppolite shows here that in Hegel the non-thought of thought, thought's double, non-philosophy or the anti-Logos (*see below*, p. 176) are nothing but the Logos emerging from itself in continuity with itself by means of self-contradiction; the other (nature, for example) is always the other of the Logos, its other. For Hyppolite's Hegel, there is only sense; Hyppolite therefore calls Hegel's logic a "logic of sense" (*see below*, pp. 170, 175).

In 1969, Deleuze adopts this phrase from Hyppolite's *Logic and Existence* as the title of one of his own books.[11] Echoing Hyppolite, Deleuze says, "The logic of sense is necessarily determined to posit between sense and nonsense an original type of intrinsic relation, a mode of co-presence."[12] But, the intrinsic relation that Deleuze will formulate will not be based in contradiction. More importantly, for Deleuze, nonsense enacts a donation of sense such that sense is always an effect, always an event.[13] Thus Deleuze's book should really be called *The Logic of Nonsense*, because in Deleuze's logic it is not the case that sense differentiates itself into its other, into nonsense (as in Hegel's logic of sense); rather, in Deleuze's logic, sense is differentiated by nonsense. This reversal of priority is why Deleuze specifies the definition of nonsense so precisely; he says, "nonsense does not have any particular sense, but is opposed to the absence of sense rather than to the sense that it produces in excess. . . . Nonsense is that which has no sense, and that which, as such and as it enacts the donation of sense, is opposed to the absence of sense. This is what we must understand by 'nonsense'."[14] This discussion

---

11. Gilles Deleuze, *Logique du sens* (Paris: Minuit, 1969); English translation by Constantin V. Boundas as *The Logic of Sense* (New York: Columbia University Press, 1990). All citations to *The Logic of Sense* hereafter will contain the reference to the French page number in parentheses after the English page number.

12. Deleuze, *The Logic of Sense*, 68 (85).

13. Deleuze, *The Logic of Sense*, 69–71 (87–89).

14. Deleuze, *The Logic of Sense*, 71 (89).

of nonsense by Deleuze occurs within the context of a discussion of structuralism. Similarly, Derrida says in his 1968 essay, "The Ends of Man," that the recent attention given to system and structure in France "is a question of determining the possibility of sense on the basis of a 'formal organization' which in itself has no sense, which does not mean that it is either the non-sense or the anguishing absurdity which haunts metaphysical humanism."[15] Finally, Foucault in his 1970 "L'ordre du discours," after rejecting the name *structuralism* for his own work, asks "if [philosophy] is in repeated contact with non-philosophy, where then lies the beginning of philosophy? Is it already there, secretly present in that which is not philosophy, beginning to formulate itself half under its breath, amid the murmuring of things? But, perhaps, from that point on, philosophy has no *raison d'être*, or, maybe, philosophy must begin on a foundation that is simultaneously arbitrary and absolute. We thus see the theme of the foundation of philosophical discourse and the theme of its formal structure substituting itself for the Hegelian theme of the movement proper to immediacy."[16] Foucault claims that Hyppolite brought about this substitution, this new thought of non-sense, of non-philosophy, of the other.

What makes *Logic and Existence* one of the great works of our time is Hyppolite's constant attempt to circumscribe the originality of Hegel's thought, an originality which lies in the relation of thought to the unthinkable. Hyppolite says, "Some have reproached Hegel for having spoken of a 'weakness of nature,' for having shown the resistance of the brute existent to the Logos; it seems to us, on the contrary, that this reproach brings to light the originality of his thought. Hegel does not construct the world with the pseudo-concepts of the academy; he takes seriously 'the pain, the work, and the patience of the negative.' His

---

15. Jacques Derrida, "Les fins de l'homme," in *Marges de la philosophie* (Paris: Minuit, 1972), 161; English translation by Alan Bass as "The Ends of Man" in *Margins of Philosophy* (Chicago: University of Chicago Press, 1982), 134. Although Derrida never mentions Hyppolite in this essay, Derrida's reading of Hegel here (especially on p. 121 [144]) seems indebted to him. Cf. also "The Pit and the Pyramid" (in the same volume, p. 71 [81]), in which Derrida says, "Certain of these texts already having been examined by Jean Hyppolite in *Logique et existence*, most notably in the chapter 'Sens et Sensible,' we will be making an implicit and permanent reference to the latter."

16. Michel Foucault, *L'ordre du discours* (Paris: Gallimard, 1971), 78–79; English translation by A. M. Sheridan Smith as "The Discourse on Language" in *The Archaeology of Knowledge* (New York: Pantheon, 1972), 236. Hereafter all citations to "The Discourse on Language: will have the page reference to the French edition in parentheses after the English reference.

concept is not the rational in the ordinary sense of the term, but the enlargement of thought, of reason which turns out to be capable of sublating itself as mere thought, as mere understanding, and to be capable of continuing to think itself in the beyond of mere abstract thought. Across spirit, the Logos thinks itself and its other" (*see below*, p. 103). Again: "Hegel's originality lies in the rejection of this merely human explanation of negation—an explanation that we find for example in Bergson—as well as in the rejection of the particular privilege granted to the thought that would nevertheless maintain that 'Being, the thing, is in a sense always positive'" (*see below*, p. 108). Finally: "Hegel's originality . . . lies in the rejection of this calling forth by the end. Dialectical evolution is attraction and instinct; it starts from immediate being and returns to immediate being. It is truth only as engendered truth. On the other hand, it is indeed *also* dualistic, but this dualism is not, as in Spinoza, the parallelism of Logos and Nature which never encounter one another. It is the dualism of mediation. Nature and Logos are simultaneously opposite and identical. This is why the Logos can think itself and the other, contradict itself in itself. And Nature, which is the anti-Logos, can appear as Logos" (*see below*, p. 163). By means of its precise examination of Hegel's *Logic*, *Logic and Existence* therefore started what has to be seen as the attempt by French philosophers to escape from Hegel. As Foucault says,

> But truly to escape Hegel involves an exact appreciation of the price we have to pay to detach ourselves from him. It assumes that we are aware of the extent to which Hegel, insidiously perhaps, is close to us; it implies a knowledge, in that which permits us to think against Hegel, of that which remains Hegelian. We have to determine the extent to which our anti-Hegelianism is possibly one of his tricks directed against us, at the end of which he stands, motionless, waiting for us. If, then, more than one of us is indebted to Jean Hyppolite, it is because he has tirelessly explored, for us, and ahead of us, the path along which we may escape from Hegel.[17]

If the task of philosophy remains today one of becoming the "the philosophy of non-philosophy, or perhaps the non-philosophy of philosophy itself," then, just as before, *Logic and Existence* remains an unavoidable text to read.

---

17. Foucault, "The Discourse on Language," in *The Archeology of Knowledge*, 235 (75).

Leonard
Lawlor and
Amit Sen

TRANSLATORS'
NOTE

When Hyppolite uses the words *dépasser* and *supprimer* to translate Hegel's technical term *aufheben* (and its inflected forms), we have translated these words as *to sublate* (and its inflected forms); in other contexts, we have rendered *dépasser* as *to overcome* or as *to surmount*. (Cf. Hyppolite's French translation of *Phänomenologie des Geistes*, vol. 1 [Paris: Aubier, 1939], 94n7 and 107n35.) Since the theme of this book is reflection in Hegel, almost all reflexive verbs have been rendered in English as reflexive verbs and not in the passive voice. In order to maintain the ambiguity of the French word, *sens* (an ambiguity which is also found in the German, *Sinn*), we have used the word *sense*, rather than *meaning*; the English *sense*, however, does not capture the meaning of *sens* (and *Sinn*) as direction. Going back to Hegel's German, we have translated

Hyppolite's *être-là* as *Dasein*; we have chosen this rendering (instead of the more standard English translation as determinate being) in order to make the literal meaning—being-there—explicit; see especially page 242; such a translation also indicates Hyppolite's attempt at a rapprochement between Hegel and Heidegger. For the most part, we have translated the reflexive verb *se confondre* as *to coincide*, but one should also keep in mind the similarity of this verb with Heidegger's *Gleichursprünglishkeit* (equiprimordiality). We have rendered Hyppolite's *egalité* and *inegalité* (which he uses to translate Hegel's *Gleichheit* and *Ungleichheit*) as *similarity* and *dissimilarity*. The reader should also keep in mind that, although we have translated the verb *comprendre* as *to understand* and, in contexts where it is necessary to distinguish it from *l'entendement* (the Kantian understanding), as *to comprehend*, this verb also means *to include*. Hyppolite uses the word *manifestation* liberally to translate *Erscheinung*, *Darstellung*, and *Manifestieren*. In general, however, the word seems to correspond to *Darstellung*. So, we have most often used *presentation* to render *manifestation*; where necessary we have also inserted the German word and used its standard English translation. Finally, we have rendered *prise de conscience* as *comprehension*, because, although this phrase literally means the taking up of something into consciousness, the becoming conscious about something, in the context of Hegel's work, this phrase signifies the transformation of experience into the concept. As much as possible, we have tried to make this translation be consistent with the existing English translation of Hyppolite's *Genesis and Structure of Hegel's "Phenomenology of Spirit"*. See, in particular, the glossary provided at the end of the English translation of *Genesis and Structure* (pp. 607–8).

LIST OF
ABBREVIATIONS
OF HEGEL
TEXTS CITED

At times, we have altered the standard English translations in order to make them consistent with Hyppolite's commentary.

DS   *The Difference between the Systems of Fichte and Schelling*, tr. H. S. Harris and Walter Cerf (Albany: State University of New York Press, 1977).

EL   *The Encyclopaedia Logic: Part I of the Encyclopaedia of Philosophical Sciences with the Zusatze (1830)*, tr. T. F. Geraets, W. A. Suchting, H. S. Harris (Indianapolis: Hackett, 1991).

ES   *Hegel's Philosophy of Mind: Being Part Three of the Encyclopaedia of Philosophical Sciences (1830)*, tr. William Wallace (London: Oxford University Press, 1971).

FK   *Faith and Knowledge,* tr. Walter Cerf and H. S. Harris (Albany: State University of New York Press, 1977).

GL   *Hegel's Science of Logic,* tr. A. V. Miller (New York: Humanities Press, 1976).

HI   *The Philosophy of History,* tr. J. Sibree (New York: Dover, 1956).

JL   *The Jena System, 1804-05: Logic and Metaphysics,* tr. John W. Burbridge and George di Giovanni (Montreal: McGill-Queen's University Press, 1986).

LA   *Hegel's Aesthetics: Lectures on Fine Art,* 2 vols., tr. T. M. Knox (New York: Oxford University Press, 1988).

PH   *Hegel's Phenomenology of Spirit,* tr. A. V. Miller (New York: Oxford University Press, 1977).

Other texts cited:

MM   Karl Marx, *Economic and Philosophic Manuscripts of 1844,* tr. Martin Mulligan (New York: International, 1976).

CE   Henri Bergson, *Creative Evolution* (New York: Holt and Company, 1926).

PART I

LANGUAGE
AND LOGIC

INTRODUCTION

Hegelian Logic[1] starts with an identification of thought and the thing thought. The thing, being, is not beyond thought, and thought is not a subjective reflection that would be alien to being. This speculative logic extends Kant's transcendental logic by exorcising the phantom of a thing-in-itself, which would always haunt our reflection and would limit knowledge in favor of faith and non-knowledge. Absolute knowledge means the in principle elimination of this non-knowledge, that is, the elimination of a transcendence essentially irreducible to our knowledge.

---

1. From among the contemporary works that have inspired us, let us cite R. Kroner, *Von Kant bis Hegel*, and of G. R. G. Mure on Hegel, *A Study of Hegel's Logic*.

By means of a recollection of human experience, the *Phenomenology of Spirit* demonstrates concretely that knowledge and the Absolute coincide. Undoubtedly, in order to actualize such a demonstration, it is necessary to investigate thoroughly the notion of knowledge and that of absolute being, to show concretely (that is, by means of a description of experience) the nearly naive error which turns knowledge and concepts into an intermediate medium or an instrument. The denunciation of this error, however, is not made by means of Scholastic arguments; it is made rather by a return to "the things themselves," by an authentic naivety which disperses false interpretations and is satisfied with recording their necessary birth. Absolute knowledge is not different from the immediate knowledge with which the *Phenomenology of Spirit* starts; it is only its true comprehension (*la vraie prise de conscience*). Empiricism and rationalism are not opposed to one another. The dialectical invention is nothing but a discovery of being; it is not a more or less arbitrary construction. Moreover, the dialectical demonstration is intimately united to the reality that interprets itself and reflects itself in a meaningful language. On this point, the Preface to the *Phenomenology of Spirit*—perhaps the best statement of Hegelian philosophy—provides pointers as dense as they are significant. The proper object of philosophy, Hegel says, is actuality (*Wirklichkeit*), the category of the Logic which designates the concrete unity of essence and appearance, the presentation which presents only itself and tests its necessity not in a separate intelligibility, but in its own movement and development. Actuality understanding itself and expressing itself as human language is what Hegel calls the concept or sense already immanent to the being of absolute knowledge, the being, according to Hegel, which "is reflection, which is itself simple, and which is for itself immediacy as such, being that is reflected into itself" (PH §26). Human language, the Logos, is this reflection of being into itself which always leads back to being, which always closes back on itself indefinitely, without ever positing or postulating a transcendence distinct from this internal reflection, without ever positing a beyond which would not be reflected completely, or a reflection which (although mediating) would be alongside being. Perhaps Hegel's ultimate project is the complete fusion of immediacy and mediation, of actuality and sense, a complete fusion which leads to a lived evidence, to a demonstration which is only the very movement of actuality: "for mediation is nothing other than the movement of self-similarity." Philosophy does not concern itself with extrinsic demonstrations, as those of mathematics are for Hegel, extrinsic demonstrations in which mediation, as an intermediate between inert unities, has to be composed and decomposed from the outside. Instead, philosophy concerns itself with demonstrations in which immediacy shows itself as (self-)mediation and as the mediation that proves to be genuine immediacy—the being which is sense and the sense which is being—by means of a reflection which is simultaneously a development and a return into the self. "The abstract or what is deprived of actuality is not the element and content of philosophy, but rather it is the real element, what posits itself, what lives in itself, Dasein which exists in its own concept. . . . Appearance [*Erscheinung*] is the movement of birth and death, the movement which itself neither is born nor dies, but which exists in itself and constitutes actuality and the movement of the life of truth" (PH §47). Philosophy's element is the temporality which is eternal, that is, the perpetual movement of appearance [*manifestation*] which implies the exchange of the future and the past, of sense and being, and exists as the present permanence of this exchange which is internal reflection.[2]

It seems then that the highest form of human experience (and there is nothing outside of human experience) is the revelation of the identity of being and knowledge. The highest form of human experience is the penetration into the structure of this universal self-consciousness at the heart of which being says itself, expresses itself, stating the thing of which one speaks as well as the "I" who speaks. To follow, in this way, the movement of the category diversifying itself into categories, into moments or particular nodes of a dialectical chain, is to turn philosophy into a logic, and such is really the sense of the Hegelian endeavor. This discourse that the philosopher forges about being, however, is as well the very discourse of being across the philosopher. This claim first presupposes that a philosophy—scattered throughout Hegel's texts—of human language be made explicit: "The forms of thought find their exposition and their being in human language. In all that becomes its interiority, its representation in general, we rediscover the intervention of language and in this language we discover the categories. Thus man thinks quite naturally according to the logic or rather that logic constitutes his very nature (GL 31). But how can human language be "cette voix qui se connaît quand elle sonne n'être plus la voix de personne"?[3]

---

2. For Hyppolite's use of *manifestation*, see below p. 174, notes 6 and 7.—TR.

3. This passage comes from Paul Valéry's "La Pythie," in *Oeuvres de Paul Valéry* (Paris: Bibliothèque de la Pléiade, Gallimard, 1957), 1:136: "this voice that knows itself when it no longer sounds like the voice of anyone." See also Jean Hyppolite, "Information et communication," in *Figures de la pensée philosophique*, 2:930. Our thanks to Theodore Toadvine and to Marco Cassisa (the Italian translator of *Logique et existence*) for locating this quote and the ones found on pages 23, 71, 94, 105, 112, 114, 189, all of which are left uncited by Hyppolite.—TR.

How can being say itself in man and man become universal consciousness of being through language? In order to attempt to respond to this
primordial question, one has to exorcise the phantom of non-knowledge
as well as the phantom of an ineffable. One has to show how human language is constituted as the *Dasein* of spirit and the sense of being. And
finally, thereby, one has to dispel the notion of a properly technical language which would not be at once sense and language, but rather extrinsic calculation, external manipulation of signs. Why does one have to
prefer the *logoi* to the *mathemata* as the living expression of being? This
last part of the question allows us to see in human language the very
medium of the dialectic.

CHAPTER **1**

THE INEFFABLE

What are the limits of knowledge and of language? This is the problem of non-knowledge and of the ineffable. The *Phenomenology* encounters it first on the empirical level as fatal ignorance, when Oedipus does not recognize his father in his offender and his mother in the queen that he marries, when in good conscience one acts as if one knows completely all the circumstances of an action. But this non-knowledge is relative. It does not imply necessarily an absolute non-knowledge, essentially escaping from the concept. The *Phenomenology*'s philosophical consciousness moves against such an ineffable. The strained effort of conception must allow this original truth to be expressed conceptually, this original truth about which Reinhold speaks and in reference to which Hegel writes in his work on Fichte and Schelling that, if such a truth were presupposed, it would be necessary to begin and end philosophy by forging inconceivable concepts rather than renouncing thought. To renounce discourse, to renounce the instituted community of conscious-nesses, or to give oneself up to feelings that are below language are all the same:

> Since the man of common sense makes his appeal to feeling, to an oracle within his breast, he is finished and done with anyone who does not agree; he only has to explain that he has nothing more to say to anyone who does not find and feel the same in himself. In other words, he tramples under-foot the roots of humanity. For it is the nature of humanity to press onward to agreement with others; human nature only really exists in an instituted community of consciousnesses. The anti-human, the merely animal, consists in staying within the sphere of feeling, and being able to communicate only at that level. (PH §69)

If it is true, however, that thought is a dialogue, a dialogue with another or with oneself, we can indeed wonder whether being lends itself to expression and whether it does not escape radically from the Logos which claims to signify it. In ancient philosophy, the problem is posed at the very level of the sensible world. What is merely felt is always fleeing, is in fact inexpressible, and science would not be able to remain science if it consists merely in sensation alone. The Platonist had to overcome the doxa so that human language is not objectless. Sensible being, as pure singularity or pleasure, is ineffable. Let us assume that singular things and souls exist in themselves. We would be able neither to conceive them nor to name them, since conception and language move within the universal. All the determinations through which we think things and which correspond to names are general determinations; they establish a community and a continuity between things which do not correspond to this opinion, which is, moreover, common, according to which the singu-lar alone exists, is the first genuine object of sense certainty, the certainty which believes itself to be immediate and which claims to apprehend, on the far side of all language and all sense, an individual this or an incom-parable this one. There would be therefore a "this side" of language which would be the immediate grasp of a being, of a being by nature ineffable.

There is, however, also a "far side," a "beyond" of language and of conception which appears as the object of a faith. The philosophies which Hegel studies in his Jena work, *Faith and Knowledge*, are for him philosophies of reflection which deny, more or less, knowledge in order to make room for faith. Here the expression of non-knowledge is entirely at home. Knowledge would not be able to overcome the structure of experience as it is considered by the understanding and which is already implicit reflection. But, thanks to explicit reflection, knowledge discovers its own finitude. It is therefore only capable of negating itself and of allowing faith to overcome this knowledge. The Absolute then is the object of a faith and not of a knowledge. The Absolute is beyond reflection and all knowledge. Hegel shows how these philosophies of reflection retreat to the final subjectivity of knowledge, and drive everything into the mystery of a "beyond" of knowledge, into the mystery of an ineffable Absolute. Let us pause however at the analysis Hegel provides of Jacobi's philosophy, which he studies between the philosophies of Kant and Fichte.

Jacobi's philosophy has often been considered a philosophy of feeling, but this means only that it claims to replace knowledge with an immediate apprehension of being, to which Jacobi gives the general name, faith. Knowledge is only formal; it grasps no content; it structures propositions, and the only consistent philosophy is, for Jacobi, that of Spinoza, which moreover, Hegel tells us, Jacobi understands rather badly. But faith overcomes philosophy through the direct apprehension of an inconceivable content, of an unconditioned (the immediate) that it discovers in the finite as well as in the infinite. Thus Jacobi can write: "We are all born into faith and must remain in faith. . . . It is through faith that we know that we have a body and that outside of us other bodies and other sensible beings are present." In other words, faith here does not concern merely the eternal or God, but also finite beings themselves, insofar as they are existences, and in a formula which has a contemporary ring to it, Jacobi can write: "Doesn't the greatest attainment of an investigator lie in the unveiling and presentation of existence?," but this attainment, according to Jacobi, can be acquired only by separating it from the rational form of science which is incapable of this unveiling. The inconceivable, the unnameable is the singular being in its pure singularity, the existent. It is also the "beyond" of these finite beings, the transcendent, and the mutual relation of these two existents. Hegel tried to express Jacobi's worldview: "Now, this relation of an absolute finitude to the truly absolute is faith. In faith, finitude does recognize itself to be finitude and nothingness before the eternal, yet it manages this recognition in such a way that it saves and preserves itself as a being-in-itself outside of the Absolute" (FK 137). Certainly, Hegel recognizes that Jacobi is trying to maintain a singular vitality in moral life by asserting that "the law is made for man and not man for the law." But this vitality is buried in pure subjectivity, in the unsayable, singular soul. And the heroes of Jacobi's novels, the Allwills and the Woldemars, are always tormented by themselves; they do not give themselves up to objectivity. These are beautiful souls, certainly capable of moral beauty, but incapable of forgetting themselves, of renouncing this consciousness of subjectivity, of renouncing this perpetual return of reflection upon the subject who acts: "The fundamental character of these figures is this conscious lack of objectivity, this subjectivity which is always attached to itself—the unhealthy moral character." Nostalgic suffering is the lot of beautiful souls, if, as the great poets, a Dante or a Goethe, have noted, hell is to be always self-aware, to reflect constantly on one's own action. By developing the theme of Jacobi a little, and this conception of faith that is opposed to knowledge, we would bring to light a primary silence before all language, a primary adherence to being which would be immediate and which knowledge understood as reflection and concept would disturb. This reflection, however, being capable of self-critique, of self-reflection, would discover its own nothingness and through faith would try to get back to the primary silence, the immediate contact with being. Philosophy—the expression of being in concepts or in discourse—would destroy itself. Silence, the ineffable, would be higher than speech. Like faith, non-knowledge would be the only possibility for man to overcome finite and conditioned knowledge, to overcome the knowledge which is stated in the mediation of discourse.[1]

If non-knowledge, the inconceivable, the ineffable is an absolute limit of knowledge, then there is no absolute knowledge. Now, the *Phenomenology*'s essential thesis is the establishment of absolute knowledge on the basis of the whole of human experience. Knowledge, however, is not only knowledge of being, it is also what makes the instituted community of consciousnesses possible. As the *Phenomenology* says: "The Dasein of the pure self as self." Language says things, but it also says the "I" (*le moi*) who speaks and it establishes communication among the diverse "I's." It is the universal instrument of mutual recognition: "In language, self-consciousness, qua singularity being for itself, comes as such into existence, so that it exists for others." In language, Hegel concludes, we can say that "the 'I' is this particular 'I'—but equally the universal 'I'" (PH §508). If, preparing for absolute knowledge, the *Phenomenology*'s task is really double, if it is proposing simultaneously to show that being, life, is knowledge, and that self-knowledge is universal knowledge, that is, that universal knowledge sublates and absorbs all the consciousnesses of singular selves, it has to be the case that self-consciousness not be an ineffable singularity enclosed in its own intuition. It

1. Cf. Hegel, *Faith and Knowledge*, 97–152, for Hegel's discussion of Jacobi's philosophy.

has to be the case that human discourse be simultaneously the discourse of being and the discourse of a universal self-consciousness. That implies the possibility of a universal recognition, of an intelligible discourse which is simultaneously this "I" and all "I's." Of course, the problem of recognition is not resolved immediately in Hegel's work. Violence is always possible, disdain or the haughty refusal to communicate, or even the feeling that one is unable to communicate at all. Barely having emerged from the pure self-feeling which defines animal existence, man faces a life and death battle from which spring the masters and the slaves, from which spring the workers who transform the world, a battle that lasts until thought presents itself as universal thought, conceptual thought; but discourse reproduces, in its own living dialectic, the confrontation of self-consciousnesses. It reproduces the movement of mutual recognition which is the very element[2] of absolute knowledge. Originally, what does the word *dialectic* mean, if not the art of discussion and dialogue? Socrates starts from popular opinions and forces his interlocutor to come out of himself, to confront his thought with that of another, a confrontation from which oppositions and contradictions come. Often the interlocutor is led to discover a contradiction in his own thought. He can then flee from Socratic irony, refuse to continue the debate or attempt to achieve harmony across the divergence of opinions. Thus dialectic is the moment of dicourse that elaborates the development of a universal self-consciousness, in which singularity is at the same time universal, and in which universality is at the same time singular, that is, a subject which expresses itself and is constituted from determination to determination. Every other singularity, that is, every "I" who takes refuge in silence and rejects communication, even claiming thereby to reach an absolute on this side of or beyond expression, is the dupe of an illusion. Expression of sense is the work of thought and this work does not start from an ineffable which would be given first, nor does it lead beyond to an ineffable transcendence; sensible singularity, as well as the mystery of faith, are for Hegel illusions; or rather, since he could not allow unexplained illusions, sensible singularity and the mystery of faith are the presentation of the Absolute as pure nothingness or dissolution. Human life is always language, sense, without which human life loses its character and returns to animal life, and the singularity with which it thinks it has merged gets lost immediately in universality, but this is abstract universality. No less immediately, immediate being turns back

---

2. We are taking the word, *element*, in the Hegelian sense of medium (*milieu*), as when we say the "element of water." When saying "the self," we want to note, like Hegel, the absolutely reflective character of being itself and of the "I."

into nothingness. Only the becoming, which at the level of immediacy is already mediation, prefigures what this discourse will be, the reflection of being into itself, the Absolute as universal self-consciousness or as subject, positing itself, while at the starting point it was only presupposed, an empty name. "Apart from the self that is sensuously intuited or represented, it is above all the name as name that designates the pure Subject (that is, *hypokeimenon*, substance), the empty unit without concept" (PH §66). But yet again, what is this sensuously intuited or represented self? What is this sensible outside of the sense with which language endows it? On this point, the *Phenomenology of Spirit* contains analyses which will be taken up again on the ontological level of the logic and which can help elucidate already the famous reversal of being into nothingness with which this logic begins.

The refutation of the ineffable and the proper character of human language, as the Logos of being and universal self-consciousness, can be found again at several stages of the *Phenomenology of Spirit*, from the first chapter on *sense certainty* up to one of the last in which the beautiful soul, rejecting universal recognition, sinks into nothingness, the sole expression of its failure. Of course, this development of self-consciousness seems able to be interrupted at each particular phase; it can get lost in violence (Socrates died as the victim of such violence) or it can be engulfed in boredom and dissolution. Dialectical discourse could therefore be interrupted, and skepticism is in effect always possible. What characterizes, however, this skepticism is that it always ends up as nothingness and that, in turn, it always has need of a new content in order to be able to dissolve it. This nothingness is nothing other than what is presented in living nature as death, and as pure and simple disappearance in nature in general. The consciousness which claims to live in pure singularity without thinking it or signifying it can in fact only be dissolved. In vain, it rejects language and discourse and claims to reach an ineffable absolute. What it says is the opposite of what it intends, and it is language which is right; or if it stubbornly renounces language, this consciousness can only get lost, dissolved. Let us repeat, this dissolution is always possible, and then the only virtual transcendence seems to be that of nothingness. Skepticism does not see that the discursive process is always being pursued, going from form to form, from figure to figure, from determination to determination, and that every nothingness is in a way determinate, "the nothingness of that from which it results." Skepticism itself finishes with the abstraction of nothingness; it isolates this nothingness as the ineffable, instead of thinking it as the internal negativity which allows discourse to follow its course by going from determination to determination. The consciousness, however, which claims to reach absolute being in singularity, either outside of itself or in

itself, is the victim of this claimed immediacy of being, and what it discovers instead of being is precisely nothingness, the transcendence of
supreme abstraction instead of the sole concrete mediation. This passage
from being to nothingness is the truth of immediate sense-certainty
which, rejecting mediation, is then prey to becoming. Sense-certainty is
consistent again only by accepting the determinations which establish
the connection and community of all things, the connection and community which alone turn sensible singularity into an intersection of determinations. This possibility of dissolution, which is found in almost every
phase of the *Phenomenology*, in no way implies that the development of
self-consciousness goes from nothingness to concrete and determinate
being. Dissolution is not the reverse of progression, for self-consciousness progresses in its discourse from one determinate figure to another,
from one sense to another, and not from nonsense to sense. Dissolution,
either as investigation of pure immediacy or as rejection of all commun-
ciation (which amounts to the same thing), is only that which haunts all
the particular figures of consciousness, and this dissolution, this non-
sense is then the truth of the rejection of mediation.

In sense-certainty, consciousness tests its first relation to being; it
is immediate certainty and claims to be certainty of immediacy. What it
intends therefore is singular, unique and ineffable being, the being outside of itself, this night, or this unique light, itself, this incomparable consciousness. But what it intends, that about which it has an opinion (in the
sense of the Greek doxa)—it really is unable to say it: "When science is
faced with the demand—as if it were an acid test that it could not pass—
that it should deduce, construct, find *a priori*, or however it is put, something called 'this thing' or 'this one man,' it is reasonable that the
demand should say which 'this thing,' or which 'this particular man' is
meant; but it is impossible to say this" (PH §102). Now Hegel, who here
could take sides against language, adopts this very language as what
alone has validity. He says, "Speech has the divine nature of directly
reversing the sense of what is said, of making it into something else"
(PH §110); "in other words, we do not absolutely say what in this sense-
certainty we mean to say. But language, as we see, is the more truthful"
(PH §97). We really believe that we grasp singular, immediate being as
singular, but what we say is that there is something more universal, a
"this," a "this one." But everything is a "this," every "I" is a "this one."
We believe that we grasp what is richest, but what remains of this experience for us is only the consciousness of our poverty. We see the singular
transforming itself into the universal, and unique being passing into
nothingness as the nothingness of all determinations. Of course, we can
place these determinations back into their connections and find then
again being as determinate. But we are entering into the discourse which

starts with the gesture through which we designate things, and if the universal is particularized, or is more and more closely determined, we nevertheless always remain within the universal without ever being able to say anything other than the universal. Thus the categories already sustain all of what we call sensible perception insofar as this perception is lived by a consciousness: "These elements are the cohesive power and mastery of the understanding itself. They alone are what constitute what the sensible is as essence for consciousness, what determines the relations of consciousness with the sensible and that in which the movement of perception and its truth runs its course" (PH §131). The understanding, however, which constitutes only perception or immediate sense certainty, is unaware of this character of perception or of certainty; perception and sense certainty say that philosophy merely has to do with things of thought. "As a matter of fact, philosophy does have to do with them too, recognizing them as pure essences, the absolute elements and powers; but in doing so, recognizes them in their specific determinateness as well, and is therefore the master over them" (PH §131). Immediate certainty and perception are already a sense which does not yet reflect on itself, a discourse which is not yet the discourse which recognizes itself as such, as self, and as the discourse of things.

Sensible consciousness does not therefore reach what it believes it reaches, or at least what it only intends; it is not moreover able to reach itself as a singular and unique soul. From the *Phenomenology*'s first pages, solipsism is refuted. However, is it not the case that for myself I—certainty's subject—am an immediate evidence prior to all reflection? I am, I exist, and I exist as unique and incomparable; it is I who sense, and to feel [*sentir*] is immediate only in me. But when I say "I," a "this one," I say in fact all the "I's." "When I say 'I,' this singular 'I,' I say in general all 'I's'; everyone is what I say, everyone is 'I,' this singular 'I'" (PH §102). The illusion, however, is tenacious. Certainty's subject seems to have for itself a privilege. It believes that it takes hold of an indivisible intuition of its being which is below language, but all the other "I's" claim to have the same intuition. Their confrontation makes the claimed immediacy of their viewpoint disappear. "Man," said Socrates, "you are him and me also." This "I," originary and original, is in its ground only a universal, since language states it. It is not unique insofar as it says "I"; it only believes itself to be unique. This unicity is an opinion. The "I" who intends itself as unique is really more of a "One" (*On*), who constitutes the abstract medium of experience, just as abstract being constituted the medium of the felt. Here the lived sublates language only in intention and not in fact. "The 'I' is merely universal like 'now,' 'here,' or 'this' in general" (PH §102). And this universal that language states is the poorest form of thought. It is the supreme abstraction, the implicit nothingness of determinations, the being which exists as abstraction, but as self-abstraction not as psychological abstraction. That I am unique and incomparable means as well that I am nothing and, then, it means to be anything whatsoever. As this singular, I am the abstract universal, that is, having already in itself implicitly the moment of mediation as negation: "A simple thing of this kind which is through negation, which is neither this or that, a not-this, and is with equal indifference this as well as that—such a thing we call universal. So it is in fact the universal that is the truth of sense-certainty" (PH §96). Thus sensible singularity expresses itself truly through its own annihilation. It passes away, it becomes, it negates itself, and if we want to retain it, it remains only as this abstract universal, the being identical to nothingness, this medium of all the determinations. The singular "I" also passes away; what remains is this universal name, *I*, that language states so exactly by transforming this claimed unicity into something banal. Hegel's analysis in the *Phenomenology*'s first pages is decisive for the interpretation of his philosophy. Including mediation under the form of universal negation or of nothingness, this universal is the being which is becoming, but which, removing itself from this movement of mediation, retains only the two identical poles, being, which immediately posited in its rigid immediacy negates itself (in effect, it becomes), and nothingness, which immediately posited in this same immediacy negates itself as well, that is, nothingness *is*, for being is always there, even in becoming. Far from excluding mediation, the genuine "I," authentic singularity, that is, self-consciousness, instead coincides with mediation; it is true becoming, that is, self-becoming. Hegel says, "The 'I' or becoming in general, the act of actualizing mediation is, by means of its simplicity, just the immediacy which becomes as well as immediacy itself."

Immediate singularity, which would be ineffable intuition, the "what we will never see twice," is therefore the worst of banalities. If we posit it, we see it dissolve immediately. Fundamentally, it is dissolution. If this dissolution is understood, if it is sense and discourse, it is genesis as well as annihilation; it is mediation. This is why death is the beginning of the life of spirit, because, at the level of nature, the Absolute (substance) appears as life as well as as death, and this cycle is endless. The singularity of sensible things, and of mortal living beings which are modes of the Absolute, present this Absolute in its annihilation. In nature, there is only a sketch of this true singularity which is reflected mediation, therefore the Logos as universal self-consciousness. Nature is only spirit for the spirit who knows it. Nature is in itself Logos; it is not Logos for itself. It is immediately the Dasein of the Logos, but it is posited as such only by spirit.

But organic nature has no history; it falls from its universal,
from life, directly into the singleness of Dasein, and the
moments of simple determinateness and the single organic
life united in its actuality, produce the process of becoming
merely as a contingent movement, in which each is active in
its own part and the whole is indeed preserved; but this
activity is restricted, so far as itself is concerned, merely to its
center, because the whole is not present in this center, and is
not present in it because here it is not *qua* whole for itself. (PH
§295)

Singularity as immediate being, that is, that which wants to be
abstracted from all mediation, is therefore immediately its dissolution.
This is so in nature and likewise for the consciousness that would
claim to escape from the becoming of sense, from discourse, and from
mediation. Rejecting thought, giving itself up to something it believes
to be purely lived, this consciousness degenerates into life's uncon-
sciousness. What it discovers is necessarily death, a death of all the
instants, and a death that—*ex hypothesi*—it does not understand, a
death which therefore for this consciousness is simultaneously necessity and enigma. This is the case because necessity felt as such and not
thought is the pure enigma: "for necessity, fate, and the like, is just that
about which we cannot say what it does, what its specific laws and
positive content are, because it is the absolute pure concept itself
viewed as being, a relation that is simple and empty, but also irre-
sistible and imperturbable, whose work is merely the nothingness of
individuality" (PH §363).

Let us assume, therefore, that consciousness rejects the universal
discourse that immediately reverses its opinion. Let us assume that consciousness tries to take refuge in what it believes to be a pure experience,
in order to taste there the unique pleasure of its own singularity. It
would like to live instead of think. Hegel describes this experience for us
at a higher stage of the *Phenomenology* (PH §360–63). In fact, the issue is
no longer the test of immediate certainty, in its most naive form; rather
the issue is a sort of conscious, and if we can call it deliberate, decision to
turn back. He takes the episode of Faust and Gretchen as his example of
such an experience. It is the issue of a consciousness, weary of the universality of knowledge and of the burden of mediation, that claims to
turn back completely towards ineffable pleasure. This consciousness
knows that "all theory is gray and green the golden tree of life,"[3] it

3. Goethe, *Faust*, lines 2038–39.—Tr.

despises "the understanding and science, the supreme gifts of man."[4]
But then it is delivered up to the devil and must return into the ground:
"zu Grunde gehen." The expression *zu Grunde gehen* must be taken literally. This ground is precisely consciousness's annihiliation, an annihilation which it even refuses to be able to understand. Consciousness
aspires to immediacy, like Faust and Gretchen. This nearly amounts to
saying that this consciousness aspires to disappear without even knowing it. Like the singular consciousness which wants to live the ineffable
and refuses to think, it desires only to take life, "much as a ripe fruit is
plucked, which readily offers itself to the hand which takes it" (PH
§361). But, instead of being thrown from dead theory into life itself, it
rather rushes into death, into the dissolution of its own singularity. It
cannot understand this dissolution, since, *ex hypothesi*, it has refused to
connect the true to discourse, has claimed to descend below mediation
which alone constitutes a self-consciousness as such. It is therefore
indeed the prey of necessity and of destiny. At this higher level, this consciousness repeats the experience of the stuttering consciousness with
which the *Phenomenology* started. Sense-certainty believed that it held
onto the singular "this," but possessed only abstract being. Being able to
say only, "It is, it is," it is able to be present only at its abstract negation.
It wanted to get to the bottom of this pure singularity and it really discovers the ground of it: the dissolution which still says itself, but which
says nothing other than necessity or death, the pure enigma. Feeling
does not contain by itself the explicit sense of the event. "Consciousness,
therefore, through its experience in which it should have found its truth,
has really become an enigma to itself, the consequences of its deeds are
for it not the deeds themselves" (PH §365). It finds itself alienated from
itself, without being able to say anything about itself or to understand
itself. Already, the word, *destiny*, especially if we make reference to
Hegel's early works, means more than *necessity*. Destiny is a beginning
of comprehension accompanying the abstract movement of life. To have
a destiny is already to penetrate the sense of necessity. It is not only to
live, but also to live by elevating oneself to self-consciousness, by accepting mediation. "The transition of its living being into a lifeless necessity
therefore appears to it as an inversion which is not mediated by anything at all. The mediating agency would have to be that in which both
sides would be one, where, therefore, consciousness recognized one
moment in the other: its purpose and action in fate, and its fate in its purpose and action, that is, would recognize its own essence in this necessity" (PH §365). If we were not a little wary of being paradoxical, we

---

4. Goethe, *Faust*, lines 1850–51.—Tr.

could say, by being careful to take the word *logic* in its Hegelian sense, that, according to Hegel, human experience can be only logical (it is logical even when it is unaware of being so). The pure lived, this return to nature, means precisely nothing and consciousness is always sense, discourse. Like an absolute limit, the ineffable is nothingness.

This "turning back" is present in the *Phenomenology* not only on the level of pleasure but also on the level of knowledge. The consciousness which knows goes back down to a pure empiricism: "Consciousness, which in its very first reality is sense-certainty and intention of the 'this,' returns here to this from the whole course of its experience and is again a knowledge of what is purely negative of itself, or of things of sense, i.e. of things which immediately and indifferently confront its being-for-self. Here, however, it is not an immediate, natural consciousness; on the contrary, it has become such for itself" (PH §558). This return to empiricism is based on the comprehension of the nullity of all the other figures, on a merely negative proof. Let us return therefore to pure experience, but this pure and ineffable experience reveals itself once more as the supreme abstraction. It has been said that "Skepticism is the fruit that empiricism always brings forth again." Skepticism is at least the result of this "turning back," which aims to find again a "this side" of discourse, and to keep itself there. When self-consciousness is not the Logos for itself, it is the prey of a Logic of which it is no longer anything but the victim. Dialectic in itself exerts force on self-consciousness when self-consciousness is not this dialectic for itself.

In order to be valid, this discourse must be the discourse of a universal self-consciousness. It is such a discourse already insofar as it is language, insofar as it presupposes an established communication between singular consciousnesses who, in language, mutually recognize one another and aspire to this recognition. This recognition is the fundamental element of absolute knowledge, but language is itself this recognition and this connection of the singular and the universal which defines for Hegel the concept or sense. If, for Descartes, the mathematician cannot be an atheist without losing the guarantee of his demonstrations, for Hegel truth finds its soil and ground in this communication of consciousnesses. The beautiful soul, which encloses itself in interior silence in order not to soil the purity of its soul, which imagines that it finds at the bottom of itself the divine absolute in its immediacy, can only dissolve into nothingness. "In this transparent purity of its moments, an unhappy, so-called 'beautiful soul,' its light dies away within it, and it vanishes like a shapeless vapor that dissolves into thin air" (PH §658). It must accept the transformation of its thought into being. It must let itself be given substantiality and entrust itself to absolute difference. But then it presents itself in its particularity, in the tight node of its determinations. Its salvation, however, could not lie in this flight in the face of determination into an interior refuge where it believes it establishes a silent contact with divinity. This pure interior life is an illusion. It can neither renounce universality, nor reject the determination which alone endows it with Dasein. Such a rejection would lead it only to the dissolution which, as we have seen, always lies in wait for abstract singularity, abstract precisely by means of this rejection of determinations, and therefore revealing itself as identical to abstract universality. With less naivety, the beautiful soul accomplishes in itself the movement which immediate consciousness, believing itself unique on this side of discourse, accomplished. It ends up by coming apart into madness or by sinking into the immediacy of pure being or nothingness. The only possibility for resolving opaque determination into the transparency of the universal, to undo the node, lies in linguistic communication, in accepting dialogue. What the traditional philosophy of a Descartes or a Malebranche expects from a silent relation between human consciousness and God, Hegel expects from the expressed communication of consciousnesses who institute universal self-consciousness, which is itself the discovery of being as universal self. This is where the importance of the mutual recognition of self-consciousness in the whole *Phenomenology* comes from. This recognition finds its element in the very language which states dialectically the oppositions and the actual sublations. Language is the Dasein of spirit. Silence before the other, like interior silence, leads only to dissolution. One has to confess one's action, one's particular way of being in the world, in order to conquer one's universality, in order to make it recognizable. One also really has to welcome into oneself the particular determination of the other in order to raise it to universality, in order to promote this concrete universality which is the genuine unity of the singular and the universal. Here genuine (*véritable*) means accepting the mediation of particular determinations and not oscillating indefinitely from abstract singular to abstract universal which turn out to be identical by means of this rejection of mediation. Language states this universal mediation. I speak and I say events and things and what I say is already no longer me. "The 'I' is this 'I' and the universal 'I.'" What I say, however, insofar as I say it, insofar as it is an intelligible speech, transposes the opacity of determinations into the element of universality. Thus the Absolute as sense and as Logos appears across man but not across the one who "refuses to externalize his interior life in the Dasein of discourse, . . . [who] confronts the confession of the penitent with his own stiff-necked unrepentant character, [who] mutely keeps himself to himself and refuses to throw himself away for someone else" (PH §667). Perhaps we can see why in his early works Hegel, repeating Plato, calls Love what he now calls the concept. Both are immediate mediation.

The possibility of raising determinations to universality, the possibility of making the self that was lost in the determinations emerge, the possibility, however, of making it emerge as universal self, this possibility is the very possibility of absolute knowledge, the light of being as sense: "it is the 'I' which remains identical with itself, and, in its complete externalization and opposite, possesses the certainty of itself: it is God manifested in the midst of those who know themselves in the form of pure knowledge" (PH §671). This God, however, or this Absolute, is no longer a transcendence beyond this knowledge, the ineffable endpoint of a never attained aspiration. This knowledge becomes absolute when it knows itself as such, that is, when it is no longer only a dialectical discourse of man on being or on man's destiny, but when it is a discourse of being, an absolute self-certainty in what was revealing itself explicitly only as the other of knowledge, when it is a logic of philosophy and no longer only a phenomenology.

Christian religion had the premonition of this universal self-consciousness which finds itself as self-consciousness, as the ultimate sense of being, or rather as the dialectical identity of being and sense, when, according to a still sensible modality (but isn't everything given in human experience?), it announces: "Divine nature is the same as human nature, and it is this unity which is given to intuition in revealed religion." This intuition is, however, still an alienation, a being alien to sense, or a sense which is not a sense of self. This is why Hegel can say: "God, or the Absolute, is accessible only in pure speculative knowledge, and is only in this knowledge and is this very knowledge." The Absolute therefore is this very knowledge as absolute knowledge, the very knowledge in which substance presents itself as subject, in which being presents itself completely as sense and sense as being. That, however, does not mean that the Absolute disappears and we are left only with a Humanism, as some say. In the *Phenomenology*, Hegel does not say man, but self-consciousness. The modern interpreters who have immediately translated this term by man have somewhat falsified Hegel's thought. Hegel is still too Spinozistic for us to be able to speak of a pure humanism; a pure humanism culminates only in skeptical irony and platitude. Undoubtedly, the Logos appears in the human knowledge that interprets and says itself, but here man is only the intersection of this knowledge and this sense. Man is consciousness and self-consciousness, while at the same time natural Dasein, but consciousness and self-consciousness are not man. They say being as sense in man. They are the very being that knows itself and says itself. Only in this way can we understand that Hegel's philosophy results at least as much in a speculative logic as in a philosophy of history.

For Hegel, therefore, there is no ineffable that would be on this side of or beyond knowledge, no immediate singularity or transcendence; there is no ontological silence, rather dialectical discourse is a progressive conquest of sense. That does not mean that sense would be in principle prior to the discourse which discovers it and creates it (and that we are obligated to use these two verbs simultaneously indicates the difficulty of the problem), rather sense develops itself in discourse itself. One does not go from a silent intuition to an expression, from an inexpressible to an expressed, any more than from nonsense to sense. The progress of thought, its development, is the very progress of expression. The opposition of intuition and language no longer makes sense if language does not form thought and thought language. But if the in-formation of one by the other is common, the one is not an external translation of the other. Sense unfolds itself and determines itself without its being given previously in an ineffable form. Undoubtedly, this progress of expression is the result of an incessant battle thanks to which the universal turns itself into self-consciousness instead of falling back into nothingness. This battle, however, is the very progress of expression, its complete development. Then the universal content is said, and this speech is the speech which says this universal as well as the expression of the self who emits it and who, lost in this universal, ends up by returning to itself. The individual raises himself to the universal, while universality is presented as a self. Such is already the work of the poet and his creation:

> Spirit is present in this individual as his universal and as the power over him from which he suffers violence, as his pathos, by giving himself over to which his self-consciousness loses its freedom. But that positive power of universality is subdued by the pure self of the individual, the negative power. This pure activity, conscious of its inalienable strength, wrestles with the shapeless essence. Becoming its master, it has made the pathos into its material and given itself its content, and this unity emerges as a work, universal spirit individualized and represented. (PH §704)

Hegel adds, "Now the perfect element at the heart of which interiority is also completely exterior, just as exteriority is interior, is still once more language." How can language, however, human speech, be simultaneously that of which one speaks and the one who speaks? How can it realize within itself this unity of self and being?

Honneur des hommes, saint langage.[1]

SENSE AND SENSIBLE

In Kant's philosophy, the understanding and the sensibility constitute two different sources of knowledge. Sensible diversity seems to come from a "beyond" of knowledge or from a thing in itself while the understanding raises itself above the sensible through its concepts in order to determine the sensible universally and make it thinkable. Hegel describes the passage from the sensible to the understanding, unveils the immanence of the universal to nature. In this dialectic, the sensible becomes the Logos, meaningful language, and the thought of the sensible does not

---

1. This quote comes from Paul Valéry, "La Pythie," in *Oeuvres de Paul Valéry*, 1:136: "Manly honor, sacred language."—TR.

remain interior and mute. It is there in language. Language is not only a system of signs alien to the signified, it is also the existing universe of sense, and this universe is the interiorization of the world as well as the exteriorization of the "I." Language is a double movement that must be understood in its unity. Nature reveals itself as Logos in human language, and the spirit that appears only in a contingent way in the human face and form finds its perfect expression only in language (ES §459). The mediation reconnecting nature and the Logos is the sole Absolute, since the terms cannot exist independently of this very mediation.

This dialectic of the sensible and sense determines the proper status of human language in Hegel's *Philosophy of Spirit* (ES §446 [intuition] and §465 [thought]). It also orders the development of his aesthetics and the organization of his system of the arts. Sense and sensible; Hegel's aesthetics insists upon the revelatory relation of these words:

> Sense is this wonderful word which is used in two opposite meanings. On the one hand it means the organ of immediate apprehension, but on the other hand we mean by it the sense, the significance, the thought, the universal underlying the thing. And so sense is connected on the one hand with the immediate external aspect of existence, and on the other hand with its inner essence. Now a sensuous consideration does not cut the two sides apart at all; in one direction it contains the opposite one too, and in sensuous immediate perception it at the same time apprehends the essence and the concept. But since it carries these very determinations in a still unseparated unity, it does not bring the concept as such into consciousness but stops at foreshadowing it. (LA 128–29)

There are therefore intermediaries between the sensible and the signification, which is only present in language. The transition from one to the other presents itself in the dialectic of the arts as well as in that of spirit. But one must not let oneself be deceived by this expression, *intermediary,* since Hegel's philosophy is a philosophy of *mediation.* Signification such that it appears in language, sense as the becoming of the concept in discourse, exist first in relation to the movement which seems to engender them. There is no sense before language, any more than there is an ineffable Absolute, or any more than there would be dreams for the one who would never be awake. The arts which precede poetry in the ascending series of the fine arts, architecture, sculpture, painting, and music, give us the illusion of an ineffable which would be sense without speech, and in relation to which we could say, in a paradoxical form, that speech is itself mute.[2] Couldn't we prefer the image to speech as the carrier of sense? Poetry, however, appears as the endpoint of a movement which remolds the sensible in order to signify it. Poetry is the supreme art; preserving from the sensible only the sound that disappears as soon as it is emitted, sublating the elaboration of the world of sounds in music, poetry is the originary light of the world, because it says and narrates the world. Poetry also says the "I" who narrates and who, first thrust into his narrative with epic poetry, reflects upon himself in lyric poetry and who, with dramatic poetry, is placed within the frame of his world. But if poetry is the apex of art, it is also the sign of its decline. It is complete in the double sense of the term. The negation of the sensible is almost too complete so that there is still art and already pure signification; sense as sense, that is, philosophy, shines through. What therefore is art if there is no ineffable sense, no sense independent of language? We indeed know that a picture is in no way reducible to the discourse that people can make *about* it. But the difficulty is still greater; setting aside the discourse about the picture, or the idle talk surrounding the thing itself—although people think almost exclusively of this "discourse about" when they insist on the incommensurability of the plastic work of art and speech— it is still the case that the work of art does not say itself, does not produce meaningful speech. It does not speak, at least insofar as a work of art does not coincide with its subject and resides rather in the way the work handles its subject. If the whole movement of art ascends towards poetry, so that, on the whole, the expression is indeed signification, it is still the case that the arts prior to poetry are not signification at their particular stages. However, the picture presents itself as sense before signification; it seems to evoke for us a signification that we cannot formulate. If it does not actually speak, it seems to want to speak. Undoubtedly, there is an appearance there, but art is this very appearance, and it remains appearance or it disappears as art. It presupposes the absolute reference without which the very notion of sense is inconceivable, the universe of the Logos or of significations. Art, however, does not come back to this universe directly. Like nature, it is signification in itself, but it differs from nature in that it seems to be sense for itself. Art is simultaneously nature and the suggestion of signification. It mimes a sense without ever delivering it. Purposiveness without a purpose, it is a nature which immediately evokes signification, a signification that falls back into nature, an indefinite oscillation from one to the other. It suggests the essence in the appearance, but is reduced to this suggestion; it is deception (in a non-pejorative sense). "Art," says Hegel, "is an existence made

---

2. This expression is used by Merleau-Ponty.

out of appearances." Its truth is really the Idea, as the dialectical genesis of poetry shows. But this truth is no longer appearance, no longer art. The artwork makes mediation appear, it simulates it, and it gives a character of completeness and perfection to this pure appearance.[3]

Isn't what Hegel calls the *prophetic soul*, those gestures or expressions through which a way of being in the world prior to speech and explicit sense seems to be unveiled, the same as this? Psychology has recourse to an unconscious, as if signification existed in some unknown place, even before these very gestures. But it would more precise to speak of a sort of nature, a nature which disappears as such gradually as we go on to signify it on purpose, as we go on to untie the knot of opaque determinations, by clarifying them with the light of sense. This sense is one that has to be presupposed, a sense which then explicates retrospectively what was there as being. But would not every being be a lost sense? The movement that provides a nature exists then in this reconquest of sense and in this displacement of the origin. The prophetic soul—and every manner of being in the world which does not reflect on itself is a prophetic soul—exists only for others. Its expression becomes sense by means of actual interpretation. The real difficulty of these intermediaries, in the arts as well as in the prophetic soul, is due to the fact that we would like to engender the signification on the basis of nature by means of a series of imperceptible progressions, by means of an empirical history. We do not see that this would be to renounce the very conception of mediation, that is, the mutual position of one term by the other, each positing and presupposing the other.

It is indeed this mediation which appears in the passage from the sensible to sense, from immediate intuition to thought signification. But it also appears in the reverse passage from thought to its own alienation, to its Dasein, language. These two movements coincide. The sensible interiorizes itself, turns itself into essence, being becoming Logos; and the interiority which in itself is the nothingness of being, its disappearance, exists, however immediately, in the exteriority of language and in the exteriority of living speech. That of which one speaks and the one who speaks show themselves to be inseparable. Object and subject finally transcend themselves as such in the authentic language of being, in the Hegelian ontology. This language appears as the existence of the essence, and dialectical discourse appears as the becoming of sense. However, within natural language, how is this language, which is no

---

3. This appearance of sense is moreover not sense, because it is not sense for itself. Only language is sense and the sense of sense. There is an actual sense only through the unity of the in-itself and the for-itself. No art, except poetry, *signifies itself* by doubling itself.

longer that of anyone, which is being's universal self-consciousness, to be distinguished from human, all-too-human, language? In other words, how does the passage from the Phenomenology to absolute Knowledge work? This question is the Hegelian question *par excellence*, and the very purpose of this work lies in the attempt to pose this question by confronting Hegel's diverse attitudes concerning it.

The dialectical genesis of language, such as we will examine it here according to the *Philosophy of Spirit* (part III of the *Encyclopaedia*), already points to this problem. The sensible itself interiorizes itself into thought, and thought exteriorizes itself into language. The thought of being and the thought of thought must be unified. In the *Phenomenology*, Hegel defines genuine thought, the concept, as a thought which gives the consistency of being-in-itself, objective value, to the "I," and gives the subjective value of consciousness's for-itself to the thing thought. Thus, by thinking itself, thought always thinks being, and, by thinking being, it thinks itself: "For to think does not mean to be an abstract 'I,' but an 'I' which has at the same time the value of being-in-itself, of having itself for an object, or of relating itself to objective essence, in such a way that its value is the being-for-itself of the consciousness for which it is" (PH §197). Hegel adds that the object of thought is no longer a representation, but a concept, and that through its determination, the concept is a being which nevertheless remains a thought by means of the movement of this determination in thought. Dialectical discourse, the becoming of the categories in which being and thought are identical, is there. These categories, however, have language and speech for their medium. They exist only in this language that simultaneously negates the sensible and preserves it, sublates it. At the level of the *Philosophy of Spirit*, this dialectic of language presents the originary identity of the sensible and the understanding. Kant indeed tried to present the synthetic intermediary between the universal "I" of recognition and the sensible diversity in a subjective deduction of the categories. Perhaps he saw in the imagination this common source of the understanding and the sensibility. After Fichte, Hegel did not hesitate to see in the Kantian imagination the seed of genuine reason as mediation, as the dialectical unity of the in-itself and the for-itself. Kant, however, sought only to make accessible to knowledge a being which in its foundation escaped from knowledge. Hegel is unaware of this absolute limit. Sensible diversity refers only to this universality of the intelligence that is immanent to it. It turns itself into signification in a Dasein, man, who does not only contemplate things and is affected by them but who also himself determines them in the negativity of action. "Man's Dasein is his action." The one who speaks is involved in that about which he speaks. He is determined and he determines. He himself is this passage and this pure mediation which is actually the unity of sense and being, the concept as time. This involvement of the one who speaks in that about which he speaks presents itself in the passage from epic poetry to tragedy; by means of narrating he becomes an actor. The negativity of being is also his negativity. He plays the role of negativity at the heart of necessity or of destiny which then becomes his destiny at the same time as it is universal destiny. Now, absolute knowledge is this universal destiny that says itself as a self identical to being, and includes within itself the one who speaks and that about which one speaks, their unity and their opposition, the unity of their unity and of their difference. As the *Phenomenology* shows, absolute knowledge assumes also the man of action, because he is not only the given signification, necessity, but also engendered signification, self-signification: "The Absolute is subject."[4]

The sensible therefore turns into sense by negating itself as sensible. This negation (*Aufhebung*) is its position as signification stated in the universality of the "I." In *intuition*, the universal "I" appears to itself first as affected from the outside. It finds a particular being and apprehends it, but already this affection in its concrete particularity is a discernment grounded in heres and nows which constitute the universal spatiotemporal horizon. The intuition of the being always sublates itself. It fixes itself thematically by paying attention, but its marginal sublation is the index of its still immediate universality. Space and time are the universal forms of intuition, are the "I" outside of itself. *Memory* is the essentialization of this immediate intuition that exists only through recognition. The spatiotemporal datum passes away and becomes. It no longer is there, as soon as it is there, like the night about which the *Phenomenology* speaks. The "I" remembers; the interior of things is the pure knowledge of the "I" which includes everything in its simple universality. This "I" is universal intelligence, the night of preservation. Pure memory is the interiorization (*Erinnerung*) of the world. It is not a divisible and spatial, localizable image. In vain, we look for traces and fibers in the brain where it might be housed (ES §452). This interiorization is however the undivided seed, "the potential coming to free existence in its development, and yet at the same time collecting itself in its inwardness" (ES §453). Immediate Dasein, the found sensible, is negated, and this first negation allows imagination to have the datum

---

4. It is important to recognize this negativity of action preserved in absolute knowledge. This negativity of preserved action nevertheless poses a formidable problem in Hegelianism. What is the relation between this negativity of action and the negativity of thought in the dialectic of the categories? Hegel believed that he surmounts this difference because the Logos is more than itself. It is the dialectical identity of being and sense.

available in its absence, and to evoke it as absence: "It is no longer the thing itself which is there, but me, the one who remembers the thing, interiorizes it. I no longer see, I no longer hear the thing, but I have seen it, I have heard it." In this way, memory is like the interior of being, its return to the seed, its recollection; memory raises the concrete determinations of intuition to the universality of pure knowledge. By negating the sensible, the "I" still preserves it as an echo. It imagines the absence. It refers itself to what is not there in what is there, to what is there in what is not there. The *imagination* is symbolic and indicates the sense. This is why this memory, which interiorizes the world, exists only through the other memory which externalizes the "I." *Erinnerung* exists only through *Gedächtnis*: the interiorization of that about which one speaks exists only through the complete exteriority of the one who speaks. This exteriority, the open system of language and speech, is thought in itself (*Gedächtnis = Denken*), the thought that turns itself into a thing, a sensible being, a sound, while the thing itself is negated, interiorized into thought. *Language's memory*, with all its complex articulation, is the identity of being and thought. To understand the intimate connection of these two memories and their inseparability (which Bergson has not done in his *Matter and Memory*, because he starts from the opposition of intuitive sense and discourse, and because he believes that he has criticized all language by means of criticizing one specific language) is to understand thereby even the concrete identity of the immediate and the universal, to catch a glimpse already of the reason why the Logic will be able to treat immediate being, the structure of the sensible, while remaining in the universe of significations. Hegel therefore insists with justification on the speculative importance of this exteriority of thought in language, and not only on its practical and pedagogical importance. Language is learned and lived; it is the being of thought. Through this objective memory (*Gedächtnis*), the existent, sonorous language, and signification are unified.

> Memory is in this manner the passage into the activity of thought, which no longer has a sense, i.e. its objectivity is no longer severed from the subjective, and its interiority does not need to go outside for its existence. . . . To comprehend the position and sense of memory and to understand its organic interconnection with thought is one of the hardest points, and hitherto one quite unregarded in the theory of spirit. Memory *qua* memory is itself merely the external mode, or merely existential aspect of thought, and thus needs a complementary element. The passage from it to thought is to our view or implicitly the identity of reason with its

existential mode: an identity from which it follows that reason only exists in a subject and as the function of that subject.
Thus active reason is thought. (ES §464)

The memory interior to things exists only in and through this exteriority
of narrative, or through the one who says the things themselves—and,
without knowing it, still says himself—since he says the things as
thoughts. The one who speaks has transposed all sensible diversity into
the element of its universality. He knows, still without knowing it explicitly, that he recognizes himself in this knowledge, "Intelligence is recognition" (ES §465), although he is heard and he hears himself. The epic
poet, become universal consciousness, narrates his world which is the
world: "His pathos is not the stupifying power of nature but *Mnemosyne*,
awareness and a gradually developed interiority, the recollection
through memory of the formerly immediate being" (PH §729). This recollection is the first universality, the primordial language, the *epos*.
    Imagination therefore raises itself from intuition to actual repre-
sentation through the *symbol* and the *sign* in which the sensible transcends itself. Objective memory posits at the same time the identity of
the sign and the signification. In the symbol, the present intuition and
the absent symbolized content still have something in common. They
resemble one another, just as onomatopoeias suggest what they designate, just as symbolic writing (or hieroglyphs) preserves fixed represen-
tative elements, elements that are abstract by means of an arbitrary
slicing up of the sensible. Intelligence is still the prisoner of the external
datum, and of an analysis in invariant notions, an analysis which is the
opposite of the mutual relation of determinations, the opposite of the
totality immanent to the particular determinations. Hegel says somewhere that natural language, the child of intelligence, actually makes
possible the dialectical discourse in which conceptual determinations not
only are characterized by their context but also are apt to enrich their significations by means of the discourse which posits them and sublates
them. The passage from the symbol to the sign, whose history we could
follow in an anthropology, presents the dialectical negation of the sensible, of the pure datum affecting the "I" in intuition. Already the *enigma* is
more than the symbol. The pyramid has no relation to the dead pharaoh.
It invites the imagination to sublate itself towards an unknown secret,
but there is no particular secret: "The Egyptian enigmas were enigmas
for the Egyptians themselves." The sensible is not what it appears to be;
by itself, it negates itself, like the sounds of the voice which are no longer
there as soon as they are there, and which nevertheless extend themselves into one another. In the pure sign, however, in pronounced words,
or in written words which are signs of signs, the sensible is reduced

down to the minimum. It does not count for itself. The ideal is to speak without accent, and, for the educated man, reading is deaf and writing is mute. The sensible has no resemblance to the represented content; it signifies the content but is not itself what it signifies. The sensible becomes the signified by means of language's creative memory which, at first pure arbitrariness, fixes then this Universe of language and gives to it the solid consistency of the being that is found and always taken up. "In its pure state, the sign is first an immediate intuition which represents a content wholly other than what it is itself" (ES §458). In principle, this arbitrariness is an essential moment. It must be the case that the sensible completely transcends itself as sensible, that intelligence finds itself in an exteriority which is completely *its own*, a being which, while remaining entirely being, is nevertheless its creation, an alienation of itself into itself. This is why the anthropological origin of language, the existence of onomatopoeias for example, is not the essential problem for Hegel. With Hegel, the issue is not exactly that of a history. In contrast to the symbol, and even to the sensible suggestions of the enigma, in the sign as such, the proper content of intuition, which is a "here now," and the content of which it is the sign in no way agree. Likewise, one will have to forget the sign's musicality in order to see or hear in it the signification alone. Insofar as intelligence becomes signifying intelligence, it raises itself above symbolic imagination. It masters the sensible, although it turns itself into being and exteriority. It posits absolutely as *its own* this intuition of the sign and it posits *itself* in this intuition. It does not however exist elsewhere; it is this position. Language is not a translation. Memory exercises therefore a new negation upon the sensible sign as such. What it is itself disappears, is no longer heard or seen, and in its place we hear and see signification. In the sentence, we hear and see the becoming of sense. Signification is there in the exteriority of language. For us, the signs are the significations themselves. Thus intelligence is rendered external to itself, objective. It has even sublated its arbitrary creation since it finds itself in language and lives in it. Intelligence finds sense, interiority, the opposite of being, as a being, and it finds the being, the opposite of sense, as a signification. It is as if a natural thing were completely becoming signification and the life of sense, visible and audible sense, without any alien support. It was becoming the life of sense by yet remaining something natural and by reflecting itself.

The universal "I," interiority, exists only in language; there is no interior sense which subsequently would be expressed. "In sensible intuition, the 'I' finds determinations; in language what is its own comes to be for it like something found" (ES §463). Language precedes the thought of which it is nevertheless the expression, or if you like, thought precedes itself in this immediacy. Language refers only to itself, sublates itself only in language, and it is in this sense that we can call it natural. Symbolic imagination is in relation to language what the dream is in relation to wakefulness. "The world, nature, are no longer a realm of images which have no Dasein, but a realm of names. This realm of images is spirit dreaming which concerns itself with a content which has no reality, no Dasein. Its wakefulness is the realm of names. . . . Now alone do the images have a truth. The one who dreams cannot distinguish himself from the one who is awake, but the one who is awake can distinguish himself from the one who dreams." If, in the sign's arbitrary creation, the represented content seems to be something other than the intuition which represents it, this difference disappears in objective memory. "Making its own this connection which is the sign, intelligence, by this memory elevates the single synthesis to a universal, i.e. permanent, synthesis, in which word and sense are for it objectively united and renders the intuition (which the word originally is) a representation" (ES §461). This elevation from an arbitrary creation to a permanent system which is the "I" itself in its self-exteriority indeed therefore sublates the intended difference between the signification and the name.

> We think things in words without having recourse to sensible images. The name is thus the thing so far as it exists and counts in the realm of the understanding. In the name, memory has and recognizes the thing, and with the thing it has the name apart from intuition and image. . . . Given the name lion, we neither need the actual vision of the animal, nor its image even: the name alone, if we understand it, is the simple and unimaged representation. We think in names. (ES §462)

Moreover the name does not refer to the sensible, but the sensible refers to the name, to the universe of expressed and expressible significations:

> Through language we say the true being of the thing. What is this? We respond by saying, it's a lion, something wholly other than what is in the intuition. There is its true being, its essence. Through the name, the object, as being, is born a second time. Such is the creative power that spirit exercises. Adam gave a name to everything. Man speaks to things in the same way as he does to what is his own, and lives in a spiritual nature, in his world, and such is the being of the object, being as sense.[5]

---

5. Hegel, *Jenenser Realphilosophie*. 1805–6, p. 183. Ed. Lasson, Hoffmeister. [Translated from Hyppolite's French.—TR.]

It is language which reveals this being as sense on condition of understanding thereby the system that sublates itself, the discourse that anticipates logical thought,[6] and that constantly enlarges the name-concept—already an originary proposition—through its connections with other determinate concepts. In order to specify a signification, this discourse refers not to a sense which would be behind language but to other significations, themselves expressed and expressible. Like universality, the "I" is immanent to the totality of discourse. The "I" sub-tends it, but without ever distinguishing itself from it, because the insufficiencies of language are as well insufficiencies of thought, and vice versa. As we have already said, words are then no longer external to one another. They are structured in a way that can be more or less contingent or necessary according to the nature of this language; but in philosophical dialectic this language tends towards the unity of intuitive understanding and discursive understanding, towards the unity that is the soul of Hegelian logic. Language as life is thus the intellectual intuition which exists only through its discursive development, the dialectical structuring of all the determinations as moments of this unique intuition. This is why Hegel calls this universe of discourse the space of names: "As the existence of the content in intelligence, the name is the exteriority of intelligence itself. The memory of the name is at the same time the alienation into which theoretical spirit posits itself outside of itself. Thus it is being—a space of names. There is a multiplicity of names, of multiple connections among them. The 'I' is their universal being, their power, their connection."[7] But this "I," the one who speaks, finds itself only in and through language. It does not exist elsewhere as a true or universal singularity. To understand the name is to go from signification to signification. It is to transcend language with language. Intelligence in its entirety is in this system to which it has given birth, but outside of which it cannot find itself.

We have seen that this language is the supreme moment of *representation*, the passage to thought. The texts of the *Encyclopaedia* show us then how this language which is thought in itself (*Gedächtnis*) becomes thought for itself, how the thought of being which constitutes language becomes the thought of thought, without it being the case that this reflection on language itself emerges from language. The movement through which the sensible, across the symbol and the sign, raises itself to

---

6. *Encyclopaedia, The Philosophy of Spirit*, §459: "it is this logical instinct which gives rise to grammar."

7. *Real-philosophie d'Iéna* and *Encyclopaedia, The Philosophy of Spirit*, §463.

thought, is the same as that through which the universal "I" exteriorizes itself. It is there, in language. This is why the alien content, that of which one speaks, has become a thought, that of the one who speaks. By thinking being, thought therefore thinks itself. Its discourse on being becomes a discourse on itself, a discourse on its discourse.

> In the name, intelligence knows the thing: but now it finds its universal in the double signification of the universal as such, and of the universal as immediate or as being—finds that it is the genuine universal which is its own unity overlapping and including its other, being. Thus intelligence in itself knows for itself; in it the universal, its production, the thought is the thing: it is the simple identity of the subjective and the objective. It knows that what is thought, is, and that what is, only is in so far as it is a thought; for itself, the thinking of intelligence is to have thoughts: these are its content and object. (ES §465)

However, this identity of thought and reflection is at this level still only a formal identity. As the reflection of its identity, thought is opposed to its thoughts insofar as they are determinate, and attributes to them an alien source for the content. Hegelian logic as ontology will be concerned with sublating such a distinction.

It is quite remarkable, however, to see reflection, the thought of thought, appear in the *Encyclopaedia*'s dialectic in a form different from that in which it appears in the *Phenomenology of Spirit*. In fact, reflection, this passage from thought in itself to thought for itself, is considered in the *Encyclopaedia* as a necessary passage. After an opposition of reflection to the thought of the content, it will lead to the dialectical identity which is the soil of the Logic (which this philosophy of language prepares), to an identity which will show that reflection is the very reflection of being in thought, and as well that thought is the thought of being. In contrast, the *Phenomenology* studies the anthropological conditions of this reflection; it starts from human, properly subjective, reflection in order to sublate it, in order to show that this *Phenomenology*, this human itinerary, leads to absolute knowledge, to an ontological reflection which the *Phenomenology* presupposes. If we just stayed with the *Phenomenology*, by separating it from its conclusion as well as from its preface, we would remain at a humanism, at a philosophical anthropology, and the Logic, the Logos of Being, which is of such importance to Hegel, would be incomprehensible. In the *Encyclopaedia*—where, moreover, the *Phenomenology* is replaced as an introduction to absolute knowledge by a study of "the diverse positions of thought in regard to objectivity"—absolute knowledge is introduced directly. But Hegel does not disavow the *Phenomenology*, which he mentions in this study (EL §25, addition). The two works correspond to one another. The one, the *Phenomenology of Spirit*, is a theory of experience which presents the content of experience, as if its source was alien to knowledge, but which shows that this experience presupposes absolute knowledge. The *Phenomenology* establishes the soil of absolute knowledge, the universal consciousness of being on the basis of human experience and on the basis of the finitude of this experience. The other starts from universal self-consciousness which *is* at the same time as it *thinks*, whose language is the identity of this being and this reflection. It no longer makes the distinction characteristic of experience, the distinction between truth and certainty. The concept, such as it appears in this dialectical discourse, is simultaneously truth and certainty, being and sense; it is immanent to this being which says itself. This is why it appears, at the end of the Logic, not only as the being which is sense through the mediation of reflection, but also as the sense which is. But this mediating reflection is no longer an external or subjective reflection; it is the very reflection of being. In the *Phenomenology*, with the figures of consciousness and in a concrete form, experience discovers the determinate moments which are found again in the *Logic*'s dialectical discourse. But this discourse is no longer a discourse on experience, tarnished with subjectivity, always reflecting on its own subjectivity, a still-human discourse; it is the discourse which says universal being in itself and for itself. It is the Absolute itself which says itself as universal self-consciousness. In the *Phenomenology*'s Preface and in the chapter on absolute Knowledge, Hegel specifies this correspondence between the theory of experience and philosophical Logic:

> Whereas in the phenomenology of spirit each moment is the difference of knowledge and truth, and is the movement in which that difference is sublated, science on the other hand does not contain this difference and the sublation of it. On the contrary, since the moment has the form of the concept, it unites the objective form of truth and of the knowing self in an immediate unity. The moment does not appear as this movement of passing back and forth, from consciousness or representation into self-consciousness and conversely: on the contrary, its pure shape, freed from its appearance to consciousness, the pure concept and its onward movement, depends solely on the its pure determinateness. Conversely, to each abstract moment of science corresponds a shape of manifest spirit as such. (PH §805)

Absolute knowledge is the immediate knowledge which is reflection into itself, the being which is universal self-consciousness, universal self-consciousness as being. This is why it can appear to itself in a Phenomenology when, starting from immediate knowledge, it becomes knowledge *of* the immediate and shatters the concept, the Logos, into its internal moments, that of truth, of the in-itself, and that of certainty, of the for-itself. "Science contains within itself this necessity of externalizing the form of the concept, and it contains the passage from the concept into consciousness" (PH §806). The spirit that knows itself turns into, as difference, certainty *of* immediacy. The *Logic* therefore explains the *Phenomenology*. Philosophy, Hegel says, must alienate itself. Experience and the Logos are not opposed. The discourse of experience and the discourse of being, the *a posteriori* and the *a priori*, correspond to one another and mutually require one another. There would be no possible experience without the presupposition of absolute knowledge, but the path of experience points ahead to absolute knowledge. It is true that the historicity of this absolute knowledge poses at the very heart of Hegelianism new and perhaps unsolvable problems.

This absolute knowledge is the intellectual intuition immanent to the dialectical discourse which in language is the identity of determinate thoughts and of the thought which thinks itself in them, and thinks itself only by fixing itself at these determinate thoughts, by stopping at these determinations in order to penetrate them and see them become. In this discourse, being itself reflects itself and expounds itself as intelligible speech. This philosophical logic assumes therefore that the thought which is there in language is at the same time the thought of thought, the discourse of the self in the discourse of being, and that this discourse of the self, this reflection, remains at the same time the discourse of being. If this unity is not realized, only a formal reflection that opposes itself to the content exists. Dogmatism, Empiricism, Skepticism are the diverse attitudes that Hegel describes and presents at different stages of the *Phenomenology*. Sometimes thought strays into sensible experience as such and it happens that it does not raise itself up out of this immediacy; at other times, it reflects on its own subjectivity and always raises itself up over that of which it speaks:

> [F]ormalistic thinking . . . argues back and forth in thoughts
> that have no actuality. . . . [A]rgumentation is freedom from
> all content, and a sense of vanity towards it. What is looked
> for here is the effort to give up this freedom, and, instead of
> being the arbitrarily moving principle of the content, to sink
> this freedom in the content, letting it move spontaneously of
> its own nature, by the self as its own self, and then to contem-

plate this movement. This refusal to intrude into the immanent rhythm of the concept, either arbitrarily or with wisdom
obtained from elsewhere, constitutes a restraint which is itself
an essential moment of the concept. (PH §58)

Pure empiricism and formalism that is idle talk complete one another.
The *Logic*'s dialectical discourse is neither the discourse of experience
(with its reflection which assumes the concrete relation of human self-
consciousnesses), nor formal discourse about discourse, which is empty
or which is the idle talk of conversation. It is the authentic unity of that
of which one speaks and of the one who speaks, of being and of the self,
the sense which appears only in the medium of intelligible language. We
have tried to show, with Hegel, the strict unity of "that of which one
speaks" and of "the one who speaks," the dialectical transposition of the
sensible into the "I," and the exteriorization of the "I." However, this
unity is expressed in different ways in the *Phenomenology* and in the
Logic. At the level of the *Phenomenology*, there is a sort of debate between
the one who speaks and the world of which he speaks, a debate with
those to whom he speaks and who hear him as he hears himself. This
debate constitutes the very dialectic of human experience. There is, however, a permanent ambiguity concerning the variable limit of the two
terms. The one who speaks reduces that of which he speaks to his own
human subjectivity, or he projects it into an in-itself which turns out later
to be in-itself only for him. At the level of formalism and of idle talk, the
one who speaks always withdraws from that of which he speaks; he
attempts to save his subjectivity by withdrawing from all objective content. In relation to philosophical dialectic, this idle talk is inauthenticity
itself. It is no longer the debate with the world or with others and it is
not the authentic language of being such as Hegel's Logic tries to present it.

   This Logic says being—a little like the epic poet saying the
world in his primordial language—but it says being by replacing merely
representational thought with the rigor of the concept. How does this
language of the concept differ from two other fundamental languages,
that of the poet and that of the mathematician?

Donner un sens plus pur aux mots de la tribu.[1]

CHAPTER 3

PHILOSOPHICAL DIALECTIC, POETRY, AND MATHEMATICAL SYMBOLISM

In language, being says itself across man, but all language is not authentic. Beyond the language of experience and beyond inconsistent and subjective idle talk, philosophy must also be distinguished from poetry and mathematical symbolism. In order to avoid the one, it is always tempted to move closer to the other. The poet speaks the language of representation which seems to be a middle term between the sensible and the

---

1. This quote comes from Stéphane Mallarmé, "Le Tombeau d'Edgar Poe" in *Oeuvres Completes* (Paris: Bibliothèque de la Pléiade, Gallimard, 1945), 70: "To give a purer sense to the words of the tribe." This translation is by Mary Ann Caws (Stéphane Mallarmé, *Selected Poetry and Prose* [New York: New Directions, 1982], 51).—Tr.

concept. Poetry is the very birth of language, the elevation to thought. Representation mixes that of which one speaks with the one who speaks, the objective with the subjective. It is not genuine mediation and this is why it occupies an ambiguous position. Like the symbol or the enigma, poetry refers to an alien in-itself that shines through without appearing completely. It mixes particular being with universal sense. It does not conceive the genuine unity which will be, for Hegel, speculative unity. Poetry, however, is prior to the severe and divisive distinctions of the understanding. The poetical world is a world in which the abstract universal and the distinct particular are still not separated as they will be in the *prose of the world*, this prose which Cervantes's work depicts so well by opposing the understanding's cold, stripped world to Don Quixote's objectless imagination.[2] The primordial unity of the universal and the particular, of the objective and the subjective, is felt and foreshadowed by the poet. He is nostalgic for it. Poetry, which encompases literature in general for Hegel (the novel is for him the modern form of the epic and what is novelistic is the survival of the poetic in the prose of the world), lives in the medium of language. And yet, like the prior arts whose truth poetry is, it seems to be also like a sort of dream in relation to the sense which would exist as such. Poetry's existence refers to this sense, but, when this sense exists in turn as such, poetry stops existing. The dialectical discourse of the logic is no longer poetry, although it is closer to poetry than to the understanding's abstract discourse. The prose of the world, which claims to delimit very exactly an empirical truth and a subjective illusion, begins with the understanding. The empirical sciences are the work of the understanding, and history, which was at first poetry as memory, becomes an exact science, or at least claims to be one.[3] While poetry tends to rediscover reflectively the primitive magic of language, the understanding smashes the concrete representation into its elements which are fixed and determinate. The poetic mixture and literary symbolism are dissolved. Language wants to be then the expression of a thought which has for its guarantee the subtle fixity of the "I" in each considered determination. The one who speaks guarantees the permanence of these determinations. He is himself this formal permanence, this abstract tautology of a content which holds in the particularity of its distinct determination. As always, empiricism and formalism are

---

2. Cf. Jean Hyppolite, "Le Tragique et le rationnel dans la philosophie de Hegel," in *Figures de la pensée philosophique*, 1:260. For Hegel's use of the phrase, "the prose of the world," or "the prose of life," see *The Philosophy of History*, 288 and *Hegel's Aesthetics: Lectures on Fine Arts*, 150.—Tr.

3. On this point and on the different forms of history, see Hegel's introduction to the philosophy of history.

complementary. The understanding subsumes determinations under determinations, or coordinates them; the formal "I" ties all these determinations back together, the external order. But precisely thereby it remains alien, just as abstract unity remains alien to multiplicity. Characterized in this way, the understanding always distinguishes that of which it speaks (the content), from the one who speaks (the form). The understanding is finite because it refers to a content whose origin is transcendent, and because it surveys this content from above, either in order to constitute empirical sciences with it or in order to talk idly about it, and thus to preserve the "I" in its sterility by always keeping the "I" outside of the content.

In these two cases, poetic discourse and the discourse of the understanding, the philosopher is in inauthenticity. The cause, however, of this inauthenticity must be sought in the very condition of man, simultaneously natural Dasein and universal self-consciousness. This condition defines representation as the equivocal mixture of that of which one speaks and of the one who speaks; it defines as well the understanding as the divisive distinction between a diversified content and a form. The one who speaks in poetry is the universal destiny of which he speaks as well as the man who narrates. Representation sublates man and falls back into man. It springs from its natural Dasein. Like the Pythian sayings, it expresses the primary unity or attempts to rediscover it; it is closer to immediate knowledge than to the understanding. In the *Phenomenology* therefore Hegel follows—before taking it up again in *The Lectures on Aesthetics*—the development of poetry from the epic up to comedy, passing through tragedy (PH §§699–747). In comedy, the mask is thrown away, and the universal falls back into man. This disappearance of all transcendence, however, results only in the platitude of the prose of the world in which the man who becomes the center—but center as natural Dasein—is seen as the prey of a new dialectic, a dialectic which does not amuse its victim, but amuses rather the one who happens to be the spectator of it. Certainly, ancient comedy was a happy consciousness since it represented "the return of everything universal into self-certainty" (PH §747). Connecting itself, however, to natural Dasein and wanting to confer on it an arbitrary fixity, this certainty is in turn comic for the spectator. Modern comedy is this very dialectic, that of the man who gives the seal of the Absolute to the finite as such, to the loved woman, to propriety, to particular contracts, to health, and is powerlessly present at the dissolution of all of what he took as assured, a dissolution that is tragic for him, comic for the others.

Such as it appears in absolute knowledge, speculative philosophy too will indeed be the disappearance of all transcendence, the return "into self-certainty," but self-certainty as universal self, the self of the content and not the merely human self. With equal reason, it will be neither an anthropologism nor a humanism. It will be a philosophy of the Absolute which exists as the Logos only in language. It will think and say the genuine unity of the being of which one speaks and of the one who speaks, of truth and of certainty, but after a sublation of the human, a sublation similar to the one in which the sensible sign passes away into signification. It will be a *reduction* of the human condition. The Logic's dialectical discourse will be the very discourse of Being, the *Phenomenology* having shown the possibility of bracketing man as natural Dasein. The discourse of the understanding is, on the one hand, a human discourse on being since it grasps content as alien to the "I," and since this formal "I" coincides in fact with the particular determinations of an empirical "I." Abstract person and contingent individual are opposed only in appearance because they coincide at the base and because the one is merely the formal lining of the other. The understanding, however, is an essential moment, as Hegel indeed shows in the *Phenomenology*'s preface. Philosophy would not be able to remain at poetry's primitive prophecies, at this primordial unity which resists dissociation; it must pass through the understanding's analysis. After having shown the defects of the understanding, the *Phenomenology*'s preface praises its power, which is the very power of dividing and distinguishing. The understanding, however, which triumphs in mathematics, is a reflection external to the very thing of which it speaks. This is why its language becomes mathematical symbolism. Sense—which is the concept itself—is erased in favor of a calculus. Philosophical demonstration, dialectical discourse, is of a wholly other order. It is the movement of the demonstrated thing, and it does not function by means of rules applied to the content from the outside. The "I," the one who speaks, is not then fixed in each determination, or beyond all the determinations as a formal "I." Rather, the "I" gives itself up to the life of the content whose self it becomes. Determinations stop being alien to the "I" since it is immanent to them, and it itself stops being separate from these determinations. As in poetry's primordial language, the universal and the particular are gathered together, but this is no longer an ambiguous mixture because each determination is posited for itself, with all the rigor of discursive understanding, and yet by being reflected into itself, the determination becomes. Reason states this mediation. Its sense is there. This is why Hegel considers the reduction of reason to a calculus a misunderstanding of the nature of the concept, just as every return to poetry or to literature seems to him the abandonment of conceptual rigor. The philosopher's dialectical discourse passes over these two abysses, poetry and mathematical manipulation. What is essential is the unity of the "I" and its determinations as mediation and as sense.

Thoughts become fluid when pure thinking, this inner immediacy, recognizes itself as a moment, or when the pure certainty of self abstracts from itself—not by leaving itself out, or
setting itself aside, but by giving up the fixity of its self-positing, by giving up not only the fixity of the pure concrete,
which the 'I' itself is, in contrast with its differentiated content, but also the fixity of the differentiated moments which,
posited in the element of pure thinking, share the unconditioned nature of the 'I.' Through this movement the pure
thoughts become concepts, and are only now what they are
in truth, self-movements, circles, spiritual essences, which is
what their substance is. (PH §33)

How can language become the medium of this dialectical discourse? It *is prior to thought*, in the precise sense that Hegel gives to this
word. It is the supreme moment of representation and this is why poetry
precedes prose, precedes the prose of the world as much as that of the
understanding. But also *it expresses* the thought which is known or
reflected only in it. In language, thought insofar as it is signification is
there immediately; it exists as a thing. It finds itself outside of itself. This
is why the logical dialectic will be a dialectic of being. It will say immediate being before it says essence, which is reflection just as signification is
reflection in relation to the sign. But reflection in its turn is; it is immediately as sense within the totality of discourse. As we have described it,
language presents the passage from the sensible to the sense which
makes being say itself, which makes being be self-consciousness.
However, this passage, as much as this reflection of thought in language,
allows one to understand poetic discourse as well as the illusion of the
understanding which believes itself able to create an adequate system of
signs in order to resolve or dissolve problems. Language *precedes and
expresses thought*. This contradiction is the source of poetry and the exag-
gerations of symbolic calculation (whose development Hegel could only
foresee and whose claim to replace conceptual sense he condemns in
Leibniz). To say that language is prior to thought means that thought is
not a pure sense which could exist somewhere else, outside of its expression, like an essence beyond appearance. Thought is only by already
being there, only by preceding itself, in this speech which refers to nature
and to anthropology by means of its sonorous material, in this speech
which precedes the understanding by means of its grammatical structure, sketching in a way, at times prolifically, at other times insufficiently,
the understanding's forms. This speech, in which the sensible sign disappears so that we hear the signification, is still in its form submerged in
the sensible, while in its depth it gathers together that of which one

speaks and the one who speaks, without distinguishing them clearly. One of Hegel's disciples, Benedette Croce, said that the first word was a poetic word and turned language into intuition-expression, the first aesthetic moment of theoretical activity. He thus developed certain aspects of the dialectical genesis of language that we have described. Poetry precedes philosophy, just as music in principle precedes poetry in the Hegelian system of the fine arts. Music, however, like all the arts is pure appearance of signification; poetry reveals this by saying something. "In Orpheus's miracles, sounds and their movements were really sufficent to tame the wild animals that came to lie about him, but not the men who require the content of a more elevated doctrine." Still as a reminiscence, poetry preserves this musicality in the signification. In its content, poetry, primordial language, the epic, which one has to distinguish from a reflective poetry opposing itself to prose, makes no claim to the understanding's exactitude-truth; it naively mixes that of which one speaks with the one who speaks. It does not distinguish the real from the imaginary, the poetic narrative from the understanding. This distinction begins with the fable or the comparison which is indeed careful to put the signification, the spiritual sense, on one side, and the particular content which serves as its example on the other. The prose of the world is born, and with it this separation instituted by the understanding, between an essential interior and an inessential exterior. It is still the understanding which claims to delimit the fictive narrative and the true narrative. Poetry then exists for the philosopher as a nostalgia, an immediate language which evokes an authentic, but lost, language of being. Moreover, it was not naturally immediate in the signification because it assumed already the technical concern of expression as such, the elaboration of a discourse molded out of human memory.[4]

Hegel does not consider language to be exclusively poetic; in the representation, it already announces the understanding. Since it is existing signification, language appears as the negation of the sensible in the sign itself; it is really the signification itself that I hear in speech and that I see in writing. Language's progress, at the heart of representation, is this disappearance of the sensible which manifests it. Onomatopoeias disappear, grammar is simplified and becomes more general, a mass of trivial distinctions which gives rise to direct symbolism coalesce when the symbol becomes solely a sign. The same happens in written language; hieroglyphs are merely primitives. The return to a symbolic writing, like Leibniz's dream of a universal characteristic, is not only utopian

---

4. Hegel considers poetry to be pre-reflective. There is, however, a poetry that strives to reconstruct primordial language after reflection.

but also absurd according to Hegel, because the progress of thought continually changes the nature and the relation of the objects of thought. One would therefore constantly need new symbols corresponding to new discoveries and to new relations of thought. This universal characteristic, which would assume an empirical analysis of things, would always be lagging behind these advances. The illusion of the understanding, however, is tenacious. It pushes the negation of the sensible to the limit and takes into consideration only the *expression* of thought in language, as if signification could be an interiority without exteriority. It imagines then the pure creation of a system of signs, or rather of symbols which would be better adapted than verbal language to the significations. It repairs language on the basis of a thought isolable in principle and claims thereby to eliminate all the equivocations and ambiguities of language and of speech, as if thought did not precede itself or did not presuppose itself in being. This presupposition appears to the understanding to be contradictory; in certain respects, it is in fact contradictory and this is why language is speculative. The understanding, however, misunderstands the speculative. Its critique of language can be valuable only up to a certain point beyond which, the external and the internal being separated, thought (under the pretext of expressing itself adequately) ends up losing all sense and being reduced to a calculus which is an exterior manipulation of symbols. These symbols can indeed designate or signify something, but they are treated only as sensible elements external and indifferent to one another. Thus according to Hegel, this requirement of purity results in an external manipulation, in a blind thought, for which we could substitute a machine. This illusion, however, is sustained by the example of the rigorous demonstrations and the exact calculations of mathematics, demonstrations and calculations which make the philosopher jealous. A mathematical algorithm exists. Why couldn't philosophical thought imitate the rigor of mathematical demonstrations? Why couldn't logic present itself as a calculus with symbols similar to those found in algebra? In this way it would avoid the equivocations of natural language. Hegel tries to make the distinction between mathematics and philosophy precise. Dialectic has nothing to do with mathematical demonstrations, and the authentic logic has nothing to do with algebraic calculations. Although Hegel could not foresee the development of formalism and contemporary logistics, or the importance of this formalism which tends to envelop logic and mathematics in one single discipline, his premature critique remains valuable, at least against the claim of this formalism to replace verbal language for the purpose of stating philosophical problems. Hegelian logic is the opposite of this formalism; it looks for the sense of the very form. For Hegelian logic, to treat the concept, the judgment and reason, by replacing the words of language with symbols and by applying to these symbols operational rules from the outside, is to descend from the sense which is immanent to them to a prior domain; it is to return to immediate being. For Hegel, even mathematics is only the category of quantity which is expressed in nature by indifferent diversity. The *logoi* however are different from the *mathemata*. Philosophical dialectic is *logos*; it is the discourse to which sense is always immanent, a sense which is there, in an external way in speech's being, and which expresses itself through the development of words into a discourse. *Being, reflection, sense,* are three moments of language. To stay at language's immediate being is not to sublate the sensible in language itself and to return to poetry which is the premonition of sense in the immediate; but, to attach oneself to reflection is to negate language's substantial element, which allows language to be a language of sense across reflection.

Reflective understanding extends therefore the negation of the sensible already achieved in the verbal sign. Let us suppose in fact that the signification can be isolated from its sensible sign, that it stops being exterior. Language will appear then as a set of clothes covering a body. But, just as clothes can disguise the body, the external form of language will be able to disguise thought. Language dresses up a thought which could receive another, more appropriate set of clothing. We could therefore separate a problem from the language in which it is stated. We could look for more adequate signs in order to formulate it; we could in particular avoid those variations of signification arising from context, that perpetual equivocation and ambiguity of the sense of words. The understanding would like a fixity and an exactitude that is not found in existing language; the idea of creating a pure language, a system of symbols which remain absolutely invariant over the course of the diverse combinations they undergo, comes from this. Perhaps philosophic problems would be posed differently or would be dissolved since they come from certain verbal confusions, from the shiftings of sense found so often in a discourse. A symbolic language would avoid these transformations of a word's signification. By making itself the pure creator of its system of signs, the "I" of the understanding would not find significations already there; it would not be engaged in them as one is already in life when alive. It could take the things up at their base and replace an explicit convention for what is present to it as already agreed upon, for what appears to it as an alienation of its own interiority. The words of language, however, are the "I" outside of itself, finding itself there before actually being there. The "I" continues to be in their mutual relation, in their past arrangement as in their present transformation. It embraces the language which seems to it to be an alienation of itself, and now makes it say what it had never said, with words that were existing in the past. Self-expression makes progress because, across the expressed content (what was there earlier), sense announces itself and states itself in a universal way. The self can never withdraw from this language, from this universal reference which nevertheless, in its exteriority, remains reflection and sense. We read a philosopher and we first take his words in their usual sense; little by little the context constrains us to make imperceptible changes, and the use he makes of context ends up affecting the words with a new signification proper to him, a signification proper to him but nevertheless universal since we understand it. Language, Hegel says, is the self existing as self, and it does not exist anywhere else than in language as singular self and universal self at the same time.

When the understanding claims therefore to strip a problem of its language, it is already the dupe of an illusion; it inevitably leads us to ask this question: What would the problem be without the clothing of its language? There is, however, no naked problem when the issue is philosophical problems; it is impossible to pose Plato's problems differently without changing them radically, without posing different problems. The progress of thought is parallel to the progress of its expression; the one is strictly unified with the other. This is where the difficulty of a translation comes from—and translation is executed as a transposition in the very medium of universal language without passing through a naked sense—the necessity of following the genesis of sense in the very language in which it has been stated in order to seek in another language what is approximately equivalent. What therefore is the word such that it is so indispensible to dialectical discourse, such that we cannot replace it with arbitrarily created symbols, while preserving the fixity of an invariant signification throughout the whole discourse? The word is the concrete universal, the Hegelian concept which is totality. This is why the word does not exist without the proposition whose seed it is, and why the proposition does not exist without the set of propositions which reconstitute this totality as a result. To say that the Absolute is subject is to say that the concept-word is what it is only in the predicates which confer on it its content, only in its relations, but this means as well that these relations constitute a totality, a sense which is a *support* and not a fixed and immobile being. Even when it is not yet explicitly intended as the philosophical dialectic, language indicates this dialectic. It prefigures philosophical dialectic. By considering the different ways in which one can understand the proposition and the relations of propositions among themselves, Hegel can characterize philosophical discourse, in the *Phenomenology*'s preface, in relation to colloquial discourse or in relation to the understanding's discourse. The word, the verbal sign, is not at first arbitrary despite the in principle arbitrariness of the sign. The "I" finds the sign and takes possession of it as an immanent signification which sublates what it seems to be in a singular consciousness. The word *gold*, Leibniz said already, is not only what supports the determinations that the common people attribute to it, but also what supports those that the educated discover. The word expresses a universal harmony which nevertheless is never constituted as such, which is already there. Like the sign, the word remains invariant, but its determinations become precise by means of the diverse relations which are established at the very heart of language. As such, a name is something which is identical in different contexts, but this identity is not a dead identity; it is not an identity of the understanding. The sign exists in the same way; the signification is modified by means of the context. This becoming is certainly the source of equivocations and one can abandon oneself to it, when one is a poet, abandon oneself "to the friendly similarities which shine out from among the words." But we can also seek the coherence of discourse, resist what seems easy, get hold of the determinations again; such is the proper function of the understanding. This coherence, however, cannot be pushed to the limit. The understanding isolates a signification in the proposition which endows the word with its content, the content without which it would be a simple name, a *flattus vocis*. But the understanding sees this signification, immediately asserted, enriching and transforming itself constantly. Although it is necessary to maintain unity and invariance, we maintain this invariance only as mediation, as total sense. This is why the word is the concrete universal and is already discourse, concept, judgment, reason. The immediate being of thought, reflection, mediation, is present naively in colloquial discourse and in the empirical discourse where the word seems to receive its enrichment from the outside, while formal understanding avoids contradiction as much as it can by reconciling its formalism with the heterology of experience. "Just as when I say 'all animals,' this expression cannot pass for a zoology" (PH §20). The word is the universal which still awaits its development, which will be what it is in truth only at the end of the development. In dialectical discourse, however, in the philosophical Logic, the Absolute displays itself as result, as mediation. "The only transition to a proposition contains a becoming other which must be reassimilated or is a mediation." Taken as Logos, language is this totality which is such only through discourse, in which thought, completely immanent to its development, posits itself as sense, stretched across the reflection of its determinations.

This becoming of sense in the diversity of significations is a banal observation. "Go over the list of senses of the word, *Eidos*," Bergson says, "in the Aristotelian dictionary. You will see how much they differ. If we examine two of them which are sufficiently distant from one another, they will seem nearly to exclude one another. They do not exclude one another because the chain of intermediary senses reconnects them. By making the necessary effort to embrace the whole, we notice that we are in the real and not before a mathematical essence that could be summed up in a simple formula."[5] Bergson, however, would like to grasp this reality in an intuition, or express it through an image—an image is already a relapse into intuition—instead of apprehending it in discourse itself, in the development of the signification. For him, verbal language is already the beginning of mathematical symbolism. Verbal language is less pure, but it is also artificial, external to the growth of a thought which could in principle be separated from language. "It is of the essence of science," Bergson writes again, "to handle signs, which it substitutes for the objects themselves. These signs undoubtedly differ from those of language by their greater precision and their higher level of efficiency; they are nonetheless tied down to the general condition of the sign, which is to denote a fixed aspect of reality under a stable form" (CE 329). The creation of these signs by the understanding (or rather the creation of these symbols, for they were first symbols in the strict sense of the term) allows for the permanence, the absolute fixity, the exactitude, which is not found in natural language. But what is thereby gained occurs at the expense of the mobile signification, at the expense of sense. Language's sign *is* signification; it disappears as sensible sign. In contrast, the symbol had value by means of the sensible intuition which represented something; but then the understanding was working simultaneously on the signification and on the sensible. This is why Hegel considers symbolism—in this sense—like a "turning back":

> Since man has in language a means of designation peculiar to
> reason, it is an idle fancy to search for a less perfect mode of
> representation to plague oneself with. . . . If, however, one
> should seriously propose to employ [symbols] for expressing
> and knowing the concept, then the external nature of all sym-
> bols is inadequate to the task; the truth about the relationship
> is rather the converse, namely, that what in symbols is an
> echo of a higher determination, is only truly known through
> the concept and can be approximated to the concept only by
> separating off the sensuous, unessential part that was meant
> to express it. (GL 618)

To turn back from language to the symbol is to manipulate the sensible as such while believing oneself to be manipulating significations, and

---

5. Henri Bergson, *The Creative Mind: An Introduction to Metaphysics*, tr. Mabelle L. Andison (New York: The Philosophical Library, 1946), 34.

what is produced here is a sort of dialectical reversal. In order to create a more pure language, in order moreover to negate the sensible, the understanding ends up considering only the sensible and manipulating it as such. While in language the signification is there, while in the imagination's symbol (which Descartes, for example, uses when he represents all magnitudes by means of lines in the *Regulae*) the signification is an interior, in symbolism pushed to its extreme limit what the symbol represents is no longer important, is not taken into consideration. We indeed still speak of the symbol, but thought intends nothing; thought considers the sign as an immobile, sensible content and no longer as a sign. The signification of the signs which figures in the axioms is not taken into account. We merely manipulate the content by virtue of preestablished rules without coordinating any sort of objects to them. It is a manipulation that presents itself as a tautology, the understanding always conserving the fixity and invariance of its content. The combinations brought about *ex hypothesi*, however, add nothing to those from which we started. The problem of signification is certainly posed at the beginning and at the end, but it is not posed in the middle. There is where the complete separation of the one who speaks from the determinate content of which he speaks takes place. This content is determinate and fixed because it is purely objective. The one who speaks performs only formal operations, operations which add nothing to the content, even though they posit it differently, because the one who speaks is purely and completely subject, distinct from the object, acting from the exterior, without being at the same time the sense of that of which he speaks. The self, however, of which Hegel speaks in philosophic dialectic is the very sense of the content. It inhabits the determinations; it is these determinations in their becoming. The issue could not be, for Hegel, to deny the importance of this symbolism, of this algebra of logic. He would not be able to deny the importance of what this algebra can do for the empirical sciences; he would not be able to deny the importance—perhaps even through the difficulties encountered, through the obstacles never completely surmounted in formalization—of the sense that philosophy can discover in this very formalization. By discovering the principle of this formalization, the issue is only to contest its possible application to philosophical discourse which, for Hegel, is mediation and which, with the help of language, is always concept and sense. What is at issue is to critique the calculus that would claim to replace the investigation of sense that Hegel makes. "[The] operations of arithmetic are an external combining or separation [of numbers], a mechanical operation—indeed, calculating machines have been invented which perform these operations; whereas it is the harshest and most glaring of contradictions when the form determinations of the syllogism, which are concepts, are treated as conceptless material" (GL 684). For Hegel, "the operation of calculus is reduced to a purely external unification or separation." "Leibniz," he says, "makes much of the usefulness of the analysis of combinations for ascertaining not only the forms of the syllogism but also the combinations of other concepts. The operation by which this is ascertained is the same as that by which it is calculated . . . how many throws are possible in a game of dice, . . . , etc. . . . the rational is taken as a dead and conceptless thing, and the characteristic feature of the concept and its determinations as spiritual essences to relate themselves and through this relating to sublate their immediate determination, is ignored" (GL 685). The critique that Hegel addresses to Leibniz's project of a universal characteristic indeed shows that, for him, determinations are a becoming, that they could not remain unchanged like a meaningless, objective content. "Connected with this was a pet idea of Leibniz, . . . the idea of a *characteristica universalis* of concepts—a language of symbols in which each concept would be represented as a relation proceeding from others or in relations to others—as though in the rational combination, which is essentially dialectical, a content still retained the same determinations that it possesses when fixed in isolation" (GL 685). Philosophical dialectic is not, therefore, for Hegel, reducible to a panlogicism in the Leibnizian sense. It is a life already immanent to language as such where sense appears in the mediation. The ontological logic is the antithesis of a formalism. In immediate being, it discovers the thought of being which is immanent to it, and sees in reflection as well a moment which sublates itself and is there immediately as sense. Being itself posits itself and says itself across discourse. And the forms of this discourse are to be considered in their sense and not to be isolated as formal rules exterior to their content. The thought of thought is speculatively the thought of being, just as much as the thought of being is a thought of thought.

Hegel opposes this dialectical discourse to mathematics, the *Logoi* to the *mathemata*. For him as for Kant, mathematics concerns only the sensible world—insofar as this world is space in which is "it is all same whether it increase or diminishes itself"—concerns only the category of quantity, synthesis of indifferent differences. This conception of mathematics lets Hegel see an operation external to the thing itself, an alien reflection, in mathematical demonstration. The thing itself is not demonstrated; the thing itself does not become what we assert about it. Reflection lets us see its properties by means of the constructions that it adds to the thing, and which are not found again in the naked result. Certainly, this result is seen as true, as necessary, but it does not contain its own genesis. Necessity is established through the subject who demonstrates; necessity is therefore really there but not the mediation itself which remains in the subject. The process of the demonstration is a process of knowledge distinct from its object; it is not a movement of the object itself. This is why the dialectic interior to the thing itself is opposed to demonstration; Hegel revalorizes the *Logoi* against the *mathemata*. The *mathemata* are only one moment of the Logoi, the moment of the category of quantity in the logic of being (that is, in the logic of immediacy).[6]

---

6. The Hegelian conception of mathematics, science of magnitudes and of quantity in general, again throws into relief the originality of the dialectic of the logic, which is an autonomous development of the Idea, consciousness being lost in its object. Perhaps, however, the internal development of mathematics is not foreign to such a dialectic; through a curious paradox, Jean Cavaillès speaks of this development of the *mathemata* in his work, *On Logic and the Theory of Science* ["On Logic and the Theory of Science," tr. Theodore Kisiel, in *Phenomenology and the Natural Sciences*, ed. Joseph J. Kockelmans and Theodore Kisiel (Evanston: Northwestern University Press, 1970)] in nearly Hegelian terms. Opposing himself to a transcendental subjectivism that he attributes to Husserl, he writes: "If transcendental logic truly founds logic, there is no absolute logic (that is, governing the absolute subjective activity). If there is an absolute logic, it can draw its authority only from itself, and then it is not transcendental" (400–1). He shows as well the limits of formalism in mathematics: "The mathematical structure possesses an internal coherence which cannot be treated abruptly. Its progressive character is essential and the decisions which neglect this lose themselves in the void" (403–4). Finally the tautological conception of mathematical systems is smashed to pieces: "Only the theories smaller than arithmetic, that is, the theories which may be called quasi-finite, can be nomological. Their development is indeed of a combinatory order, and their domination through the sole consideration of axioms is truly effective. But genuine mathematics begins with the infinite" (405–6). In contrast, Hegel does not grant to mathematics the *comprehension* of the infinite, "a truly conceptual relation, an infinite which escapes from mathematical determination." Cavaillès speaks of a deductive structure, creator of the content that it attains: "The possibility of assembling some privileged assertions at the outset is a source of illusion if we forget the operational rules which alone give them a meaning" (406). As in Hegelian dialectic, there is therefore an internal progression from singular content to singular content. "There is no consciousness which generates its products or is simply immanent to them. In each instance it dwells in the immediacy of the idea, lost in it and losing itself with it, binding itself to other consciousnesses (which one would be tempted to call other moments of consciousness) only through the internal bonds of the ideas to which these belong. The progress is material or between singular essences, and its driving force is the need to surpass each of them. It is not a philosophy of consciousness but a philosophy of the concept which can provide a theory of science. The generating necessity is not the necessity of an activity, but the necessity of a dialectic" (409). If a dialectic proper to mathematics exists in this way, where would it fit in a Logic of being like that of Hegel? Perhaps however, in Hegel, the self is

Natural language appears therefore as the proper medium of philosophic discourse; in natural language, this absolute genesis will be able to be said. This can be done by sublating the purely poetical language that still belongs to representation, by maintaining the understanding's determinations and fixations, but as well by dissolving them or rather by following their own internal dissolution, in a dialectic which engenders the totality of sense. This philosophical discourse indeed recognizes the understanding, but it also displays this understanding's contradictions and their own sublation. "Thus the understanding is a becoming and, as this becoming, it is rationality" (PH §55). We could only say finally that this philosophical language preserves from the total poetic impulse the creative power and the immanence of the whole, and that from the understanding, it preserves the weight and force which restrains the whole movement and stops it from dissipating one sole profound intention into a dispersed extension. Thus the intellectual intuition that is the Logos is simultaneously this total impulse and the permanent weight which restrains and fixes the impulse by allowing it to be realized in a continuous progression. This is why it is also discourse.

---

more immanent to the content than in Cavaillès; on this point, the rapprochement of Cavaillès with Spinoza would be more precise than the rapprochement of Cavaillès with Hegel. Cavaillès makes us think less of the unity of subject and object resulting in sense than of God's infinite understanding in Spinoza and of the passage from true idea to true idea. It is important to consider, however, that we could describe the development of mathematics in dialectical terms, but the question would still concern the relation of this dialectic of *mathemata* (the intermediaries in Plato) with that of the *logoi*. Nevertheless, it is remarkable to note that Cavaillès speaks of a dialectic of *mathemata* in such Hegelian terms.

PART **II**

SPECULATIVE THOUGHT AND REFLECTION

CHAPTER **1**

THE TRANSFORMATION OF METAPHYSICS INTO LOGIC

Descending from the mountain, Zarathustra comes across a hermit who has broken with the human world; while leaving him, Zarathustra whispers: "This old saint does not yet know that God is dead." At the beginning of his *Logic*, Hegel too records the death of metaphysics and compares it to the disappearance of those monks who formerly withdrew from the world in order to offer themselves up to the contemplation of the Eternal: "Who still cares about rational theology? The old proofs of God's existence are cited only for their historic interest or for the purpose of the edification and elevation of the soul. It is an incontestable fact that all interest in the old metaphysics, either for content or for form, or for both simultaneously, has disappeared" (GL 25).

Commonly interpreted, the current Kantian philosophy means that spirit cannot overcome experience. Only on the soil of experience can we think of conquering truths; but these truths are only phenomenal, and the place for an absolute truth remains vacant. At least Kant is still attached to this empty place. In 1772, he proposed to write a theoretical philosophy which would be broken down into Phenomenology and Metaphysics. The Phenomenology has been written—this is *The Critique of Pure Reason*—but the Metaphysics is impossible. Phenomenal truth, however, cannot be set up as absolute truth without contradiction. A mysterious *thing*-in-itself remains, therefore, that will never be the *object* of knowledge. "I have limited knowledge in order to leave room for faith."

Nevertheless, Kantian philosophy is not a positivism *avant la lettre*. It is a transcendental philosophy. If it does not unveil a ground of things which would be susceptible to being known by reason, it deals with the ground of the knowledge of phenomena. The investigation of this ground, the bringing to light of the categories, is the discovery of a logicity of being which replaces the being of logic. The question of the second world, of the intelligible world, remains open, but the world of phenomena is constituted like our understanding, and the conditions of experience are the very conditions of the objects of experience. These categories hold only for experience; they are not categories of the Absolute. Nevertheless, the transcendental logic is already the seed of Hegel's speculative logic, which no longer recognizes the limit of the thing-in-itself. This logic of being replaces the old metaphysics that opened out upon a transcendent world. Hegel does not return to the prior dogmatism; he extends transcendental logic into speculative logic. The categories become the very categories of the Absolute. Lived as sense in this logic, being is not beyond knowledge; it is knowledge itself. The Logos, as speculative life, replaces dogmatic metaphysics. In the object of the old theology, this life was living an alienated existence. Hegel rediscovers it in the immanence of this dialectical discourse of being.

The transformation of the old metaphysics into Logic implies the negation of a transcendent being that reason could know, but which would be an intelligible world over and against this reason. "The Absolute is subject," and not substance. The Absolute is the speculative knowledge of the Logic. "God is accessible only in pure speculative knowledge, and exists only in this knowledge, and is only this very knowledge" (PH §761). Theology was realizing the intelligible beyond intelligence. Hegelian logic recognizes neither the thing-in-itself nor the intelligible world. The Absolute is not thought anywhere else than in the phenomenal world. Absolute thought thinks itself in our thought. In our thought, being presents itself as thought and as sense. And Hegel's dialectical logic, like the logic of philosophy, is the expression of this doctrine of complete immanence which Spinoza had not been able to realize.

The two propositions which bring this reduction of metaphysics to logic into focus, and whose reconciliation is difficult, are the following: *there is no second world; there is however a Logos and an absolute speculative life.* In all of its aspects, the *Phenomenology* presents the critique of the second world that would be behind the first. The Enlightenment was correct, when it was opposed to faith by showing that "believing consciousness has two weights, two measures, it has two eyes and double ears, two languages. To it, every representation is double without any possible confrontation . . . faith lives in two kinds of perception: the one is the perception of sleeping consciousness; the other is the perception of wakeful consciousness" (PH §572). Although a moment of absolute spirit, religion itself is not yet in "the spiritual light of presence." It oscillates between "the colored appearance of the sensible side and the blank night of the supersensible beyond" (PH §177). "The in-itself of the unity proclaimed by revealed religion is not realized or not yet become absolute being-for-itself" (PH §787). This critique of the second world leads one already to think of Nietzsche's critique of the other world, but Nietzsche, in this way, is the adversary of a philosophy of essence. In contrast, Hegel speaks of the Logos, and this Logos, this speculative life, is distinct from nature or finite spirit as it is from empirical knowledge. How are we to reconcile this critique of the second world with the distinction between the Logos and nature, or with the distinction between the ontology (of the Logic) and the *Phenomenology*? Doesn't the Logos look like the essence of this existence realized in nature and in history; doesn't speculative logic, that is, absolute knowledge, look like the essence of phenomenal or empirical knowledge?

At the level of the understanding, the *Phenomenology* criticizes the second world as the world of essence. The understanding sublates the sensible phenomenon. It understands it; it apprehends it according to its truth. But it turns this truth into a being beyond the phenomenon at the same time as it distinguishes this truth from its investigation of the truth, from its subjective certainty. Where there is only one reflection, which is the reflection into the Phenomenon—which is completely phenomenon without remainder: "The supersensible is the sensible and the perceived posited as they are in truth, but the truth of the sensible and of the perceived is to be phenomenon. The supersensible is therefore the phenomenon as phenomenon" (PH §147)—the understanding distinguishes its subjective reflection from the truth itself. The understanding does not see itself in the phenomenon which is still objective for it. It does not see the phenomenon express itself for itself in the understanding itself. This is why the understanding projects the truth into an essence distinct from the appearance and from the understanding itself. This is like a mirage. The phenomenon as phenomenon is the concept, but the understanding does not yet know the nature of the concept:

> This interior is for consciousness an extreme, but, to it, it is also the true, because in it, as in the in-itself, it has at the same time self-certainty and the moment of its being-for-itself. But it is not yet conscious of this ground, for the being-for-itself that the interior should have in itself would be nothing other than the negative movement. Now, to consciousness, this negative movement is still the *objective* vanishing phenomenon; it is not yet its own being-for-itself. For it, the interior is really the concept, but consciousness does not yet know the nature of the concept. (PH §143)

Only when the understanding becomes reason as self-consciousness does it know that "behind the so-called curtain which must cover the interior, there is nothing unless we ourselves penetrate behind it so as to be able to see as much as to have something to see" (PH §165). Through transcendental reflection, Kantian philosophy has really understood that the truth of the phenomenon lies in the for-itself of consciousness, in its categories. It maintained the Interior, however, as an empty place. It has folded its reflection back into a subjectivity which, in order to be transcendental, is nevertheless subjective and even human. This empty Interior is a dream:

> If no further significance attached to the inner world and to our close link with it through the world of appearance [that is, the understanding], then nothing would be left to us but to stop at the world of appearance, i.e., to perceive something as true which we know is not true. Or, in order that there may yet be something in the void—which, though it first came about as devoid of *objective* Things must, however, as *empty in itself*, be taken as also void of all spiritual relationships and distinctions of consciousness *qua* consciousness—in order, then, that in this *complete void*, which is even called the *holy of holies*, there may yet be something, we must fill it up with reveries, *appearances*, produced by consciousness itself. (PH §146)

But this truth of the phenomenon which expresses itself in self-consciousness really looks like the essence in relation to appearance. In the Logos, this truth is the essence of nature and finite spirit, the essence, as absolute knowledge, of empirical or phenomenal knowledge. Hegel does not absolutely reject this consequence; he only does not want to be held to this duality, which belongs to the understanding. There would be on the one side essence, on the other existence, on the one side Logos, on the other nature, on the one side absolute knowledge, on the other empirical knowledge. This separation neglects the living relation that posits each term and reflects it into the other. The Absolute is mediation. Hegel's originality is to put reflection into the Absolute, and, consequently, to surmount the dualism without supressing it. The *rational minimum* is the triad: thesis, antithesis, synthesis. There is no primacy of the thesis which alone would be positive. One has to think the *reflection* of the thesis in the antithesis as much as the antithesis in the thesis, and the synthesis does not make the opposition disappear into a dead unity. A dead unity would be like such a return to the abstract thesis and not "this infinity or this absolute restlessness of pure self-movement" (PH §163). The Absolute is the *appearance* (that is, the reflection) of the thesis in the antithesis and of the antithesis in the thesis, and immediacy, the self-similarity of this infinite reflection. This is why we can think only the entire triad as the rational minimum. The understanding separates the terms, for example, Logos and nature, because it rejects contradiction. Reason, however, thinks the concrete identity that admits the contradiction in the heart of the Absolute. The Logos is the Absolute that negates itself as nature, therefore that contradicts itself in itself and bears in itself this other, *its* other, without which it would not be. Nature therefore appears in the Logos as the alterity of the absolute Idea. But nature is the appearance of the Logos as well as the becoming of spirit. Their identity is posited across their contradiction and this identity that posits itself is absolute spirit. The distinction of the Logos and of nature as essence and existence is not therefore the superposition of two worlds, but is the Absolute as mediation, as contradiction and identity. "There really are two different terms which subsist, they are in itself, they are in itself as opposites, that is, each is the opposite of itself, they are their other and they are only one single unity." We can reproach Hegel for having only stated the difficulty, but not for refusing to see it. He makes logic go through a torsion in order to make it capable of expressing this duality in unity and this unity in duality. Thus, the logic is not only the logic of immediate being, but still the logic of essence or of the reflection of being which appears (*videtur*). And finally it is the logic of the concept or of sense, that is, of the identity of immediate being and its reflection. The Absolute is mediation or internal reflection, identity of itself to itself in its contradiction.

If, in the constitution of his system, Hegel was concerned with the relation of the Logos and nature (to which we shall return in particular), the problem of the relation of empirical knowledge and absolute knowledge concerned him in the *Phenomenology of Spirit*. This problem is that of the coexistence of two knowledges, that of naive or natural consciousness which insofar as it is consciousness is immersed in the exteriority of experience, and absolute knowledge which knows the identity of being and the self. How can consciousness sublate itself? How can it say being without distinguishing itself from this being? How can it live a reflection that is no longer a reflection on the self, no longer a reflection external to the things, and instead live the pure reflection identical to immediacy? *Absolute knowledge is indeed immediate knowledge as universal self-consciousness,* but it is not the knowledge of immediacy; it is not what natural or sensible consciousness is. It does not divide itself, according to the general form of the concept, into (subjective) certainty and (objective) truth by making itself the object of experience for consciousness understood as certainty. Absolute knowledge allows sensible knowledge to be understood just as wakefulness allows sleep to be understood. But that is still not sufficient; one would have to show that sensible knowledge is the becoming of absolute knowledge, that it shows itself as identical to absolute knowledge since it unveils, in the form of experience (what we call the *a posteriori*), the categories that the logic will present in their proper form (what we call the *a priori*). The two knowledges look like they are opposed as philosophic consciousness—what Hegel calls Science—and empirical consciousness. "The standpoint of consciousness which knows objects in their antithesis to itself, and itself in opposition to them, is for Science the antithesis of its own standpoint. The situation in which consciousness knows itself to be at home is for Science one marked by the absence of Spirit. Conversely, science's ether is for consciousness a remote beyond in which it no longer possesses itself" (PH §26). Absolute knowledge cannot be imposed on empirical knowledge:

> When confronted with a knowledge that is without truth, Science can neither merely reject it as an ordinary way of looking at things, while assuring us that its Science is a quite different sort of cognition for which that ordinary knowledge is of no account whatever: nor can it appeal to the vulgar view for the intimations it gives us of something better to come. By the former assurance, Science would be declaring its power to lie simply in its being; but the untrue knowledge likewise appeals to the fact that it is, and assures us that for it Science is of no account. One bare assurance is worth just as much as another. Still less can science appeal to whatever intimations of something better it may detect in the cognition that is without truth, to the signs which point in the direction

of Science. For one thing, it would only be appealing again to what merely is; and for another, it would only be appealing to it itself in the mode in which it exists in the cognition that is without truth. In other words, it would be appealing to to an inferior form of its being, to the way it appears, rather than to what it is in and for itself. (PH §76)

Empirical knowledge—the one that is studied, described as such in the *Phenomenology*—experience in general with its development, is the Phenomenon of absolute Knowledge, absolute Knowledge insofar as *it appears*; and absolute Knowledge is phenomenon only insofar as it does not yet know that it itself is what is *appearing* to itself, that its appearance is universal self-consciousness: "In this connection, it makes no difference whether we think of Science as the phenomenon because it comes on the scene alongside another mode of knowledge, or whether we call that other untrue knowledge its mode of presentation" (PH §76). By following phenomenal consciousness in its itinerary, philosophical consciousness, which has already travelled the path, shows that absolute Knowledge already shines through in experience, that experience is absolute Knowledge, but only when it knows itself as absolute knowledge. The difference lies in the fact that absolute knowledge no longer needs to go beyond this experience towards some unknown hidden essence, a sleeping consciousness which would remain somewhere in the background. The difference lies in the fact that universal self-consciousness in the Logos nevertheless is the sought identity of Sense and Being, of the for-itself and the in-itself, and that there reflection is identical to Being.

Speculative logic therefore replaces dogmatic Metaphysics—the metaphysics which was thinking an absolute world of essence, an intelligible world—insofar as speculative logic constitutes itself as the language of being. We must, however, insist upon this point: the illusion of this intelligible world is a sort of inevitable illusion, it corresponds to a moment—but only to a moment—of all dialectic. *Being negates itself and becomes essence, that is, it appears.* Just as the Logos is distinct from nature (and from finite spirit), just as absolute Knowledge is distinct from empirical knowledge, essence, distinct from the phenomenon, is an appearance that is sublated insofar as this Logos *appears* in nature, and nature in the Logos (as alterity), or absolute Knowledge in empirical knowledge. But what is important is that essence appears and it is this fact of *appearing*—the ontological notion corresponding to consciousness—that defines the moment of essence. Every *appearing* refers from one term to another. Every appearing is reflection; but reflection is not only subjective, it belongs to the in-itself, to the being which is subject.

This difference, however, is sublated when this reflection shows itself precisely in this movement of appearing as internal and not as external reflection, as mediation or absolute reflection. Henceforth, appearance is not opposed to essence; it is essence itself. The essence is an appearance just as the appearance is the appearance of essence. As speculative life, the Logos is *Selbst-bewußt-sein* with its three moments: being as immediacy (*sein*), the appearing of being (*bewußt*), and the sense or the self (*selbst*).

Hegel uses an exoteric language when he says of the Logos: "Accordingly, logic is to be understood as the system of pure reason, as the realm of pure thought. This realm is truth as it is without veil and in its own absolute nature. It can therefore be said that this content is the exposition of God as he is in his eternal essence before the creation of nature and a finite spirit" (GL 50). The exoteric character of this language can be seen already in the *it can therefore be said* as well as in the equivocal nature of this priority of the Logos over nature and finite spirit. In fact, for Hegel, there is no divine thought, then a nature and a created, finite spirit. The word *creation* is a word belonging to representation. It states simply that nature and finite spirit (consciousness as such) are always posited in the element of alterity. Just like the Logos, nature is really in itself divine, is in its totality the Absolute, but this totality exists only for the spirit that identifies nature and Logos, which grasps their concrete identity. To replace the old metaphysics with Logic is also to sublate the viewpoint of a substrate prior to its predicates such as, for example, a transcendent God. "For this reason it may be expedient, e.g., to avoid the name 'God,' since this word is not immediately also a concept, but rather the proper name, the fixed point of rest of the underlying subject; whereas, on the other hand, e.g., 'Being,' or 'the One,' 'Singularity,' 'the Subject,' etc. themselves at once suggest concepts" (PH §66). The dialectical discourse of the logic is not a discourse about one thing, about an Absolute which would pre-exist. The dialectical discourse is the Absolute itself insofar as it exists as concrete Universal, insofar as it presents itself freed from this self-exteriority (which is nature or empirical knowledge), but also contains in itself the conception of this very exteriority, the ground of appearance. Since this appearance is, this moment would no more be able to erase itself than the sensible sign would be able to disappear completely in the signification. It disappears as sign, but the signification then appears; the signification is there in a sensible way and it itself comprehends its own appearance. This movement of mediation makes it exist without it having *pre-existed* its own appearance in the form of a completely constituted essence which would be behind the appearance. Here we have a sort of necessary illusion, a sort of ontological unhappy consciousness. "Religion, for example, is the spirit which thinks, but which does not think about itself nor of itself. Therefore this spirit is not self-similarity, not immediacy."[1] Philosophy, in contrast, "is re-established immediacy." It comprehends itself and its alienation in nature and finite spirit. This comprehension does not, however, refer to a transcendent beyond. It does not exist elsewhere than in this absolute knowledge which is, for itself, the certainty "that nature and spirit are in itself one sole being," but they are so only in itself. Spirit becomes the knowledge for itself of this in-itself. This in-itself appears, posits itself, and this position of reflection in immediacy is equivalent to a self-presupposition. The Logos posits itself as presupposing itself in order to get posited. The Absolute presupposes itself but is there only as self-positing. "Of the the Absolute it must be said that it is essentially a result, that only in the end is it what it truly is" (PH §20). Appearance refers to this in-itself which appears, hence the inevitable mirage that the understanding congeals into an irreducible duality. But, by comprehending this mirage, the logic comprehends that the Absolute is this very appearance of one of the terms in the other, and comprehends as well that this appearance, this absolute reflection, is the rediscovered immediacy of sense in the movement of reflection. The congealed duality is then sublated.

Absolute knowledge therefore is a result which presupposes itself in nature and finite spirit. Likewise, the Logos appears first to healthy human understanding "as the realm of shadows." The sciences of the real seem to add their concrete riches to it. However, by returning from these sciences of the real to the Logos, the understanding discovers that the Logos is the light which illuminates every particular truth and makes it exist as truth. "Philosophy is frequently taken to be a purely formal kind of knowledge, void of content, and the insight is sadly lacking that, whatever truth there may be in the content of any discipline or science, it can only deserve the name if such truth has been engendered by philosophy. Let the other sciences try to argue as much as they like without philosophy—without it they can have in them neither life, Spirit, nor truth" (PH §67). We live in the cave without taking into consideration the determinate categories that sub-tend all of our actions and all of our knowledge. We do not make them the theme of our reflection. "What is well-known is badly known" (PH §31), but the supreme interest of thought is to sublate this sensible immediacy, to be raised up to the determinations of the understanding, and to grasp these particular determinations as moments of the absolute form of thought or of the Universal. "As impulses the categories are only instinctively active. At first they enter consciousness separately and so are variable and mutually confusing;

---

1. *Jenenser Realphilosophie* [ed. Lasson-Hoffmeister], 1805–6, p. 272. [This passage is translated from Hyppolite's French.—Tr.]

consequently they afford to spirit only a fragmentary and uncertain actuality; the loftier business of logic therefore is to clarify these categories and in them to raise spirit to freedom and truth" (GL 37). The truth and freedom, however, that are at issue here no longer have anything to do with empirical truth or freedom, as we think of them in everyday life as well as in the particular sciences. They are the absolute form, the universal in itself "which immediately contains being and therein all reality" (PH §299) so that the determinations of this universal are no longer sensible determinations but moments of this unique form, and so that the determinations resolve themselves into the universal just as the universal explains itself in them. "Since immanent self-moving universality is the *sundered* concept, the latter thus has in itself a *content*, and one which is all content, only not a sensuous being. It is a content which is neither in contradiction with the form nor is separated at all from it; rather, it is essentially the form itself, for the latter is nothing else but the universal dividing itself into its pure moments" (PH §299). These moments are ordinarily apprehended as logical laws, as formal laws, which would be related therefore to an alien reality. In fact, they have a determinate content. They are observed in their isolation, but the observation which fixes them and isolates them does not know them as moments of the total form. It does not notice their dialectical character; it does not notice what situates them in a total genesis of thought thinking being while thinking itself and thinking itself while thinking being. "Observing is not knowing itself, and is ignorant of it; it converts its own nature into the form of being" (PH §300).

Speculative logic therefore takes up all the nodes of determinations experienced in their isolation. But it does not turn them into rules or instruments. Speculative logic grasps them in itself and for itself, as moments of the universal, which is the base and the soil of their development. These determinations are no longer object (*Gegenstand*), as in the sensible world, the *a posteriori of experience*; they are phases of an absolute genesis (*Entstehen*). Their necessary and *a priori* character consists in this absolute genesis. But this *a priori* is identical to the *a posteriori*. This *a priori* encloses alterity and determination within itself, without being sensible. In its universality, it contains the intellectual structure that supports all of the sensible, of which it is the truth for-itself. Hegel opposes this philosophical logic to mathematics which resides in an exterior calculation; but he cannot stop himself from comparing the structure of these categories to the development of mathematics itself.

> No subject matter is so absolutely capable of being expounded with a strictly immanent plasticity as is thought in its own necessary development; no other brings with it this demand

in such a degree; in this respect the science of logic must sublate even mathematics, for no subject matter has in its own
self this freedom and independence. Such an exposition
would demand that at no stage of the development should
any thought-determination or reflection occur which does
not immediately emerge at this stage and that has not entered
this stage from the one preceding it—a requirement which is
satisfied, after its fashion, in the process of mathematical
reasoning. (GL 40)

One has to recognize therefore the human difficulty of this task; constantly, the philosopher who expounds this logic adds to it historical
commentaries, reflections external to the thing itself. He indeed strives to
rediscover all the categorial nodes in their immanent order. But, in this
regard, his work will be perfectible, since the nodes are moments of an
infinite (and yet closed upon itself) network. The philosopher should be
present at this dialectic without mixing his particular reflections into it.
The distinction, however, between this dialectic and these reflections is
always uneasy. This is why it will be necessary to distinguish the truth of
this speculative Logic from the human errors involved in its realization.

Anyone who labors at presenting anew an independent
structure of philosophical science may, when referring to the
Platonic exposition, be reminded of the story that Plato
revised the *Republic* seven times over. The remembrance of
this, the comparison, so far as such may seem to be implied
in it, should only urge one all the more to wish that for a
work which, as belonging to the modern world, is confronted
by a profounder principle, a more difficult subject matter and
a material richer in compass, leisure had been afforded to
revise it seven and seventy times. However, the author, in
face of the magnitude of the task, has had to content himself
with what it was possible to achieve in circumstances of
external necessity, of the inevitable distractions caused by the
magnitude and the many-sidedness of contemporary affairs,
even under the doubt whether the noisy clamor of current
affairs and the deafening chatter of a conceit which prides
itself on confining itself to such matters leave any room for
participation in the passionless calm of a knowledge which is
in the element of pure thought alone. (GL 42)

Nevertheless, Hegel does not doubt that this Logic is the
absolute truth. The imperfection of its realization can be caused either by

the insufficient plasticity of the dialectical presentation, or by the particular nodes that constitute the determinate categories, but not by the very character of this Logic. The Logos is in effect the thinking apprehension of all the determinations insofar as they are moments of one sole and unique concept. What turns these determinations into moments is the internal reflection of the universal, its exposition as mediation and not as substrate. Thus, this universal is a life, and a reflective life, but one in which the reflection engenders moments instead of being opposed to them. It is this immanent reflection—which identifies the content of each determination with the form that absorbs the content into it—that stops us from distinguishing the logic's method from its very development. This identification allows us to distinguish absolute Knowledge from all other types of knowledge—the method and the content are not separate—and shows in what sense, despite the possible imperfection of this or that exposition, it is absolute knowledge. *On the one hand, absolute knowledge has no pre-existing base*; on the other hand, it is necessarily *circular*. And these two characteristics are strictly connected.

Every empirical science first assumes a content; empirical science receives it from the outside and then treats it according to a particular method. Mathematics does not escape from this requirement of a special origin. It starts from definitions and axioms. It begins on the basis of a certain subject matter posited by these axioms which are not at the same time a product of its reflection. This is not, however, possible for the logic or speculative philosophy; the latter no longer has a fixed and special base; it could not have one because such a base would be alien to its reflection. The beginning of the Logic is therefore a beginning unlike any other; it is itself the pure reflection, which is being as well; the mediation is already there in the immediacy of its origin. "We will say only that there is nothing, nothing in heaven or in nature or spirit or anywhere else which does not equally contain both mediacy and immediacy, so that these two determinations reveal themselves to be *unseparated* and inseparable and the opposition between them to be nullity" (GL 68). This surmounted opposition is the result of consciousness' finite knowledge—the result of the *Phenomenology*—which leads to absolute knowledge, which has no other base than itself, which refers to nothing other that would have to be justified, but which, in itself, is diremption or reflection as much as it is immediacy. The requirement of a beginning is an illusory requirement if it claims to attain an absolute beginning, a first immediacy which would not be itself mediation. However, absolute knowledge starts from being, but this being is at the same time implicitly the knowledge of being. It is the mediation which presents itself as the passage from being to nothingness and from nothingness to being, the determination of one by the other. It does not start therefore from an origin but from the very movement of starting, from the *rational minimum* which is the triad *Being-Nothingness-Becoming*, that is, it starts from the Absolute as mediation, under its still immediate form, that of becoming. Yet this origin which is reflection justifies itself in its own development: "The essential requirement for the science of logic is not so much that the beginning be a pure immediacy, but rather that the whole of the science be within itself a circle in which the first is also the last and the last is also the first" (GL 71). That being is at the same time its own sense, knowledge of being, is what is presupposed but not posited at the start. Being is in itself the knowledge of being. Its intelligibility is at first its nothingness, its pure and simple disappearance as being without ground, as substrate which would be there without being posited. The very negation of this fixed base is the element of absolute knowledge. Thus this knowledge has no base; it is, however, and it is this internal contradiction which makes it move. Its being, however, is only a self-presupposition; only at the end will its being be what it is in truth. It is only this absolute genesis—this speculative life that Parmenides had started to describe—which posits the totality of the Universal's determinations in the element of sense, in the element of the *a priori*. Thus the Universal knows nothing other than itself, and in itself all of being; it is a decentered and infinite reflection. It is there before being there, and this is its contradiction, that of its being and of its reflection which makes it move without making it come out of itself (therefore developing itself analytically and synthetically). It reflects itself, that is, it posits itself, but its being is only this internal reflection, that is, it posits itself as presupposing itself, and by reflecting itself turns back upon itself. Its progress is an involution, a retrospective justification of its prospective being. This element, this ether of immediate reflection, is speculative knowledge, the transposition of all the *a posteriori* into the *a priori* of an absolute self-genesis. This transposition is metaphysics itself as Logic, speculative life which is the light of every being particularized in space and in time. There are two ways for humans to err insofar as man is that through which truth states itself. The first is to remain near the particular objects, hypnotized by them, without being able to be raised to the universal which transcends them, to this open milieu which, however, alone makes the apprehension of these objects possible. The second is to escape from, to reject these determinations and to remain at this Universal, to remain at a sort of intuition without form, in which "all cows are black." This Universal is then only the nothingness of all existents. One has to think, however, the Being in the Nothingness, the determination in the Universal. Speculative Logic is this concrete Universal at the heart of which all the determinations dissolve themselves and explicate themselves. Speculative Logic is simultaneously the intuitive understanding that Kant attributed to God, and the discursive understanding that he reserved for man. Speculative logic is the dialectical discourse which contains these three moments within itself.

"With regard to its form, the *logical* has three sides: (a) *the side of abstraction* or *of the understanding*, (b) *the dialectical* or *negatively rational side*, (c) *the speculative* or *positively rational* one." (EL §79). The first is that of the distinct determination that the understanding grasps and abstracts; it is a position which is unaware of itself as negation. The second is that of the annihilation of determinations; it grasps the first moment as negation and merely as negation. Every determination is in itself a negation. A determination appears upon the ground of nothingness. And skepticism would be the apparent result of this second dialectical moment, if the opposition of being and nothingness, which is still an opposition of the understanding, were to be permanent. But the Absolute is mediation, and "every nothingness is the nothingness of that from which it results" (PH §79); this is why the third moment reveals dialectic's positivity. It is the sole absolute affirmation because it is the negation of the negation and grasps the being in the nothingness, the particular in the Universality of absolute knowledge.

This element of absolute knowledge does not exist without nature and finite spirit—for philosophy must alienate itself—but it comprehends its own alienation. By comprehending itself, it comprehends all alterity; but it comprehends them in the relation of the Universal, which exists also in space and time as the realized absolute Idea. We return to the dialectic of the Absolute, as Logos, Nature, Spirit. But this dialectic also belongs to speculative philosophy.

Je te rends pur à ta place première. Regarde-toi.[1]

CHAPTER 2

REFLECTION AND REFLECTIONS

The Absolute is reflection, which is to say that philosophic knowledge, for Hegel, is self-knowledge as well as knowledge of being. Fichte's philosophy of the Ego [*Moi*] (which, at least in its first form, is still a philosophy of reflection), and Schelling's philosophy of Nature, are really in certain regards the historical presuppositions of Hegel's philosophy. Even if it is superficial and insufficient, the schematic vision of history which classifies systems and speaks of a subjective idealism, an objective

---

1. This quote comes from Paul Valéry, "La Cimetière Marin," in *Oeuvres de Paul Valéry*, 1:148. English translation by David Paul, *Paul Valery: An Anthology*, ed. James Lawler (Princeton: Princeton University Press, 1977): "I give you back pure to your primal place: / Look at yourself" (p. 271).—Tr.

71

idealism, and an absolute idealism, is nevertheless convenient for grasping what Hegel understands by speculative knowledge. He himself
referred to this subjective idealism and to this objective idealism in the
Phenomenology's preface and in its final chapter on *absolute knowledge*.

As subjective, as the movement of the Ego, the reflection that
wants to know only its own activity, and seeks always to disengage its
activity from its products, that seeks always to free the positing act from
what is posited, is an attitude that Hegel rejects insofar as it always
results in the primacy of a thesis which allows an irreducible antithesis
to subsist. In principle, this Idealism asserts that there is nothing other
than the Ego, that *the Ego is everything*; in fact, if it constantly displaces its
limits, it cannot ignore them. They are the permanent obstacle that the
Ego encounters and that it sees constantly reborn. It posits itself only by
opposing itself, but this opposition is irreducible. "This idealism therefore becomes the same kind of self-contradictory ambiguity as
Skepticism, except that, while this expresses itself negatively, the former
does so positively; but it fails equally with Skepticism to bring together
its contradictory thoughts of pure consciousness being all reality, while
the extraneous impulse or sensations and ideas are equally reality.
Instead of bringing them together, it shifts from one to the other, it is
caught up in the bad, i.e. the sensuous infinite" (PH §238). The error of
this Idealism lies in restraining the Ego's activity, for fear of seeing it be
engulfed in the content, lost in its product. This is why it always discovers the *Other* over against the *Mine*; it preserves from nature only the
knowledge of nature because in this knowledge the Ego finds itself,
reflects on itself. But in its depth there is always a residue in nature
which escapes from the reflective Ego, a limit to its self-positing activity.
"Since reason is all reality in the sense of the abstract *Mine*, and the *Other*
is for it something indifferent and extraneous, what is here made explicit
is that kind of knowing of an Other by reason which we met with in the
form of intending, perceiving and the understanding, which apprehends
what is intended and what is perceived" (PH §238).

"This idealism," Hegel tells us, "is involved in this contradiction because it asserts the abstract concept of reason to be the true; consequently, reality directly comes to be for it a reality that is just as much
not that of reason, while reason is at the same time supposed to be all
reality" (PH §239). This abstract concept is that of the Ego which clings
to itself as Ego, that identifies itself without contradicting itself. In fact,
what characterizes the Ego or the self is this self-positing movement,
this movement of self-reflection, of finding itself. I = I, such is the formula that states self-consciousness, which Hegel indeed admits is "the
native realm of truth" (PH §167). But in its abstract form, self-consciousness must go though the test of its dependency. It must recognize "the

universal power and objective essence in its totality" (PH §196). In contrast, objective idealism, if we understand by that Schelling's idealism, overcomes the abstract Ego and the philosophy of knowledge in order to discover not that the *Ego is Everything*, but that *Everything is the Ego*, that is, that nature also exists, that the Ego is present there immediately. Schelling balances the philosophy of the Ego with a philosophy of nature and arrives at a philosophy of the Absolute in which knowledge and nature, thought and being, are transcended as in Spinoza's substance.

Hegel rejects this philosophy of the Absolute as well as the philosophy of the Ego.

> The I has neither to cling to itself in the form of self-consciousness as against the form of substantiality and objectivity, as if it were afraid of the externalization of itself: the power of spirit lies rather in remaining the selfsame spirit in its externalization and, as that which is both in itself and for itself, in making its being for self no less merely a moment than its in-itself; nor is spirit a *tertium quid* that casts the differences back into the abyss of the Absolute and declares that therein they are all the same; on the contrary, knowing is this seeming inactivity which merely contemplates how what is differentiated spontaneously moves in its own self and returns into its unity. (PH §804)

Speculative knowledge is indeed self-consciousness, but it is being's universal self-consciousness. And being is not an Absolute which is beyond all reflection; it is itself what reflects, what thinks itself. *Being and the self are identical, and their identity is dialectical.* Dialectic excludes the primacy of a thesis, the subordination of an antithesis, and what would turn synthesis into an indefinite effort to join back up with the thesis. *The Absolute is subject*: its self-identity, its reflection, is at the same time its contradiction. The self finds itself in all reality. *Everything is the Ego*, but it is found there, it is found there as in an alien content, a self-alienation; and conversely this content clarifies itself, reflects on itself like a self. Clarifying itself as speculative knowledge, reflecting itself, this Universe is philosophy's supreme interest, but this reflection is not external. It does not reflect an Absolute which would preexist its reflection. It is not the operation of an Ego that would be distinguished from what it reflects. If the Absolute is reflection, reflection is itself absolute. It is not a subjective operation which would be juxtaposed to being, and the self of reflection is no longer the human self which is taken into consideration in an anthropology or in a phenomenology. The reflection of self-consciousness in the *Phenomenology of Spirit* is still a human reflection; it lets the

Ego see itself in another Ego, to discover itself in the life which is its very being and which however does not depend on it, as well as in social power realized as dominion or wealth. This reflection, however, is not the reflection of the Absolute, speculative knowledge as such. The self must be decentered from the purely and solely human in order to become the self of Being. That Being is the self is already included in the formula that posits Being, "Being is Being," since it posits itself, since it doubles itself and relates itself to itself. This concrete identity is the self as itself and the same (*autos* in its double sense, ipseity). To say that the Absolute is subject does not mean (despite certain post-Hegelian interpretations) that the Absolute is man, but that man is the natural Dasein in which the non-resolved contradiction of nature (that of being simultaneously Logos and non-Logos) is made explicit and sublated. Man is the house (*la demeure*) of the Logos, of the being which reflects on itself and thinks itself. Man, insofar as he is man, reflects on himself also as man, and the humanity of the *Phenomenology* engenders the universal self-consciousness which is this house, across (*à travers*) an anthropological itinerary; the reflection, however, that it reaches is the very reflection of the Absolute which as being grounds itself in its own Logos. As we have shown, the character of absolute knowledge and of the Absolute as infinite mediation lies in the fact that this ground of what is presents itself as a result, a result which presupposes itself in what is. Speculative knowledge rediscovers this paradox in the relations that it establishes between the knowledge of nature and of spirit and the Logos. We cannot speak of the place of speculative Logic in the system without contradicting ourselves. In a sense, this Logic is everything; it is the being of all that is. In another sense, it is a part of the system which extends itself into a philosophy of nature and of spirit, but this contradiction is based in the fact that the Logos is necessarily more than itself. It is itself and its other in an unity. We can consider it, insofar as it is a part, as the empire of shadows; then, returning to it as totality, we can see there the light which, alone, allows one to understand nature and finite spirit and contains them in itself.

In the *Enneads*, V, Plotinus examines Aristotle's thesis: "Either thought (*nous*) thinks itself or it thinks something other than itself, and if it thinks something other than itself, either this thing is always the same or else it varies (it is multiple and changing)."[2] Aristotle chooses the first of the alternatives, leaving the thing which varies to its destiny and which is for him the world—a thought which does not think itself suspended from a thought which thinks itself. It is not the same with

---

2. Aristotle, *Metaphysics* XII.9.1074b22–23.—Tr.

Plotinus. By thinking the intelligibles, thought thinks itself; thought thinks itself in all thought. However, the skeptics had formulated an objection that they thought was decisive against this self-knowledge. Plotinus responds to it in *Enneads* V.3. The objection is stated by Sextus Empiricus in this way:

> If thought perceives itself, either it is thought completely which perceives itself, or else it perceives itself by some part of itself. Now, the first case is impossible, because if it is thought entirely that perceives itself, it will be entirely perception and perceiving, and if it is entirely perceiving, there will no longer be anything to be perceived. Thought cannot moreover make use of a part of itself in order to perceive itself, for how will this part perceive itself? Does this part perceive itself entirely? It then no longer has anything to perceive. Does it do this through a part of itself? We ask then how this part of itself will be perceived and so on to infinity.[3]

This aporia illuminates the contradiction of a thought which thinks itself. In effect, it never knows the Other except through its intentional structure, and when it reflects on itself, it can never know itself but as other, or *remain formal*. As Bergson does later, Plotinus responds to this objection by speaking of a *torsion* of the soul, ascending to *nous*, and from there to the ineffable, transcendent One. In contrast, Hegel, however, accepts the contradiction. He turns it into a moment of the thought which contradicts itself in order to identify itself. *To know oneself is to contradict oneself*, since this is simultaneously to alienate oneself, to direct oneself towards the Other and to be reflected into it, or more exactly, to be reflected into oneself in the Other. Similarly, this Other is itself revealed to be itself the self in this concrete identity. The self is the self of the content as well as the self of thought.

The empirical observation of the world is still more valid than formal idealism, which always remains in the Ego in its sterility: "Consciousness *observes*; i.e., reason wants to find and to have itself as object, as actually real mode having a sensible presence. The consciousness that observes in this way means, and indeed says, that it wants to learn, not about itself but, on the contrary, about the essence of things *qua* things" (PH §242). This empirical attitude is unaware of the identity of the reflective self and being. It is merely guided by what Hegel calls the *instinct of reason*. This reason, however, which knows itself, is not the

---

3. Translated from Hyppolite's French.—TR.

pure abstract Ego; it is the thought of being which contradicts itself in order to think itself, and by thinking itself, thinks all the determinations in its universality. This reason that thinks itself and contradicts itself is the Logos: "That this consciousness [that of observation] means and says this, is implied in the fact that it *is* reason; but reason as such is not as yet object for this consciousness. If it knew that reason is equally the essence of things and of consciousness itself, and that it is only in consciousness that reason can be present in its own proper shape, it would go down to the depths of its own being, and seek reason there rather than in things" (PH §242). This universal knowledge however—the Logos—could illuminate in turn only a philosophy of nature and of spirit: "If it did find it there, it would be directed to the actual world outside again, in order to behold therein reason's sensuous expression, but at the same time to take it essentially as concept" (PH §242).

Speculative knowledge can be simultaneously knowledge of being and self-knowledge only because *to know oneself is to contradict onself*, only because these two moments that we ordinarily separate in order to attribute one to the object, the other to the subject, truth and reflection, being and the self, are *identical*. Their identity in their contradiction is the very dialectic of the Absolute. The dialectic of the Absolute implies the synthesis of the dogmatic (or naively empirical) attitude and the critical attitude such as Kant presents it in his transcendental philosophy. The *intentionality* of consciousness which directs itself towards preexisting being, and relegates reflection to its subjectivity, and *transcendental reflection* which reflects on the self of knowledge by relegating being to the thing in itself, must coincide in *speculative knowledge*. This speculative knowledge is knowledge of the self in the content, knowledge of the content as self, for which the torsion of the soul, which by looking at being looks at itself and conversely, expresses itself through a new logic—a torsion logic—a logic which allows an identity which is a contradiction, a contradiction which is an identity. This speculative knowledge does not result mechanically from a synthesis of two moments that would precede; it is the *a priori spontaneity* that the two assume, that we discover in them on this ground. This *a priori* spontaneity is that of the Absolute which posits itself and clarifies itself with its own light. In this way, universal self-consciousness is really then "the native realm of truth" (PH §167).

EMPIRICAL REFLECTION AND THE DOGMATISM OF BEING

Natural knowledge perceives or observes what is. Observation overcomes the perception in which it collects the sensible and seeks its permanent determinations. But it would never reflect upon itself, if it did not

encounter the scandal of illusion or of error. It apprehends the objects of
the world by abstracting from the position as such in its apprehension of
being. This position, however, is the form of the truth which will be distinguished from the posited content, because this content is multiform
being. It is determined and varied, while the position or the affirmation is
universal; by describing things, by analyzing them, by stating their
diverse relations, natural or empirical knowledge must always preserve
the self-similarity of its object. But this diversity, which requires a comparison in order to establish relations, is the source of illusion and error. In
effect, it includes in itself, as diversity, being other or negation. Empirical
knowledge, however, wants to know only the positivity of its object; it
will attribute, therefore, illusion and error to itself, to an empirical subjectivity which it will not know how to locate within the economy of its
world. The being of the world is already there before I posit it and this
being-already-there is its immediacy. "I have only to take the object and
to confine myself to a pure apprehension of it" (PH §116). If error
appears, that is, if a dissimilarity, a contradiction presents itself in the relations established among the diverse elements of experience, this contradiction can only be my doing, and I must throw it back into an inessential
subjectivity, into a history which does not concern the object itself. Thus
empirical knowledge is led to reflect on itself and to discover that it was
already reflecting on itself without knowing it in its apprehension of
objects. It was reflecting on itself already, in effect, since it was deceiving
itself, that is, since it was mixing its reflection into its apprehension of
being. The stick cannot be simultaneously crooked and straight; it is
crooked for me and straight in itself. The error arises from my viewpoint,
from my particular situation, which is attached to my particular engage-
ment in the world. An empirical subjectivity is there, an empirical subjectivity which one must be able to subtract and explain in turn objectively.
Undoubtedly, this explanation is possible, but it reveals to me the possibility of being-other, of a contradictory relation among the diverse elements that I apprehend. This is why this discovery of a reflection
unaware of itself leads me to a reflection which brings out the universal
position of being, the dogmatic thesis, and opposes it to the multiform
content on the basis of which error is possible. This conscious reflection is
properly formal reflection. It *contradicts the contradiction* and makes clear
therefore the position of a truth, of a being which must remain similar to
itself if the perceiving and observing subjectivity takes contradiction
upon itself. Thus the law of non-contradiction appears which, like an
absolute defense, rules over all empirical knowledge. What is false is the
contradictory. The place of error is the subjective Ego simultaneously
empirical and formal, empirical by means of its particular situation which
causes it to reflect falsely upon being, formal by means of this second

reflection, which excludes the contradiction and raises to clear consciousness the dogmatic thesis of being's self-similarity which was
already there in immediate apprehension. "[The percipient's] criterion of
truth is therefore self-similarity, and his behavior consists in apprehending the object as self-identical. Since at the time diversity is explicitly
there for him, it is a connection of the diverse moments of his apprehension to one another; but if a dissimilarity makes itself felt in the course of
this comparison, then this is not an untruth of the object—for this is self-
similar—but an untruth in perceiving it" (PH §116). This dissimilarity
being produced,

> consciousness has determined how its perceiving is essen-
> tially constituted, viz. that it is not a simple pure apprehen-
> sion, but in its apprehension is at the same time reflected out
> of the true and into itself. This return of consciousness into
> itself which is directly mingled with the pure apprehension
> [of the object]—for this return into itself has shown itself to
> be essential to perception—alters the truth. Consciousness at
> once recognizes this aspect as its own and takes responsibil-
> ity for it; by doing so it will obtain the true object in its
> purity." (PH §118)

Nevertheless, the discovery of error, of illusion, the deceptions
of empiricism, which depend on the content presented immediately,
indeed lead consciousness to a sort of critique, but to a formal critique,
in the margins of its apprehension of the real. It is the judge of what is,
it is the measure, but it is not noticed as such. It sees itself rather as
untruth, "consciousness recognizes that it is the untruth occuring in
perception that falls within it. But by this very recognition it is able at
once to sublate this untruth; it distinguishes its apprehension of the
truth from the untruth of its perception, corrects this untruth, and since
it undertakes to make this correction itself, the truth, *qua* truth of perception, falls of course within consciousness" (PH §118). Thus, however, it does not know the place of truth any more than the place of
error. It rectifies, corrects, in such a way as to maintain the object and
the totality of objects of the world in self-similarity only by attributing
dissimilarity to itself; but this self-similarity is, for consciousness, form
without content.

Consciousness goes, therefore, from the naive, prepredicative
presupposition of existents to the dogmatic position of being by passing
through the empiricism of the particular sciences. Its reflection can only
be formal. It is the reflection of the position as universal position which
excludes contradiction, and which, by contradicting this contradiction,

posits identity or at least preserves alterity by assenting to the content while evading contradiction.

In empiricism, as in the dogmatism of being, the content or being is essentially positive. Negative judgment is a subjective judgment that dispels an error. It does not say what the thing itself is but merely predicts what could be said of it: "Water does not boil at 50 degrees Centigrade under the atmospheric pressure of 76 centimeters of mercury." In this way, I learn nothing. Only the affirmative judgment is the form of truth; it says what the thing is. Contradiction and negation belong to a subjectivity "which is nothingness," which is in the margins of being. The contradiction attributed to the object would be a dissimilarity, a negation in itself. To state that the water is hot as well as cold would be to attribute to the object, which can only be what it is, a self-dissimilarity, a difference of the self to itself, which is an impossibility given its absolute position. In the contradiction, empirical thought grasps nothing other than itself as subjectivity, and not the object. It becomes dialectical, it is confronted with itself, reflects instead of posits. When it contradicts itself, it stops being knowledge of the content, and it becomes merely formal. It refutes itself, it is contentless, nothingness from the empirical viewpoint and, consequently, without truth. It can indeed play with its contradictions. It becomes then a formal skepticism replacing empirical dogmatism. The rule of empirical knowledge lies in not contradicting itself in its object, and, since this rule is merely negative, the rule amounts to looking for the truth in the content, which is alone considered positive. But to say that A is B is already to contradict oneself, because this is to come out of the A in order to affirm something else about it; it is to say that it is not-A and not merely A. It is to say either that, for us, there is a history of knowledge, but that in itself there is only being identical to itself, *praedicatum inest subjecto*, or else it is to say that the only thing that can be done is, like the Megarics, to enclose oneself in incommunicable essences. There is indeed a diversity, but this diversity exists without mutual relation.

The naive empiricism which reflects upon itself following the discovery of error and illusion, falls into a formalism. In effect, it does not know any reflection other than formal reflection, no other positive criterion other than the content which is given to it. This formalism could lead it to an empty identity. In general, it is content to flee from contradiction and to look for its truth in the content. The encounter with contradiction is, for it, the sign of error and of subjectivity, and it cannot be otherwise since it does not recognize itself in this content. It does not reflect itself into the content and the content is not reflected into it. Like the dogmatism of being or of incommunicable beings, empirical knowledge opposes the position of the content to the subjectivity of the Ego. This is why it always oscillates between an unformed content and a formal reflection. However, the empirical sciences—which state synthetic judgments, which ascend to an understanding of nature—require that a reflection presenting the immanence of the understanding's form to the content be brought to light. Thereby, they uncover the transcendental and not merely the formal character of this form. Empirical thought must be made into authentically critical thought, formal reflection must become transcendental reflection.

TRANSCENDENTAL REFLECTION AND EMPIRICAL THOUGHT

Empirical thought is naively dogmatic. For empirical thought, the content is always a *content alien* to the thought which apprehends it. It is merely positive. When this thought reflects on itself, when it criticizes itself under the shock of error, it is only a *formal* thought which can merely dispel the contradiction of its object. "Self-contradiction" belongs only to the subject, to its illusory dialectic, alien to all content. The opposition of the formal, as merely formal, to the content, as merely content, is characteristic of this thought.

But Kantian critique—transcendental philosophy—overcomes this merely formal reflection. Transcendental reflection is a reflection into the content. It is opposed to the formal reflection "which abstracts from all content of knowledge"; it determines this content according to the categories of the understanding. In experience, it grasps the relative identity of the form and content, of the *a priori* and the *a posteriori*. The triplicity of the categories must, Kant admits, have a transcendental signification, when formal thought recognizes only the "yes" or the "no." The determinable immediacy of the sensibility appears determined by the pure concepts of the understanding. The object seems to us to be really already constituted, empirical knowledge believes that it finds it; but transcendental reflection ascends back up to the source of this constitution (and this could not be, for Kant, the issue of a psychological source). The reflection *upon* the content of experience therefore is presupposed in what Kant calls the Phenomenon. This Phenomenon is not appearance, but it is inserted in principle into a coherent totality; it thereby acquires an objective value. *Experience*, which overcomes singular perceptions and situates them in a unique context, has its ground in this transcendental reflection. This context is nature, which, at the end of the analytic of principles, is defined as "the connection of phenomena as regards their existence according to necessary rules, that is, according to laws. There are certain laws which first make a nature possible, and these laws are *a priori*. Empirical laws can exist and be discovered only through experience, and indeed in consequence of those original laws through which experience itself first becomes possible" (A216/B263).[4] The principle of all synthetic *a priori* judgments identifies the conditions for the possibility of the objects of experience with the conditions for the possibility of experience. It is therefore the understanding itself which is *recognized* in nature, this nature realizes and simultaneously limits transcendental understanding. The transcendental is not an empirical, merely human, subjectivity, any more than it is an objective essence. As possibility or ground of experience, it expresses the logicity of being. It is beyond the notions of subject and object. It states their *original identity* which *appears* in the judgment of experience. "How are synthetic judgments *a priori* possible? This problem expresses nothing else but the idea that subject and predicate of the synthetic judgment are identical in the *a priori* way. That is to say, these heterogeneous elements, the subject which is the particular and in the form of being, and the predicate which is the universal and in the form of thought are at the same time absolutely identical" (FK 69). This identity, that only the transcendental imagination truly develops, is, for Hegel interpreting Kant, the original synthetic unity, different indeed from the abstract Ego. "Thus Kant himself distinguishes the abstract Ego or the abstract identity of the understanding from the true Ego, the absolute, original synthetic identity" (FK 71–72).

> The whole transcendental deduction both of the forms of intuition and of the category in general cannot be understood without distinguishing what Kant calls the faculty of the original synthetic unity of apperception from the Ego which does the representing and is the subject—the Ego which, as Kant says, merely accompanies all representations. [Secondly,] we must not take the faculty of [productive] imagination as the middle term that gets inserted between an existing absolute subject and an absolute existing world. The productive imagination must rather be recognized as what is primary and original, as that out of which subjective Ego and objective world first sunder themselves into the necessarily bipartite appearance and product. (FK 72)

Hegel rethinks Kant in his own way. He suspects "that reason is more profound than the abstract Ego," but he extends critical thought in a direction indicated by Kant himself.

---

4. English translation taken from Immanuel Kant, *Critique of Pure Reason*, tr. Norman Kemp Smith (New York: St. Martin's Press, 1965), p. 237.— TR.

Kantian philosophy, nevertheless, remains a merely critical philosophy, a philosophy of *external reflection*, less external than empirical reflection which locates only the abstract Ego and its empty identity. It ends up lowering the transcendental back down to anthropology in order not to have to dare to raise it up to the speculative. The identity which Kantian philosophy reaches is a relative identity, the one which shines through in the Judgment of experience; it is not an absolute identity which is merely presupposed in the transcendental deduction and exiled into the transcendental dialectic. Since the idea, the totality of the condition and conditioned, is not able to be thought without contradiction as an object, it is merely an idea condemned to unreality. The contradiction of this totality thought as object, in the form of the substantial soul, of the world, and of God, is a subjective contradiction that leaves the thing in itself completely outside of it. In vain, Kant spoke of a natural illusion that would be really different from ordinary, dialectical illusions; nevertheless, he folded the whole transcendental back into an unsurpassable subjectivity. His idealism falls back into a formal and psychological idealism. However, Kant had sown "the seed of speculation [which] lies in this triplicity alone. For the root judgment, or duality, is in it as well, and hence the possibility of the *a posteriori* itself, which in this way ceases to be absolutely opposed to the *a priori*, while the *a priori*, for this reason, also ceases to be formal identity. We will touch later on the still purer idea of an understanding that is at the same time *a posteriori*, the idea of an intuitive understanding as the absolute middle" (FK 80). Kant's critical reflection which through the transcendental dimension presents itself as the absolute reflection of being, ends up being a reflection as subjective as that of Locke. Self-knowledge is formal since it is not a knowledge of being.

This is so because Kant, according to Hegel, behaves naively in regard to his own critique. He does not reflect on his reflection; he does not see that his critique is at the same time a position; he does not notice in it the new metaphysics as Logic. He therefore separates his (transcendental, but subjectively transcendental) reflection from metaphysics; he maintains the thing in itself, but beyond knowledge, and folds knowledge back into subjectivity. However, he runs into a difficulty specific to his own reflection, one not recognized by empirical and formal reflection. Empirical and formal reflection is alien to all content, but transcendental reflection grounds experience. It constitutes the content which presupposes it. It is not only analytic (abstract self-knowledge), but also synthetic (knowledge of being), not only formal but also transcendental. The identity upon which it reflects (the identity which is the reflection itself as concrete identity) is no longer the analytic identity, but the transcendental identity, the identity of the universal self (of thought) and of experience. Transcendental reflection is therefore a reflection into the content. This is why it is indivisibly a "self-recognition" and a "self-contradiction." Transcendental reflection, since it grounds experience, is a knowledge of the self in the content, a subjectivity at the heart of objectivity. Conversely, the contradictions of this reflection, insofar as it is transcendental reflection, are a knowledge of being as much as a knowledge of the self. In other words, if empirical reflection, when it contradicts itself, is only formal, says nothing, then Kantian reflection, when it contradicts itself, says the Absolute. This reflection would be then simultaneously analytic and synthetic. The transcendental analytic, which is a self-recognition of the understanding in experience, would be at the same time a transcendental dialectic, a self-contradiction. In fact, these categories, becoming categories of being and not of human experience, would make their own limitation evident in the particular position of the self that constitutes them and would contradict themselves in this very position. The dialectic would be at the heart of the analytic, as the movement and becoming of the categories, and in its turn the dialectic, which is the seat of the antinomies, would be an analytic, a knowledge of the Absolute as much as a self-knowledge.

Because Kant does not reflect on his own reflection, he returns to the naively dogmatic position of reflection, to the opposition between the thing in itself and subjectivity. Transcendental reflection is even debased to anthropological reflection. This self-knowledge in the posited content, which is the principle of transcendental reflection, is nothing but a human knowledge of experience. Kant himself insists on the ambiguity of this constituted experience that appears at the end of the analytic of principles. In fact, this experience is *our* experience, since the forms of the sensibility are human forms which could have been otherwise and since the empirical content is sensed *hic* and *nunc*. Certainly, the categories surpass man; their speculative system, to which Kant alludes, defines a transcendental understanding. They make a claim to a transcendental employment which concerns an object, as unity of a manifold, but in fact they find their legitimate employment only within the frame and material of the sensibility. Thereby, even what we call experience presents this ambiguity of being simultaneously a human experience and an experience conditioned by a superhuman understanding. In turn, this understanding, even in its transcendental employment, is still a finite understanding since the categories are only the conditions of the unification of a manifold that they do not create. We can indeed only think an understanding which is not ours and for which the determination and the determined, the one and the many, would no longer be separated.

Thus experience really provides us with a kind of truth, but not the absolute truth (so what does truth mean?); our discursive understanding indeed recognizes itself in the nature for which it is the ground, but this nature also presents an immediate character which is not fully determined by thought. We cannot not think the totality of the condition and the conditioned; we cannot not think the idea, which differs precisely from the category not only in that it is a condition relative to something other than itself, but also in that it is the absolute, unconditioned totality. This idea, however, posited as object, shows itself to be contradictory, and contradiction, for Kant, belongs only to our subjectivity. In contrast, speculative reflection will see in this contradiction a contradiction belonging to the object as well as to the subject, a dialectic which is the very dialectic of being. Hegel insists on the difficulties proper to Kant's transcendental critique. According to Hegel, Kant baptized the understanding with reason in the transcendental deduction of the categories, which expresses the originary unity, the in-itself of the two terms, sensibility and understanding. But he considers reason in terms of the understanding in the transcendental dialectic. There is therefore an interpretation of Kantianism—to which Kant is susceptible—which lowers the transcendental entirely back down to the anthropological level. This is how Hegel summarizes it: "The manifold of sensibility, empirical consciousness as intuition and sensation, is in itself something unintegrated, the world is in itself falling to pieces, and only gets objective coherence and support, substantiality, multiplicity, even actuality and possibility, through the good offices of human self-consciousness and understanding. All this is an objective determination that man perceives and projects on things" (FK 74). The essential point to note is this reduction of the transcendental to the human. There seems to be no other way to understand Kantianism, if it is not being that reflects itself.

Kant is proud of the fact that he has not overstepped the empirical employment of the categories and for not letting himself be dragged into the *dreams of a spirit seer*. Doesn't the idea of an absolute reflection of being itself, across human knowledge, represent the metaphysical pride that must yield to critical humility? The notion of absolute knowledge, however, according to Hegel, is presupposed by transcendental reflection; it is inevitable as soon as we are engaged in transcendental reflection. The speculative thought which reunites these two moments, the moment of "self-recognition" and that of "self-contradiction," is a thought of the content like empirical thought and a transcendental thought like critical thought. It transcends the reflection which would be only a human reflection on experience and its constitution. It grasps the content itself as reflection. It is being that knows itself through man, and not man who reflects on being. This speculative reflection—or absolute reflection—replaces the old, dogmatic metaphysics. Anthropology is sublated, and yet essence is not erected as a second world, explaining and grounding the first. It is immediacy itself which reflects itself, and this identity of reflection and the immediate is philosophical knowledge itself.

Hegel considered subjective reflection as a particular case of reflection in general. He wanted to sublate the purely psychological sense of the word, *reflection*. In the *Phenomenology*, reflection appears first as subjective reflection; but it shows itself later to be reflection into the thing itself, to be internal reflection: "Our experience, then, is this, that the thing exhibits itself for the consciousness apprehending it, in a specific manner, but is at the same time reflected out of the way in which it presents itself to consciousness and back into itself; in other words, in it there are still two truths" (PH §122). However, these two reflections, subjective and objective, are for Hegel only one reflection: "For us, this object has developed through the movement of consciousness in such a way that consciousness is involved in that development, and the reflection is the same on both sides, or, there is only one reflection" (PH §132). Finally, in the Logic, Hegel considers reflection as being's own reflection. Being appears because it negates itself as immediacy; appearance is negated-being, essence. This reflection of being in essence corresponds to reflection in the psychological sense of the term; and, in this logical reflection, we find again the multiple meanings that Hegel gives to the reflection of consciousness, as external or internal reflection. Perhaps the distinction that Hegel makes in the *Phenomenology*, between self-consciousness and life, can further clarify this meaning of reflection. Life is the same thing as self-consciousness, but it is in itself what self-consciousness is for itself. Life is already reflection in itself, as Kant had seen in *The Critique of Judgment*, because it is a perpetual return-into-self; it is the movement which actualizes at the end what it is at the beginning, immanent purposiveness. Self-consciousness is the truth of this life: "the universal unity [that of life] . . . is the simple genus which, in the movement of life itself, does not exist for itself qua this simple determination; on the contrary, in this result, life points to something other than itself, viz. to consciousness, for which life exists as this unity, or as genus" (PH §172). In human self-consciousness, this life grasps itself and is opposed to itself. Life appears as the immediacy which presupposes its Essence, self-consciousness; the latter appears as the reflection which posits life. The one refers to the other and self-consciousness finds itself in life; it is this *finding itself* which is the moment of immediacy. The reflection of self-consciousness on life is therefore the very reflection of life in self-consciousness; but in order to understand that there is "only one reflection," it is necessary to pass from this reflection upon, which is external, to internal reflection, the one which is expressed in the logic of Essence.

Despite the progress it constitutes over formal reflection, Kant's critical philosophy remains a "reflection upon," or a reflection already internal, but which is unaware of itself as internal. It starts from a sensible immediacy in the transcendental *Aesthetic*; then it shows the conformity of this sensibility to the transcendental conditions of reflection in the *Analytic*. However, although this immediacy becomes then the authentic Phenomenon, although it is grounded in the essentiality of the categories, it nevertheless preserves an irreducibility. There is still in it an unresolved position of being, a something alien to the reflection which must start from it order to ground it. Kant does not understand this appearance as such, as the very structure of reflection. In the Logic of Essence, Hegel shows that it is being itself which appears, which reflects itself and grounds itself, as if the appearance refers to something other than itself. This other is, however, the very movement of appearing, of self-division. "It follows, therefore, from the foregoing considerations that reflective movement is to be taken as the absolute recoil upon itself. For the presupposition of the return-into-self—that from which essence comes, and is only as this return—is only in the return itself. The sublation of the immediate from which reflection starts is simultaneously a sublation and a return to this immediacy. The movement, as an advance, immediately turns round upon itself and only so is self-movement—a movement which comes from itself in so far as positing reflection is presupposing, but, as presupposing reflection, is simply positing reflection" (GL 402). Kantian reflection, however, remains alien to this movement of being:

> That reflection to which Kant ascribes the search for the universal of a given particular is clearly also only external reflection, which is only related to the immediate as to something given. But in external reflection there is also implicit the notion of absolute reflection; for the universal, the principle or rule and law to which it advances in its determining, counts as the essence of that immediate which forms the starting point; and this immediate therefore counts as a nullity, and it is only the return from it, its determining by reflection, that is the positing of the immediate in accordance with its true being. Therefore, what reflection does to the immediate, and the determinations which issue from reflection, are not anything external to the immediate but are its proper being. (GL 404–5)

Speculative thought understands reflection as being's absolute reflection; it understands the illusion that victimizes external reflection. Because external reflection starts from immediate content, it does not see that it presupposes itself, and that the content reflects itself into what grounds it. Speculative thought reunites therefore the positive thought of empiricism, which starts from content prior to all reflection and which distinguishes it from the form, and critical thought, which is not only a subjective thought but also a thought which recognizes itself in the position of content. And because critical thought recognizes itself in this immediate position, it contradicts itself. Speculative thought is dogmatic like naive thought and critical like transcendental thought. It reflects, but it is being which reflects itself in it.

SPECULATIVE REFLECTION

Being is to itself its own light, its own reflection. Critique is not therefore a process which delimits from the outside the power of knowledge in relation to being by marking the limits of this knowledge. This external critique is only an appearance. "Reflection," Hegel says, "*changes* something in the way in which the content is at first in sensation, intuition, or representation; thus, it is only *through the mediation* of an alteration that the *true* nature of the object comes into consciousness. . . . Because it is equally the case that in this reflection the genuine nature [of the object] comes to light, and that this thinking is *my* activity, this true nature is also the *product of my* spirit, [of me] as thinking subject. It is mine according to my simple universality as [universality] of the "I" *being* simply *at home with itself,* or it is the product of my *freedom*." (EL §22–23). This thought, however, which reflects the true nature, is not a subjective thought in the ordinary sense of the word, just as this freedom is not individual fantasy.

> Thinking immediately involves *freedom*, because it is the activity of the universal, a self-relating that is therefore abstract, a being-with-itself that is undetermined in respect of subjectivity, and which in respect of its *content* is, at the same time, only in the *matter* [der *Sache*] and in its determinations. So when one speaks of humility or modesty, and of arrogance, with reference to the doing of philosophy, and when this humility or modesty consists in not attributing any *particularity* of feature or agency to one's subjectivity, then philosophizing has to be absolved from arrogance at least, since thinking is only genuine with respect to its content insofar as it is immersed in the *matter*, and with respect to its form insofar as it is not a *particular* being or doing of the subject, but consists precisely in this, that consciousness conducts itself as an abstract "I," as *freed* from *all particularity* of features, states, etc., and does only what is universal, in which it is identical with all individuals. (EL §23)

This freedom is that of the Universal which allows thought to reflect in itself and for itself all the determinations of content. Thought behaves like the pure light that illuminates the opacity of determinations. Nevertheless, the limitation of this thought presents itself in two ways: "The *finitude* of the thought-determinations has further to be taken in two ways: first, they are *only subjective* and are permanently in antithesis to the objective; secondly, being quite generally of *limited content*, they persist both in their antithesis to each other, and (even more) in their antithesis to the Absolute." (EL §25). Hegel exerts all of his strength to reduce the first point to the second. The *Phenomenology of Spirit* which serves as the introduction to Logic, and the preface to the *Encyclopaedia*'s Logic (which concerns the different "positions taken by thought in relation to objectivity") propose one and the same task: to show that the subjectivity-objectivity distinction, the certainty-truth distinction, from which ordinary consciousness starts, can be transcended and then justified as a necessary appearance. Critical reflection is upon the point of overcoming this distinction, but it remains an external reflection. After having shown the objectivity of the thought that knows nature, it again reduces this objectivity to a subjectivity. It lets an unknowable thing in itself remain standing. In contrast, Hegel claims to show in the *Phenomenology of Spirit* and in the preface to the *Encyclopaedia*'s Logic that thought is the Universal in itself and, in the Universal, being. But then this total thought knows itself only in its determinations, which are moments of the form. Each of these determinations is finite, not because the determination is subjective, but because it has a limited content which is opposed to other determinations as well as to the absolute identity of the form. Speculative Logic, absolute knowledge, is the reflection of the determinations in the medium of the universal and not the subjective reflection of consciousness as such.

> In this [science], the moments of its movement no longer exhibit themselves as specific shapes of consciousness, but— since consciousness's difference has returned into the self—as determinate concepts and as their organic self-grounded movement. . . . The moment does not appear as this movement of passing back and forth, from consciousness or representation into self-consciousness, and conversely: on the contrary, its pure shape, freed from its appearance in consciousness, the pure concept and its progression, depends solely on its pure determination. (PH §805)

The passage from this subjective reflection to objective reflection, as from external reflection to internal reflection, is the discovery of

Hegelianism. Being itself criticizes itself in its own determinations, in its own self-positions. Speculative reflection is indeed therefore also a critical reflection, but it is an immanent critique, an internal critique. Speculative Logic is only the exposition of this critique, of this dialectic immanent to the content. It differs from naive empiricism as much as from metaphysical dogmatism in that it does not realize the determinations of the understanding, in that it does not oppose the specified content to the abstract form. Speculative Logic is rather the very life of truth in itself and for itself, being which reflects itself and by reflecting itself posits itself, shows itself as the self.

Internal reflection therefore explains external reflection, subjective reflection, but not vice versa. By starting from the external reflection which compares, abstracts, subsumes, we cannot truly bring reflection back to being as absolute reflection. "Thinking that keeps to external reflection and knows of no other thinking but external reflection, fails to attain to a grasp of identity in the form just expounded, of essence, which is the same thing. Such thinking always has before it only abstract identity, and apart from and alongside it, difference. In its opinion, reason is nothing more than a loom on which it externally combines and interweaves the warp of, say, identity, and then the woof of difference" (GL 412). For Hegel, identity is being which posits itself, which reflects itself in itself, therefore, which contradicts itself and alienates itself, in order to posit itself in its self-alienation. Such is absolute reflection "which relates itself to itself as to an other (*its* other) and to this other as to itself." We then understand subjective reflection, because it results from the very reflection of being and must be brought back to it in order to understand itself in itself. Being appears and this appearance is itself, its identity to itself and its difference from itself, its contradiction which resolves itself into its ground, but a ground that does not pre-exist this very appearance. This is why reflection and appearance are identified, if we stop grasping appearance as an immediate being. "Appearance is the same thing as reflection; but it is reflection as immediate. For appearance that has withdrawn into itself and so is alienated from its immediacy, we have the word of a foreign language, *reflection*" (GL 399).

Therefore we have to take appearance just as it is, and not as the appearance of a hidden being; what Hegel calls the Logic of Essence is this apprehension of reflection as the movement of appearance in which there is really a duality, a division, the very division of being which reflects itself. This duality, however, is entirely in the appearing; it is not beyond. Thus immediacy is reestablished in reflection, actuality as self or concept, the concrete unity of mediation. Essence would be like the secret of appearance, but this secret is itself only an appearance. Absolute knowledge means the elimination of the ontological secret:

"For consciousness, there is something secret, in its object, if this object is
an other or an alien entity for it, and if it does not know it as itself." The
only secret, however, is that there is no secret. Immediacy reflects itself
and unveils itself as the self. "The self is nothing alien. It is the indivisible
unity with itself, the immediately universal." Being reflects itself as self,
and the self is there immediately. Speculative life is therefore being's self-
comprehension which is indeed a life, but the very life of the Absolute.
This is not the contemplation of the Absolute, but the Absolute itself in
its self-comprehension, "not only the intuition of the divine, but the
divine's self-intuition" (PH §795). "Substance would pass for the
absolute only in so far as it was thought or intuited as absolute unity;
and all content would, as regards its diversity, have to fall outside of it
into reflection; and reflection does not pertain to substance, because substance would not be subject, would not be grasped as reflecting itself and
reflecting itself into itself, would not be grasped as spirit" (PH §803). The
absolute actuality that the logic reaches, and that is already the concept
in itself, Sense, is the unity of essence and existence, of internal and
external. The possible grounds the actual as much as the actual grounds
the possible. Being is its own self-position; the reflection into another
which would be exteriority, and the reflection into itself which would be
interiority, coincide in this actuality which is its own self-comprehension.

This self-comprehension, this light of being which is being, in
the universality of the absolute form, is the Logic or speculative philosophy. In it, form and content are identified. In empirical reflection, the
form was the abstract identity which left all determinate content outside.
In transcendental reflection, this form was already more than an abstract
identity; it was the determination of the content according to the categories, and sensible matter was showing itself only as the determinable.
The opposition of form and content, however, disappears. The form is
opposed first to the essence as the determination is to its indeterminate
ground, to its substance. "Just because the form is as essential to the
essence as the essence is to itself, the divine essence is not to be conceived and expressed merely as essence, i.e., as immediate substance or
pure self-contemplation of the divine, but likewise as form, and in the
whole wealth of the developed form" (PH §19). Considered on its own,
the form is not only the particular determination, but also the complete
determination, negativity; it is the movement which sublates the abstraction of its determinations in order to become perfect, in order to identify
itself completely with itself. Thus the form is essence just as much as the
essence is form. The absolute form is the Universal as identity, no longer
abstract but concrete, surmounting the proper contradiction of its
diremption. "Since immanent self-moving universality is the sundered
simple concept, the latter thus has in itself a content, and one which is all

content, only not a sensuous being" (PH §299). The content which is the already informed substance contradicts the form because it is only one of its moments. Thus all the determinations of content must be considered as phases in the form which is total, total because it is the absolute identity of the self to itself. This form is the essence, the Universal, which is actualized in all of its determinations which are posited in it, and reduces them to itself; but this essence is form because it is itself only in this movement, in this absolute self-genesis. The Absolute is not a form or a content; if this distinction is maintained, then it is valid only for empirical consciousness which does not grasp each content of thought as the differential of its integral. It is the inadequation of the determinate content that turns it into a moment. Because it contradicts itself, it becomes. The form is really the identity of being or of the self, the identity that the classical rationalists introduced into ontology, but this identity is also contradiction, diremption; it is synthetic and not only analytic. The classical rationalists, a Spinoza or a Leibniz, remained at the inherence of the predicate in the subject, and this is why Being, although identical, was not the self. It did not contradict itself; therefore it did not posit itself as determination which, being negation—a self-negation however—negates itself in turn or negates its own negation. It was not the infinite negativity that defines the Absolute as subject, the truth as a life that reflects itself within the self in order to posit itself. The Logos, dialectical identity of form and content, becomes the element of philosophy. In fact, in this element, all the determinations of thought must find their place; the Logos is the unique category, the being which is the self, which specifies itself in a multiplicity of categories each of which, as a self-position, shows itself at the same time as negation and contradiction. Each of these categories, each of these nodes, resolves itself into the others. Dialectical discourse, the true in itself and for itself, "is thus the Bacchanalian revel in which no member is not drunk; yet because each member collapses as soon as he drops out, the revel is just as much transparent and simple repose" (PH §47). This Logos is the *a priori* spontaneity, but this *a priori* does not mean the arbitrary reconstruction of being in the head of a philosopher. Philosophy thinks as genesis what presents itself in experience as object. All the universal determinations of existence present themselves as figures of consciousness in the *Phenomenology* or in the *Philosophy of History*. The Logos conceives them as the being which thinks itself in its universality, and by thinking itself, thinks also its own alienation in nature and in finite spirit.

In empirical thought, contradiction and negation were showing themselves as purely subjective. Contradiction was to be absolutely avoided, but this is no longer the case with speculative contradiction. Contradiction is inevitable if knowledge of being is at the same time self-knowledge. Contradiction then no longer comes about through a divergence from positive knowledge; it is no longer an illusion, but a necessary moment. In fact, speculative knowledge does not merely go towards the posited content, but within the content, it still goes towards itself. It is self-knowledge in the content, knowledge of the content as of the self. It is being and sense at the same time, intentional and reflective. Contradiction does not sublate the position of the content in order to save abstract identity. Rather it sublates the abstract identity of the content, the mere position, by turning it into an opposition. The posited content opposes itself to itself; in this opposition, speculative thought finds identity again, but this identity is the concrete identity of the self. Speculative contradiction is the means of transforming the empirical criterion of truth (the mere content) into a criterion which is at the same time formal, logical, speculative. It alone conceives and justifies what *The Critique of Pure Reason* does not succeed in conceiving and justifying: the synthetic character of analytic thought (absolute reason knows itself and therefore knows being), the analytic character of synthetic thought (by knowing being, it knows itself). Speculative knowledge is simultaneously *tautological*, like formal thought, and *heterological*, like empirical thought. Empirical thought is heterological, synthetic. It reconnects diverse elements, but speculative thought is reflected heterology; therefore alterity presents itself for it as the reflection of the same, as opposition; speculative thought thinks difference as reflected difference, as essential difference, the difference of itself to itself. Empirical thought does not see that synthetic judgment implies negation and contradiction; it remains at its exterior difference (for a reflection alien to the terms). Speculative thought must oppose the *heteron* to the *tauton*, as the *henantion*, the opposite. It transforms external diversity into contradiction because it thinks the categories of the Absolute, each of which is the self, as determination and therefore as negation.

Speculative contradiction is the contradiction of the Absolute itself that negates itself by positing itself; but this meaning of negation, which is not only subjective but also inherent to being, is the decisive point of the Hegelian dialectic, the characteristic of speculative thought in relation to empirical thought. Empirical thought becomes speculative thought, when it becomes thought of the universal self in every position, and remains at the same time dialectical thought, and not ineffable intuition. We are going to attempt to bring to light this ontological meaning of negation and of contradiction in the relation of the three moments of the system: Logos, Nature, Spirit.

CHAPTER 3

ABSOLUTE KNOWLEDGE AS IDENTITY AND CONTRADICTION: LOGOS, NATURE, SPIRIT

Absolute knowledge is a knowledge unlike any other. We do not pass in a continuous way from external reflection to a reflection internal to being. A new dimension has been discovered, the very dimension of being. Undoubtedly, Hegel wrote the *Phenomenology* in order to introduce self-consciousness into this ether and to allow self-consciousness to live there. In his *Logic*, he attempted to present absolute knowledge as the discourse of being, its Logos. Philosophy must avoid two dangers. It must overcome empirical reflection, or even transcendental reflection which is still a reflection external to its object; but it must as well avoid getting lost in the immediate intuition of the Absolute which is nothing but night. By writing a speculative Logic in which the dialectic is the very dialectic of being, being's self-reflection, Hegel proposes in this way to reconcile reflection and absolute intuition, to show how being coincides with its own reflection. "Reason is, therefore, misunderstood when reflection is excluded from the true, and is not grasped as a positive moment of the Absolute" (PH §24).

Kant used the dialectic in order to dispel a pure appearance. For him, dialectic, as illusion, was opposed to the analytic, to the truth of experience. Fichte turned the dialectic into the method by which to know the true insofar as the true is knowable. With Schelling, in contrast, dialectic becomes again appearance. It allows one to surmount empirical knowledge and reflection; dialectic is their critique. Dialectic is the vestibule to an absolute knowledge which coincides with an intuition that is closer to aesthetic intuition than to an authentic intellectual intuition. Thereby, Schelling has the merit of insisting upon the incommensurability of empirical or reflective knowledge and absolute knowledge:

> All the forms we use in order to express the Absolute express only the way in which they present themselves to reflection; on that everyone agrees. But, no explanation would be able to make its very essence known, an essence which, as ideal, is also immediately real. This essence can be known only through intuition. Only what is composed can be known through description; the simple can be apprehended only through intuition. In vain we will have described light (and nothing would be more correct) in its relations with nature, as an ideal element which, as such, is at the same time real. Through description, we will never make known what light is to a person born blind. Similarly, a description of the Absolute, being what is opposed to the finite (and we would hardly know how to describe it otherwise), will never be able to procure the intuition of the genuine essence of the Absolute for the spiritually blind. Since we cannot attribute a universal validity, similar to a geometrical figure, to this intuition—since it is particular to each soul, just as light is particular to each eye—we find ourselves in the presence of a purely individual revelation, and yet also one that is universally valuable as the light for the empirical sense of sight.[1]

Schelling still draws attention to the inability of human language to describe this idea of the Absolute.

---

1. F. W. J. Schelling, *Philosophie und Religion* (1804), in *Schriften von 1801–1804* (Darmstadt: Wissenschaftliche Buchgesellschaft, 1968), 611; translated from Hyppolite's French.—TR.

Schelling's philosophy, which makes use of the dialectic in order to dissolve the finite, and which claims to induce in us the conditions of this intellectual intuition that makes us transcend the human and coincide with the source of all productivity, is a philosophy that overcomes all reflection. And it is a philosophy that turns out to be incapable of understanding conceptually how the finite can emerge from the infinite, how difference can appear at the heart of the Absolute. It can only make use of images, only use analogies, myths, or symbols. This type of philosophy, which refers to intuition, is characterized by the fact that it communicates only by breaking through conceptual language and by substituting the image for the concept. Through its symbolic character, the image refers us simultaneously to the sensible and to what overcomes the sensible; it suggests rather than says. A philosopher like Bergson, who often sounds like Schelling, sees in the image the only possible mediation of intuition, and, in the variety of utilized images, the possibility of detaching spirit from the sensible weight particular to each image. However, this renunciation of conceptual language, which indeed places philosophy in a new element, makes it harmonize too much with poetry, or even with the arts prior to poetry. Is the intuition that does not say itself still sense? In fact, spirit oscillates then between the empirical and the Absolute, which turns out to be like a night prior to the light of reflection; moreover, it is like the night that is incapable of engendering light. Perhaps Hegel was already thinking of Schelling when, in his *The Difference between Fichte's and Schelling's Systems of Philosophy*, he opposes himself to a type of philosophy in which "the Absolute is the night, and the light is younger than it; and the difference between them, like the emergence of the light out of night, is an absolute difference. Nothingness is the first out of which all being, all diversity of the finite has emerged" (DS 93). Another presupposition of philosophy would be the Absolute itself: "reason produces it merely by freeing consciousness from its limitations. This sublation of the limitations is conditioned by the presupposed unlimitedness" (DS 93). But, anouncing thereby the proper task of philosophy, Hegel adds: "the task of philosophy consists in uniting these presuppositions: to posit being in non-being, as becoming; to posit diremption in the Absolute, as its phenomenon, to posit the finite in the infinite, as life" (DS 93–94). These three aspects of mediation correspond already to the three moments of the Logic. In immediate being, it is non-being which is the ground into which all particular beings disappear or from which they emerge. In essence, it is being itself which reflects itself, insofar as being appears. Existence is this very appearance: "For appearing and self-diremption are entirely the same." Finally, in the concept, it is life and thought which are the same. Speculative life is the very life of sense. Speculative life posits and, held back by the weight of understanding which gets fixed and deepened by the determination, it sublates at the same time each of these positions. It resolves them dialectically, because every position is a reflection, a contradiction; but it is in this way also led to a new position. Speculative life itself is the Sense of its own movement. Speculative negation is creative. It negates as much as it posits; it posits as much as it negates. This life of sense or of thought is the absolute life of being as Logos. But far from this Logos, as speculative life, appearing to reflect life (in the biological sense or in the sense of a philosophy of nature), it is really rather the case that this biological life and this negativity of life are a reflection of the absolute life of sense. Hegel's ownmost originality lies in his not having renounced conceptual language, in his having instead created a speculative Logic, which is to the old formal logic what the living body is to the dead. This life of thought that Hegel presents to us in his Logic, that appears in this work as a lived description of the movement of thinking, is not the particular thought of man over and against existents; it is absolute thought, the reflection of being itself across human consciousness. Thus it is indeed absolute knowledge and it implies an element in which empirical thought does not rediscover itself. But if empirical thought cannot understand absolute thought, absolute thought can understand empirical thought as its other, because it itself contains this alterity. The universal does not subsume the particular; rather, the universal expresses it and gets expressed in it, in its continuous development, in its discourse. This alterity allows absolute knowledge to understand "that philosophy must alienate itself," and that on the basis of absolute knowledge, we can embrace the existence of an anthropology, while on the basis of an anthropology, we can never raise ourselves to absolute knowledge without a kind of rupture.

Against philosophies that are merely intuitive or religious, Hegel firmly states in the *Phenomenology*'s preface:

> This prophetic talk supposes that it is staying in the center and in the depths, looks disdainfully at determinateness (*Horos*), and deliberately holds aloof from concept and necessity as products of that reflection which is at home only in the finite. But just as there is an empty breadth, so too there is an empty depth; and just as there is an extension of substance that pours forth as a finite multiplicity without the force to hold the multiplicity together, so there is an intensity without content, one that holds itself in as a sheer force without spread, and this is in no way distinguishable from superficiality. The power of spirit is only as great as its expression, its depth only as deep as it dares to spread out and lose itself

in exposition. Moreover, when this non-conceptual, substantial knowledge professes to have sunk the idiosyncrasy of the self in essential being, and to philosophize in a true and holy manner, it hides the truth from itself: by spurning measure and definition, instead of being devoted to God, it merely gives free rein both to the contingency of the content within it, and to its own caprice. Such minds, when they give themselves up to the uncontrolled ferment of the substance, imagine that, by drawing a veil over self-consciousness and surrendering understanding they become the beloved of God to whom He gives wisdom in sleep; and hence what they in fact receive, and bring to birth in their sleep, is nothing but dreams. (PH §10)

Hegel rejects this ineffable intuition, which would be immediate knowledge opposed to reflection, as well as empirical knowledge which is an external reflection. In the Jena Logic (1801–2), we can follow his attempt to conceive the Absolute as internal reflection, his attempt to translate what sublates the understanding into conceptual language. What is at issue is not to put on one side unity, infinity, universality, and on the other multiplicity, the finite, the particular. But, in order to avoid such one-sidedness, we have to twist thought, we have to force it to look contradiction square in the face and to turn it into a means of surmounting the differences onto which the understanding holds. The infinite is not beyond the finite, because then it itself would be finite; it would have the finite outside of itself as its limit. Similarly, the finite negates itself; it becomes its other. But this negation is not progress to infinity, that is, always unfinished, incomplete—this solution allows the understanding to dissimulate contradiction, while recognizing its problem. At the end of his early period, during the last years at Frankfurt, Hegel would consider the passage from the finite to the infinite as a mystery that we can only live and that is impossible to conceive. Now he tries, in contrast, to create a new logic which articulates this very passage. The central theme appears to us to be the idea that the Absolute posits itself only by opposing itself, itself to itself, by reflecting itself. The central theme is that the Absolute is the unity of this reflection, but this is a unity that does not set itself apart from reflection like a substance that would be *prior natura suis affectionibus*. This unity results from the very reflection of which it is the movement, the mediation; the unity is the becoming-similar of the dissimilar as well as the becoming-dissimilar of the similar. "There can be no talk of the going forth of the absolute out of itself; for only this can appear as a going forth: that the opposition is, yet the opposition cannot pause at its being; rather, its essence is the absolute unrest of sublating itself. Its being would be its terms, but these essentially are only as connected with each other—that is, they are not on their own account; they are only as sublated. What they are on their own account is: not to be on their own account. If the absolute opposition is separated from unity, then the latter is on its own account just as the former is outside itself, but in this case the opposition itself has only changed its expression" (JL 36). The unity is not beyond opposition. If it were, it would no longer be unity; it would be one of the opposed terms. The opposition is not the duality of two terms external to one another. If it were, it would no longer be absolute opposition, because it would no longer have its unity in itself. "According to its concept, infinity is the indivisible movement of sublating the opposition; it is not the sublatedness. The latter is the void to which the opposition itself stands opposed" (JL 37). We could translate this by saying that infinity is not transcendence, but the act of transcending, mediation as movement of passage from one of the terms into the other, their mutual reflection. However, this process is possible only if it posits the limit as much as it negates it. "The annihilating unrest of the infinite is only through the being of what it annihilates; the sublated is absolute just so far as it is sublated: it arises in its perishing, for the perishing only occurs because there is something that perishes" (JL 38). The Infinite, the Universal, is only insofar as it negates itself. It includes its limitation, its diremption in itself. Every position is negation, but it is an internal negation, a negation of the self by the self; such is the sense of the speculative category of limitation. The Universal limits itself; it still therefore has only the self outside of itself, and this identity appears by means of the double negation. The "Yes" is abstract because it is opposed to the "No," as unity is to multiplicity, the universal to the particular, the infinite to the finite; but the negation of the negation is the concrete "Yes," the one which becomes itself by sublating its own limitation, by affirming itself in its opposition as an opposition of the self to the self: "Infinity is within this immediacy, that of otherness and of the otherness of this other, or of being the first again, the immediacy of the *duplex negatio* [double negation] that is once more *affirmatio* [affirmation], self-similarity in its absolute dissimilarity. For the dissimilar, or the other, is just as much the other of itself immediately as it is an other according to its essence" (JL 36).

The fundamental contradiction is that of the Absolute which limits itself, which becomes in this way the opposite of itself. But, thereby, it determines itself (every determination is negation, as much as every negation is determination), and in this determination, in this self-limitation which is negation, it negates itself again, posits itself therefore concretely as itself in its opposite. If the infinite contradicts itself by limiting itself in order to determine itself, conversely, the finite, the determinate, is in itself its own negation. It makes itself infinite by determining itself as its other, as the opposite of itself: "This alone is the true nature of the finite: that it is infinite, that it sublates itself in its being. The determinate has as such no other essence than this absolute unrest: not to be what it is. It is not nothing, because it is the other itself, and this other, being just as much the opposite of itself, is again the first" (JL 35).

The Absolute is therefore only through this division—which is negation—this opposing duplication in which each of the terms is a determination, but such that it exists only in its relation to an other, to *its* other. The result is that the Absolute, by positing itself in each of its determinations, appears to itself entirely in each (since each refers to the other). The Absolute is their mediation, the reflection of one of the determinations into the other, which is at the same time external reflection (relation of one to the other), and internal reflection (self-relation). The Absolute contradicts itself in order to identify itself; it is the concrete identity, unity extended to duality, the being inside of the self in the being outside of the self, the being outside of the self in the being inside of the self. This absolute identity is simultaneously form and content; it is analytic and synthetic, tautological and contradictory. We see that in Hegel there is no primacy of the thesis. The dialectical triad constitutes the "rational minimum." In fact, the synthesis does not exist without its antithesis, without opposition. The Absolute is inconceivable without the three terms, or rather, it is the very mediation that distinguishes them and gathers them back together; it is what divides itself and unifies itself in this division. The synthesis separated from the opposition would be an immediacy, one of the members of the new opposition thus constituted.

The Absolute therefore is itself only in this self-division, and in the movement of surmounting it, in the identity of opposite terms. The Absolute is thus Logos and Nature. It is entirely in the Logos and entirely in Nature. It appears to itself in this absolute opposition, in this reflection of itself in itself, and, as this mediation, the Absolute is Spirit.

The division of the Absolute into Logos and Nature is the moment of determination, of negation, or the moment of the understanding. "The activity of dividing is the power and work of the understanding, the most astonishing and mightiest of powers, or rather the absolute power" (PH §32). The understanding is not only our understanding, it is also the understanding of things, of nature, of the Absolute. The immediate Whole arouses no astonishment, says Hegel, but the analysis that is negation itself, that provides a distinct Dasein to what exists only in its relation to the whole: this is the absolute power. This division is indeed negation; it is not really the separation of parts external to one another, because if they are external, there is no Whole. The division is already done. The division is therefore the Whole which

negates itself as Whole, which posits itself in a self-negation. This negation is what we call determination. In nature and in experience, determinations appear in the dispersion of space and time. They seem to be
external to one another; their relations appear to reconnect them from
the outside. By means of the external reflection performed by the knowing ego, these determinations identify themselves, distinguish themselves or oppose themselves. But it is not so in thought. "The
determination seems at first to be due entirely to the fact that it is related
to an other, and its movement seems imposed on it by an alien power;
but having its otherness within itself, and being self-moving, is just what
is involved in the simplicity of thinking itself; for this simple thinking is
the self-moving and self-differentiating thought, it is its own interiority,
it is the pure concept. Thus the understanding, too, is a becoming, and,
as this becoming, it is rationality" (PH §55).

The Absolute determines itself and negates itself as Logos and
as Nature. This opposition is absolute. Each term is simultaneously positive and negative. Each is the Whole that opposes itself to itself. Each is
in itself the opposite of itself and represents therefore the other in itself. It
presents it in its element, in its own determination that it thus surmounts. "It is itself and its opposite in one unity. Only thus is it difference as internal difference, or difference in its own self, or difference as
infinity. . . . The two differentiated terms both subsist; they are in themselves as opposed, i.e., each is the opposite of itself; each has its other
within it and they are only one single unity" (PH §§160, 161). Such an
opposition is not the empirical opposition. Logos and Nature are not
species of one genus which contains them both and on the basis of which
they are distinguished. This distinction would no longer be immanent to
them; it would exist only for a third which would compare them, which
would consider them from the viewpoint of their similarity or dissimilarity: "Identity or non-identity, like similarity or or dissimilarity, is the
viewpoint of a third that falls outside of them." If, for example, I distinguish the ellipsis and the parabola, it is for me that they are similar insofar as they are curves of the second degree or sections of one cone. It is
for me also that they are dissimilar insofar as the one is a closed curve,
the other open, and so on. It is I who compares them, and it is within me
that their similarity and their dissimilarity fall. If I want to grasp this dissimilarity and similarity together, it is then upon me that I reflect. It is I
who bears both simultaneously, and it is therefore me that I compare to
myself. It is I who opposes myself and distinguishes myself from myself.
The self is thus the genuine concrete identity which identifies itself in its
difference, and distinguishes itself in its identity. It is the self that reflects
itself. But in relation to the curves under consideration, this reflection is
external, just as it is external for empirical differences. The formula of

identity, A = A, is not the genuine identity, because it presupposes the difference of form and content. A particular content A is posited in its self-similarity; it is the Ego that sustains this position, as Fichte showed, and which also sustains the difference of form and content. The speculative opposition, however, does not exist for an external reflection. It is the self itself which opposes itself and distinguishes itself from itself. It is the self which reflects itself. There is no common point between the Logos and Nature; they differ absolutely. And this is why they are identical. Each reflects the other, bears it necessarily in itself, since it is only insofar as it is its negation. There is no common soil, no preexisting base, supporting Nature *and* the Logos. This base would be the universal self, but the self is indivisible. It is entirely in the Logos, entirely in Nature. Therefore when we set the Logos on one side, we find in it its difference as self-difference, its dissimilarity from itself, and likewise for Nature. Each contradicts itself, reflects the other, *its* other in itself; each is more than itself, is the becoming of its unity, the negation of the negation, or the affirmation of the Whole reconstituted as mediation. Hegel calls this mutual reflection spirit. We must not therefore say the Logos *and* Nature, but that the Logos *is* nature, Nature *is* the Logos. The judgment (*Urteil*) states the originary division; it is the relative identity, the still immediate mediation. It is only reason, mediation, that develops the dialectical character of this *is*, by showing simultaneously the opposition of the terms, their contradiction, and their identity. Reason alone makes spirit appear in the Logos and in Nature.

One must insist within this opposing duplication of the Absolute (which exists only by this doubling) on the ontological meaning of the negation. Position and negation balance themselves and identify themselves. Every speculative position is just as much a negation, but every speculative negation is also a position. This is not the case with empirical negation. If I negate the ellipsis, I do not determine the curve that I obtain by this negation, not even if what is at issue is the curve. The negation of A leaves the field of possibles open. If, however, I negate the Logos, I can have only Nature, because Nature is for the Logos *its* other, just as the Logos is for Nature *its* other: "That the negative is in itself as well positive, results," says Hegel, "from this determination that the term opposite to another is *its* other." Speculative negation is therefore a negation which determines; it has a creative value. By negating itself as Logos, the Absolute posits itself as Nature; it engenders itself as the opposite of the Logos, and vice versa. When the Absolute negates itself, it posits itself into positive and negative, into Being and Nothingness, Being and Essence, Logos and Nature, but the positive is as negative as the negative is positive. It is necessary therefore to grasp the negation in the position and the position in the negation. The position appears to have a privilege because it is the indivisible self, but the position is precisely what it claims to be, it precisely justifies this privilege, only when it recognizes itself as negation and negates this negation. The absolute position is then the negation of the negation, the movement that completes the determination by reflecting its other in it, that is, by reflecting it into itself within the absolute positivity of the self as mediation.

The Absolute presupposes itself in the Logos, opposes itself to itself in Nature, posits itself concretely in spirit, which is the identity of the opposed terms, and this spirit itself becomes Logos, comprehends itself as presupposing itself. The Logos is the other of Nature; it is in its determination a negation. It therefore refers itself to this other and reflects it into itself. "If there were only ideas, there would be no ideas." In this self-negation as Nature, the Logos sublates itself. It is more than itself. It surmounts this negation which is its difference from itself. This is why the Logos is the Whole in the determination of the concept or of sense. It sublates itself in its own limitation; it negates itself; it comprehends Nature in itself. It translates its very opposition with Nature into its determination; *contradiction is the logical translation of this opposition.* The Logos contradicts itself. It is being as nature, but as the universal determination of being, it is also the nothingness of this determination. The contradiction of Essence is the contradiction of nature posited as contradiction, that of being simultaneously itself and its opposite, Nature and *Logos*, being and sense.

Here perhaps we get to the decisive point of Hegelianism, to this torsion of thought through which we are able to think conceptually the unthinkable, to what makes Hegel simultaneously the greatest irrationalist and the greatest rationalist who has existed. We cannot emerge from the Logos, but the Logos emerges from itself by remaining itself; since it is the indivisible self, the Absolute, it thinks the non-thought. It thinks sense in its relation to non-sense, to the opaque being of nature. It reflects this opacity into its contradiction. It raises thought, which would be only thought, over itself by obliging it to contradict itself; it turns this contradiction into the speculative means by which to reflect the Absolute itself.

Indeed, Nature is the negation of the Logos and this negation is creative. Nature is the opposite of thought, the opacity of brute existents. The Absolute would not be itself if the Logos did not negate itself, did not reflect itself into this opposite of itself. Certainly, Nature is also what reflects its other; it contains therefore this self-difference; it points to the Logos, sense. In its non-sense, it appears as lost sense; it is "spirit hidden, it is spirit for the spirit who knows it." There is therefore in nature this non-resolved contradiction that the Logos thinks; it is Nature and Logos at the same time. This is why there are sciences of nature and a philosophy of nature. Nature is also the absolute Idea. It is divine in this totality, but it does not appear to be so to itself. Nature does not conceive itself; it is spirit that conceives it. Insofar as it is conceived, we can say that Nature is the Logos, that it is its other; but insofar as Nature does not conceive itself, it preserves this proper opacity that turns it into the anti-idea. Some have reproached Hegel for having spoken of a "weakness of nature," for having shown the resistance of the brute existent to the Logos; it seems to us, on the contrary, that this reproach brings to light the originality of his thought. Hegel does not construct the world with the pseudo-concepts of the academy; he takes seriously "the pain, the work, and the patience of the negative." His concept is not the rational in the ordinary sense of the term, but the enlargement of thought, of reason which turns out to be capable of sublating itself as mere thought, as mere understanding, and to be capable of continuing to think itself in the beyond of mere abstract thought. Across spirit, the Logos thinks itself and its other. This is why it appears in the reason that structures the moments of the triad—Logos, Nature, Spirit—as the absolute mediation.

The judgments—*Logos is Nature, Nature is Logos*—state speculative thought quite imperfectly. They present neither the opposition nor the speculative identity of the terms, nor spirit which opposes them and reconciles them in itself. These *a priori* synthetic judgments do not ground their synthesis. On the other hand, Hegel takes spirit, the third term, in two different senses. Subjective spirit and objective spirit, which is realized as history, are themselves finite. Absolute spirit is in contrast the Absolute itself, and its authentic expression is philosophy, and in philosophy, the Logos, as speculative life. At the end of the *Encyclopaedia*, Hegel examines the different ways of reconnecting these three moments; since the Absolute is mediation, each of them must be able to present itself as being mediation, but the three syllogisms which result from it are not equivalent.

In the first, it is nature which serves as the middle term. Spirit comes out of the depths of nature, and the Logos appears in it through the intermediary of nature. The concept has here "the external form of passage," the process appears as an event. Mediation is represented as immediate necessity in the element of nature. The freedom of the universal that becomes for itself in spirit appears only as a product in one of the extremes.

This immediate aspect disappears in the second syllogism where spirit serves as the middle term. This mediation is that of the reflection of one of the moments in the other, of nature in the Logos, and of the Logos in nature. It is spirit, but a spirit *which remains finite*, which clarifies the opacity of natural existents in the light of sense. But reflection does not reconcile itself with immediacy. The opposition and the identity of the moments are not completely reconnected.

This is why the authentic mediation is that of the Logos—of the reason which grasps itself—the Logos divides itself into spirit and nature. It confirms itself in knowledge and in objectivity. It was the presupposition of nature. As philosophy, it becomes the position which posits its own presupposition and comprehends itself and its other. Thus this speculative life of the Logos is the light that clarifies itself, and clarifies nature and finite spirit; it is the light that is simultaneously immediacy and reflection. The existence of the Logos reflects itself into nature and into spirit.[2]

The Absolute thought as mediation, as internal reflection, dispels all the false problems of origin. Each of the moments refers to the others. None can be isolated. It is in the existence of the Logos, however, that this reflection of the Absolute thinks itself. The Logos says itself as itself and as the opposite of itself. It knows itself as itself in its own negation. It thinks "the power of the negative." And it is through this power of the negative that the Logos divides itself and sublates each of its determinations. It is this power of negation in the speculative that we must oppose to the use and sense of negation in empirical thought.

2. For the three mediations, see the *Encyclopaedia*, §§575, 576, 577.

Jusqu'à l'Être exalte l'étrange
Toute puissance du Néant.[1]

CHAPTER 4

EMPIRICAL NEGATION AND SPECULATIVE NEGATION

Hegel's philosophy is a philosophy of negation and negativity. The Absolute is only by determining itself, that is, by limiting itself, by negating itself. The Logos is the Absolute which abstracts itself from itself, separates itself from itself as nature, and thinks itself, but this thought sublates itself. It is more than itself. It surmounts its negation or

---

1. This quote comes from Paul Valéry, "Ebauche d'un Serpent," in *Oeuvres de Paul Valéry*, 1:146. The complete phrase is the following: "Cette soif qui te fit geant, / Jusqu'à l'Être exalte l'étrange / Toute-Puissance du Néant!" English translation by David Paul in *Paul Valery: An Anthology*: "The very thirst that made you huge / Can raise to the power of Being the strange / All-probing force of Nothingness!" (p. 263). Cf. below, LE 112.—TR.

its limitation, and becomes by means of contradiction the very thought of its other. This internal sublation is the genuine affirmation of the Absolute, the one which is no longer immediate; affirmation is negativity or the negation of the negation. Hegel's philosophy is therefore a philosophy of negation in a double sense. On the one hand, it deepens Spinoza's theme "which is of infinite importance": *all determination is negation*; it apprehends the lack or insufficiency in what is presented as positive. On the other hand, it exhibits, at the very heart of this negation, a repetition of negation, a negation of the negation which alone constitutes authentic positivity. Such is the work of the negative which appears first to be dissolution and death, which turns out, however, to be the thing that reveals "the Absolute as subject." Such a proposition amounts to saying that mediation alone, and not any sort of immediate base, sustains the whole. The text of Hegel that we are going to cite perhaps condenses all of his thought. It exhibits the prodigious power of the negative (our understanding or being's understanding) that makes the determination exist and that maintains the determination in its separation, as a sort of death, since, in its limitation, it grasps itself as what is not. One can prefer immediacy or innocence to this abstraction, but immediacy dissolves itself. It passes away without comprehending the being of nothingness; it is mediation unawares. Naive thought believes in the apparent positive, and abandons the negative that is the supreme resource of life and thought. In fact, it is by passing through this abstraction that negation is, that immediacy stops vanishing into nothingness, as it keeps doing because it leaves mediation outside of itself and because it is mediation's innocent victim. Immediacy reconciles itself with mediation just as mediation stops being an alien reflection in order to turn itself into immediacy. This text of Hegel concerns real negativity, that which exhibits itself in human existence and in life, as well as logical negativity, that which turns speculative thought into an absolute reflective life. If it is the case that the text speaks of one self-same negativity, is there an equivocation here? We cannot not ask this question, and the issue is especially to discover whether Hegel has more or less transposed an ontic negativity into an ontological negativity, a real opposition into a logical contradiction. The response, similar to the one that we gave for the relations of Logos to Nature, can only evoke thought's attempt to sublate itself, the logical torsion of contradiction that allows the Logos to comprehend itself and its other. But if, depending on texts from the *Phenomenology*, we want to consider speculative life as a super-structure in Hegel, reflecting more or less fortunately vital and human conflict, it would be necessary to recall Hegel's courses on Logic at Jena which would present to us a sort of ecstasy of thought, "each time in the immediacy of the idea, lost in it, and getting lost with it, and connecting ourselves with other consciousnesses (what we would be tempted to call other moments of the consciousness) only through the internal connections of the ideas to which the ideas belong." It would be necessary to recall as well the *Science of Logic* and the conclusion of the *Encyclopaedia* on the Logos. Undoubtedly, the text that we are going to cite is colored with passion; Hegelian thought transcends the distinction between pure humanism, the one his unfaithful disciples will develop, and absolute speculative life. Without ignoring the other aspect (pure humanism) and the Hegelian texts that could justify it, we believe that Hegel has chosen the speculative conception, being's self rather than the human self:

> The circle that remains self-enclosed and, like substance, holds its moments together, is an immediate relationship, one therefore which has nothing astonishing about it. But that the accidental as such, detached from what circumscribes it, what is bound and is actual only in its context with others, should attain an existence of its own and a separate freedom—this is the tremendous power of the negative; it is the energy of thought, of the pure ego. Death, if that is what we want to call this non-actuality, is of all things the most dreadful, and to hold fast to what is dead requires the greatest strength. Powerless, beauty hates the understanding for asking of her what it cannot do. But the life of spirit is not the life that shrinks from death and keeps itself pure from devastation, but rather the life that endures it and maintains itself in it. It wins its truth only when, in utter dismemberment, it finds itself. It is this power, not as something positive, which closes its eyes to the negative, as when we say of something that it is nothing or is false, and then, having done with it, turn away and pass on to something else; on the contrary, spirit is this power only by looking the negative in the face, and tarrying with it. This tarrying with the negative is the magical power that converts it into being. This power is identical with what we earlier called the subject, which by giving determinateness an existence [Dasein] in its own element sublates abstract immediacy, i.e. the immediacy which barely is, and thus is authentic substance: that being or immediacy whose mediation is not outside of it but which is mediation itself. (PH §32)

This text opposes speculative thought, which accepts the understanding and sublates it by passing through it (thus the understanding is a becoming and, as this becoming, it is rationality), to naive and empirical thought, which believes in the privilege of the positive by repressing the negative as "if it were nothing." There is indeed also the pseudo-innocence of the aesthete who seeks refuge in immediacy, but this return to a naivety which can no longer be so dissolves itself. Empirical thought refuses to take note of the negation in being. It attempts to exclude it, or when it cannot do that, it reduces it to a subjectivity "which is nothingness." It explains the negative judgment by an attitude of human consciousness which is an attitude of regret or hope, which is dialectical in the bad sense of the term, that is, which concerns only a dialogue with other humans, a way of warning them against a possible error or a way of correcting their actual errors. This consideration of the negative, however, would concern only man and would have no ontic or ontological value. Only the affirmative judgment would be the form of truth. "Being is, non-being is not." Even when an intellectualist philosopher recognizes the value of negative thought, he sees there only a value of thought, a means for thought to liberate itself and to rejoin being by means of a detour, but this negativity would concern only thought and not being itself. "If we can say that to think is to generalize, can we not say with as much reason and more depth, to think is to oppose? What characterizes thought is the faculty of putting affirmation and negation into a parallel relation. Being, the thing, is in a sense always positive. Thought liberates itself from being by giving a sense to non-being. What is not has the same right to be an object of thought just as much as what is."[2]

Hegel's originality lies in the rejection of this merely human explanation of negation—an explanation that we find for example in Bergson—as well as in the rejection of the particular privilege granted to the thought that would nevertheless maintain that "Being, the thing, is in a sense always positive." It is, however, a paradox for empirical thought to speak of a negation at the very heart of being. Yet the things *distinguish* themselves from one another, and one has to start from this distinction in order to understand the negation in being and in thought, before we even study the meaning of the negative judgment in empirical thought and in speculative thought.

The immediate intuition of the sensible already contains negation in the form of pure becoming. If we adhere to the most elementary description of sense-certainty, we observe that the sensible "this" passes away, the day stops being the day, and the night takes its place; this perpetual passage from one sensible "this" to another sensible "this" is a disappearance and an appearance; the disappearance is incontestably a

2. Léon Brunschvicg, *La modalité du jugement* (1897), 12.—Tr.

negation. It is true that, in order to observe it, one has to admit the existence of a being that remembers and compares the past to the present in terms of the past. "To represent that a thing has disappeared, it is not enough to perceive a contrast between the past and the present; it is necessary besides to turn our back on the present, to dwell on the past, and to think the contrast of the past with the present in terms of the past only, without letting the present appear in it" (CE 295). One has to say that the night was there, and therefore that it is no longer there. It is true that Bergson thinks that for a mind that would purely and simply follow the thread of experience, there would be no emptiness, no nothingness, not even a relative or partial nothingness, no possible negation. But he adds: "Endow this mind with memory, and especially with the desire to dwell on the past; give it the faculty of dissociating and distinguishing: it will no longer only note the present state of the passing reality; it will represent the passage as a change, and therefore as a contrast between what has been and what is. And as there is no essential difference between a past that we remember and a past that we imagine, it will quickly give rise to the idea of the possible in general" (CE 294).

Undoubtedly, what is essential here is the representation "of the passage as a change," "and the faculty of dissociating and distinguishing." The two characteristics are, moreover, equivalent. Let us substitute for Parmenides's pure being, or for Bergson's continuous duration, a multiplicity of beings or a succession of phases such that the one becomes for us a past distinct from the actual phase; then it will be really necessary to speak of change, of a night which was there and which, now, is no longer there. This amounts to saying that the disappearance assumes dissociation and distinction. But does Bergson put this faculty of dissociating and distinguishing only in our minds? Are there not for him living bodies which individuate themselves more or less in the continuity of the real, directions in the evolution of life which, mixed from the beginning, accentuate then their divergences, quite while remaining complementary, for example, the torpor of the plant, the instinct of insects, the intelligence of vertebrates? Is not matter, finally, such as Bergson defines it, characterized by a tendency incompletely realized in the exteriority of the parts, in the fragmentation that our mind pushes to its extreme? But if Bergson grants that dissociation and distinction are also in the things, in being, in the duration, and perhaps in the absolute principle, he has to introduce negation into the universe and into the Absolute itself, because negation and distinction imply one another, as Hegel tried to show.

If passage is also a change, the most naive consciousness therefore recognizes negation is its immediate form. It recognizes the nothingness of being and the permanence of being in its very annihilation. It recognizes the immediate mediation which is temporal mediation, the hopes of tomorrow and the nostalgia for yesterday. This negation in the sensible, however, is not striking because it is immediate and because the perceiving understanding attempts to surmount it. In effect, it substitutes for this diversely colored becoming determinations and determinate things which sustain the change; this passage from pure sense certainty to perception and to understanding is inevitable. It leads us to a universe where there are bodies, things, determinations, to a universe that involves a multiplicity of beings and determinations. Undoubtedly, memory is indispensable in order to transpose immediacy, in order to rediscover determinations, to turn cognition into recognition. But for Hegel, this memory, which is the interiorization of the world, corresponds to the essentialization of being. Being becomes appearance; it reflects itself just as we reflect on it. Bergson speaks of the genesis common to intelligence and materiality; concerning the understanding, Hegel says not only that it is our understanding, a subjective power of dissociating and distinguishing, of reflecting determinations, but also that it is still nature's understanding. "But it is far harder to to bring fixed thoughts into a fluid state than to do so with sensible Dasein. . . . [Sensible] determinations have only powerless, abstract immediacy, or being as such" (PH §33). In other words, change, negation, are obviously in sensible immediacy. They no longer present themselves in the same way in the reflected determinations that preserve their fixity and their independence, because they are sustained by the understanding or because, subjectively, the ego posits itself in them and maintains them in their identity. This reflection of immediacy into a universe where there are diverse beings and relations among these beings leads us directly to the mutual implication of diversity and negation, to empirical thought's stubborn rejection of the recognition of this implication, while speculative thought takes possession of it, justifying thereby the identity that it establishes between being's reflection and thought's reflection.

Before posing the problem in all its generality, it is interesting to show that Bergson, who criticizes the ideas of nothingness and negation by seeing there only a human illusion, explicitly admits that there is negation not only in things, in life, but also in the absolute principle itself that he places at the source of creative evolution. Actually, this principle inverts itself when it is interrupted. Thus there are two movements, two possible orders, and merely two, because the one is the inverse of the other. However, Bergson starts with the primacy of the thesis. One of the orders, the creative and living order, is the positive order in itself; the other, which results from the interruption of the first and which is its inverse, is the negative order in itself. The only possible mediation then shows itself as an effort at the heart of the second in order to rediscover the first. This effort, however, this negation of the negation which is life itself, is for Bergson a synthesis very inferior to the thesis which, alone truly positive and alone immediate affirmation, justifies for him the primacy of the positive over the negative. Nevertheless, there is in Bergson something negative, because the inverse order of the creative order is defined precisely by this inversion or this negation. Bergson himself says it explicitly:

> All of what appears positive to the physicist and to the geometer would become from this new viewpoint an interruption or inversion of the true positivity which one would have to define in psychological terms. Certainly, if we consider the admirable order of mathematics—the perfect agreement of the objects with which it concerns itself, the logic immanent to numbers and figures, our certainty of always getting the same conclusion, however diverse and complex our reasonings on the same subject, we hesitate to see in properties that are apparently so positive a *system of negations*; the *absence* rather than the presence of a true reality." (CE 208)

If Bergson refuses to grant an ontological significance to the negative judgment, he does not therefore fail to recognize negation, to recognize the negative in the real. He admits that an order, the order of the understanding, is a determination which is negation; he admits that it is sufficient therefore to overcome, to negate, the creative movement, in order to discover in its very absence an actually negative determination. He goes farther still when he recognizes that this determination presents itself as positive and turns out to be negative. He initiates the reversal of the positive into the negative, which is the transition to speculative thought because empirical thought knows only positivity. Empirical thought admits that there is a diversity of things, a diversity of determinations, but it deprives itself of discovering the negation in this existence of diversity. Hegel expresses the way of seeing that characterizes empirical thought by saying: "The distinguished terms subsist as indifferently different towards one another because each is self-identical, because identity constitutes its ground and element" (GL 418). "Now because in this manner they are not different in themselves, the difference is external to them" (GL 418–19). However, experience reveals at times that this external difference exhibits itself in one of the things as a lack, as an absence, through which a negation of this negation or a negativity appears. In Bergson's philosophy, which is a philosophy of life, this negation and this negativity are also evident. Instinct lacks intelligence— it could solve problems that it does not pose—but intelligence especially lacks instinct or intuition and seeks to overcome this deficiency. Desire, finally, is a lack. In the *Phenomenology*, Hegel shows us the living in the presence of the other that it lacks: "the essence of desire is an other that is not self-consciousness." Self-consciousness, however, also seeks self-certainty in the annihilation of the other, or in pleasure, but the other always returns as long as life lasts. And desire is a lived and permanent contradiction: "Cette soif qui te fit géant."[3]

The examples at which we just looked are still too particular. They are especially important in a philosophy of life or consciousness, in which a determination is actually felt as a negation, as a determinate emptiness, because it the emptiness of something. But how are we to extend this conception of determination as negation to all that presents itself immediately as positive? Isn't the consideration of the negative, then of negativity, a way of taking things upside down instead of considering them right side up, that is, as they present themselves to empirical thought, in positivity alone: "But this passive intelligence, mechanically keeping step with experience, neither anticipating nor following the course of the real, would have no aspiration to negate. It would not be able to receive an imprint of negation, because, once more, what exists can be recorded, but the non-existence of the non-existent cannot" (CE 292). It would still affirm, Bergson says, in the endpoints implicitly contained in the flow of the real; but, once more, if there are endpoints, it is the case that in nature there is not only being or continuous duration; rather, there is a multiplicity of beings, a multiplicity of more or less distinct determinations.

The problem of this distinction of things, of this diversity, is the very problem of the other: "Each thing is what it is, and is not what it is not."[4] Thus a negative aspect which could not be eliminated is stated in the thing. "Around each form, there is therefore a multiplicity of being and an infinite quantity of non- being."[5] Plato, who sought to resolve this problem in the *Sophist* in such a way as to make predication possible, as to make the harmonious mixture of genera and beings possible, without falling into inextricable confusion, attempted to substitute the other for the opposite of being. By admitting negation, he wanted to avoid falling into contrariety and contradiction: "So when it is asserted that a negative signifies an opposite, we shall not agree, but admit no more than this— that the prefix 'not' indicates something different from the words that follow, or rather from the things designated by the words pronounced

---

3. "The very thirst that made you huge." Cf. note 1, above.—TR.

4. Plato, *Sophist*, 256d.

5. Plato, *Sophist*, 256e.

after the negative."⁶ Not-A signifies all of what is not A. Among beings, Plato looks for the relations and the non-relations that are capable of defining a true discourse. The dialectician is to these relations what the musician is to his sounds: "And is there not something similar for all the sharps and flats? To possess the art of recognizing the sounds that can or cannot be combined is to be a musician."⁷ By recognizing alterity, Plato hopes to discover the eternal measure that allows the different genera to participate with one another in a true order; in his own way, he excludes contradiction from these mutual relations. In contrast, Hegelian dialectic will push this alterity up to contradiction. Negation belongs to things and to distinct determinations insofar as they are distinct. But that means that their apparent positivity turns out to be a real negativity. This negativity will condense the opposition in negation; negation will be the vital force of the dialectic of the real as well as that of logical dialectic. In the *Phenomenology*'s preface, speaking of the difference that exists between the ego and its object, Hegel writes: "The dissimilarity which exists in consciousness between the ego and the substance which is its object is the difference between them, the *negative* in general. This can be regarded as the defect of both, though it is their soul, or that which moves them. This is why some of the ancients conceived the void as the principle of motion, for they rightly saw the moving principle as the negative, though they did not yet grasp that the negative is the self" (PH §37). The meaning of this negative thought is really brought to light in this passage. Platonic alterity allows for an immobile dialectic, a dialectic that still does not have the self for its driving force. Hegelian dialectic, however, deepens alterity into position and opposition into contradiction. This is why dialectic is not merely the symphony of being, being in its measure and in its harmony; dialectic is the creative movement of the symphony, its absolute genesis, the position of being as self. Thus between Platonic dialectic and Hegelian dialectic, there is the same difference as between a symphony heard and the creation of the symphony. The one is being contemplated in its harmony and consonance; the other is the progression of being which posits itself and comprehends itself by positing itself, by identifying with itself in its internal contradiction. This movement expresses the transformation of diversity into opposition, and of opposition into contradiction.

This is what empirical thought observes: diversity, the things being distinct from one another, also one thing being as positive as the other. One has to reflect already in order to discover that a thing that

---

6. Plato, *Sophist*, 257b–c.

7. Plato, *Sophist*, 253b.

differs from another, and from all the others, is thereby a thing that contains negation. Empirical thought, all the same, recognizes difference as well as identity, but it still does not recognize internal or essential difference, no more than it recognizes concrete identity. For empirical thought, difference becomes therefore the indifferent diversity of things. It is "immediate difference. . . . In diversity the different things are each individually what they are, and indifferent to the relation in which they stand to each other. This relation is therefore external to them" (EL §117). Just as light is dispersed through the prism, so being shows itself broken into multiple fragments; the difference which is the difference of identity gets scattered into a multiplicity of terms external to one another. Difference realizes itself. The Logic knows this scattering as the Logos of diversity, a diversity that nature realizes with superabundance.

> Il se fit celui qui dissipe
> En conséquences son principe
> En étoiles son unité[8]

This diversity is the unity of identity and difference; difference is taken into identity which becomes its base. Each thing is what it is, and it is even so a determinate thing. But empirical consciousness takes this unity as immediate: "Difference as thus unity of itself and identity, is in itself determinate difference. It is not transformation into another, not relation to an other outside it: it has its other, identity, within itself, just as identity, having entered into the determination of difference, has not lost itself in it as its other, but preserves itself in it, is its reflection-into-self and its moment" (GL 418).

The existents are therefore there, each for itself, each identical to itself and different, but different from other existents. The moments fall "not in the same thing, but in diverse things. The contradiction which is present in the objective essence as a whole is distributed between two objects. In and for itself the thing is self-identical, but this unity with itself is disturbed by other things. Thus the unity of the thing is preserved and at the same time the otherness is preserved outside of the thing as well as outside of the consciousness" (PH §123). Hegel is going to do everything he can in order to reduce this indifferent diversity to opposition and to contradiction. We would find it impossible to accept this too-often formulated criticism of Hegelianism, that it neglects quali-

---

8. This quote comes from Paul Valéry, "Ebauche d'un Serpent," *Oeuvres de Paul Valéry*, 1:139. English translation by David Paul in *Paul Valery: An Anthology*: "He became the one who fritters away / His primal Cause in consequences, / And in stars his Unity" (p. 247).—Tr.

tative nuances in order to bury itself in opposition: the arbitrary translation of alterity into contradiction. "We grasp here vividly the particularity and perhaps the profound vice of Hegel's thought; it wants to
recognize only the difference of positive and negative and it fails to recognize the differences of quality. When comparing them, it does not say
that they are simply other; it limits itself to finding them contradictory
because they are not identical."[9] Hegel perfectly recognizes dispersion in
space and time, and his logic involves the moment of indifferent diversity, but only as a moment. Opposition is inevitable not because there is
only a multiplicity of things, of finite modes, or of monads, but because
each is in relation with the others, or rather with all the others, so that its
distinction is its distinction from *all the rest*. The complete distinction of a
thing reconnects it to the whole Universe, reduces differences to essential
and internal difference, to the difference between a thing or a determination and *its other*. This duality is the speculative duality, the fundamental
double; that is what we still vaguely catch a glimpse of in the dissolution
of finite things. "There is no individual thing in nature, than which there
is not another more powerful and strong. Whatsoever thing be given,
there is something stronger whereby it can be destroyed."[10] We catch
sight of this speculative duality in empirical oppositions, which are
always incomplete because nature is the element of exteriority, the element in which the absolute Idea, subtracting itself "from the relation of
self-certainty" (PH §807), earns its full freedom. What is at issue therefore is not the rejection of varied nuances and concrete dissimilarities of
existents. Natural science *observes* these existents, classifies them and
reconnects them to one another, but its observation can never grasp *passage itself*, mediation. Observation transforms what is engendered and
made, what comprehends itself, into static being. It superficially displays
the authentic genesis that concerns the emergence of the self-relation in
the relation to an other, the emergence of identity in difference. Empirical
thought recognizes only exteriority or separated interiority. Without sublating itself, it cannot discover that "the object is in one and the same
respect the opposite of itself: it is for itself, so far as it is for another, and
it is for another, so far as it is for itself" (PH §128).[11]

---

9. Andler, *Revue de Métaphysique*, article on Hegel, July–September
1930. [Translation based on Hyppolite's French.—TR.]

10. Spinoza, *Ethics*, tr. R. H. M. Elwes (New York: Dover, 1955), 191
(Axiom, book IV).

11. Some will notice Hegel's pantragism, which condenses the scattering of the existent into a fundamental duality. Diversity is a consequence of
essential difference, but essential difference always returns.

Diversity is reduced to opposition insofar as it is reduced to duality, in which each term is reconnected essentially to its other, and difference becomes *their* difference. We have seen Bergson spontaneously rediscover something like this speculative principle when he places a duality at the creative source. Then the other of the creative principle is *its* other; it is therefore the negation of it. But, for Bergson, reciprocity is not genuine. This is why his philosophy is sometimes a monism, sometimes a dualism, without any conceivable reconciliation. Experience provides us with examples, and something like images of speculative opposition, images of the positive and negative. And we know indeed, because of Kant's essay on negative magnitudes, that the negative is positive just as much as the positive is negative. Real opposition, however, is always imperfect, because it is incomplete (the father and the son are not just a father and a son, the high and the low are also places determined otherwise). Real opposition does not take into account all of the experience. The Logos, however, thinks this very incompleteness. It comprehends diversity as diversity. It situates diversity and sees it necessarily concentrate itself into a series of oppositions and contradictions, because there is *only one thing in itself*; this is absolute self-genesis, the positing of its own identity in self-difference.

The transition from diversity to opposition can be shown in two ways. On the one hand, diversity reflects itself into the knowing subject, which becomes the base and soil of opposition; on the other hand, external, quantitative diversity concentrates itself into intrinsic difference, Leibniz's *discernible*, and this intrinsic difference becomes the very opposition of the thing, its internal contradiction. Diversity is such only for a subject external to the diverse things. "In consequence of the distinct things being thus indifferent to the difference between them, it falls outside them into a third thing, which *compares*. This external difference, as an identity of the objects related, is similarity; as a non-identity of them, is dissimilarity" (EL §117). Identity transposes itself into the similarity of diverse things, difference into dissimilarity, but the measure falls outside of them. It is the knowing self which becomes this measure in a self-alienated reflection. "Whether or not something is like something else does not concern either the one or the other; each of them is only self-referred, is in and for itself what it is; identity or non-identity, as similarity and dissimiliarity, is the verdict of a third party exterior to the two terms of comparison" (GL 419–20). Letting things subsist in their unaltered positivity, thought takes upon itself the movement of comparison: "In the self-alienated reflection, therefore, similarity and dissimilarity appear as mutually unrelated, and in relating them to one and the same thing, reflection holds them apart by the introduction of 'insofar as,' of sides and respects. The diverse, which are one and the same, to which both similarity and dissimilarity are related, are therefore from one side similar to one another, but from another side are dissimilar, and in so far as they are similar, they are not dissimilar. Similarity is related only to itself, and likewise dissimilarity is only dissimilarity" (GL 420–21). But in this case, the external difference sublates itself, because similarity is such only in relation to dissimilarity and vice versa. The viewpoint of similarity never encounters the viewpoint of dissimilarity, and each of these viewpoints means nothing but itself. Insofar as they are dissimilar, things can be similar; insofar as they are similar, they can be dissimilar. Thought becomes taut and relaxed in similitude and dissemblance; it supports its own opposition. This is why the contradiction that we forbid to the things gets folded back into the mere, subjective activity that compares them.

> The effect of this is to remove the unity of similarity and dissimilarity from the thing, and to adhere to what would be the thing's own reflection and the merely implicit reflection of similarity and dissimilarity, as a reflection external to the thing. But it is this reflection that, in one and the same activity, distinguishes the two sides of similarity and dissimilarity, hence contains both in one activity, lets the one show, be reflected, in the other. But the usual tenderness for things, whose only care is that they do not contradict themselves, forgets here as elsewhere that in this way the contradiction is not resolved but merely shifted elsewhere, into subjective or external reflection generally, and this reflection in fact contains in one unity as sublated and mutually referred, the two moments which are enunciated by this removal and displacement as a merely posited. (GL 423–24)

However, this external reflection does not reflect on itself; it is beyond the compared things, it is subjective. Empirical thought does not emerge from the diversified content; it does not posit the content, although it calls it positive. The relations that it establishes in its comparisons are tautological or heterological. When it raises itself up to the explanation of things and presses its own contradiction, either it reduces the contradiction by means of linguistic devices (while talking about things, it speaks only about itself, and therefore repeats itself without any advancement), or it dissolves these relations and results in skepticism. The contradiction brought to light in this last case remains a formal and subjective contradiction. In the *Phenomenology*'s chapter on understanding, Hegel insists on this formalism of explanation, this play of thought with itself which ends up by losing all seriousness (the nothingness of subjectivity).

Contradiction stops being formal and subjective when it is *the contradiction of the things themselves*. The content then is no longer received as an alien datum; it is posited. The self of reflection and the self of the content become identified. Thought is no longer a game about or around the content for which skepticism always lies in wait; it is the very thought of the *Thing*. Explanation coincides with reality itself; it is reality's development. But for that to happen, thought must sublate empiricism, as much as the formalism which is empiricism's complement. It must apprehend the content as a moment of the form and the form as the universal form of the content, that is, it must see in the things this activity of comparison that was only external reflection. This subjective activity, which in one single act was reflecting similarity into dissimilarity, must be understood as the very activity of the real. Then reflection is no longer subjective; it becomes the content's reflection. External reflection must see its contradiction in the content itself.

It does this by considering the transition from diversity to opposition, no longer merely subjectively but objectively. Subjectively, the reflection of similarity in dissimilarity, and, reciprocally, the reflection of dissimilarity in similarity, is the opposition of the self to the self, but this opposition is also immediately the opposition in the thing; the latter is similar in its dissimilarity, dissimilar in its similarity. The things reflect one another, and this reflection is their opposition. "Similarity is an identity only of those things which are not the same, not identical with one another: and dissimilarity is a relation of things dissimilar. The two therefore do not fall on different aspects or points of view in the thing, without any mutual affinity, but one throws light into the other. Diversity thus comes to be reflective difference, or difference in itself, a determinate difference" (EL §118). Subjective reflection and objective reflection then coincide, because difference has become internal difference or essential difference. It appears as the opposition of the positive and the negative.

Each thing differs from all the others, but this difference is not only a quantitative difference, an external difference. "Philosophy has to do, not with unessential determinations, but with a determination in so far as it is essential; its element and content is not the abstract or non-actual, but the actual, that which posits itself and is alive within itself— Dasein within its own concept" (PH §47). Unessential difference is merely quantitative difference, the surface of being, that which does not allow the thing to be distinguished by its *absolute characteristic*, that by which it is made to be what it is. A thing is for itself, reflected into itself, insofar as it is discernible from *all the others*; this is the principle that Leibniz has brought to light as the principle of indiscernibles. Such an absolute characteristic, however, is no longer the result of an external comparison; it belongs necessarily to the thing; it constitutes its being. Leibniz indeed insisted on the necessity of overcoming the thing's exteriority in order to reach its uniqueness. "That everything is different from everything else is a very superfluous proposition, for things in the plural immediately involve multiplicity and wholly indeterminate diversity. But the proposition that no two things are completely like each other, expresses more, namely, determinate diversity" (GL 422). If identity suits things, dissimilarity or intrinsic difference also suits them, since they must be distinguished or differentiated in themselves from all the others. This difference (found within them) is essential difference, because it is the difference posited in the identity of the thing; this difference is what puts the thing in opposition to *all the rest.* "We are therefore presented with this determination, that both moments, similarity and dissimilarity, are different in one and the same thing, or that the difference, while falling asunder, is at the same time one and the same relation. This has therefore passed over into opposition" (GL 423). Undoubtedly, Leibniz, who stated the principle of indiscernibles, does not himself reach this consequence. By positing the monads for which spontaneity is the absolute form, he limits them in themselves, limits them from the outside by a preestablished harmony. This representation, however, is inadequate to the position of the self that he has granted to his monads. The principle that attributes an intrinsic and qualitative difference, a precise determination to each thing, is also what dissolves the thing in universal mediation, resolves it into the ground. Thereby, the principle opposes the thing to all the rest. "It is just through the absolute character of the thing and its opposition that it relates itself to others, and is essentially only this relating. The relation, however, is the negation of its self-subsistence, and it is really the essential property of the thing that is its undoing" (PH §125). Each distinct thing is opposed therefore and is opposed to all the rest insofar as it is actually distinct. Opposition is the result of this absolute distinction in the things, as it was in the subjective reflection of the unity of similarity and dissimilarity of the measuring self. It is the universal self which, in its determination, is opposed to itself, is itself and its other, the universal and the particular. If Leibniz had not limited the monads' reflection from the outside, if he had not alienated the absolute position of the self into a God external to the monads themselves, he would have seen this principle of distinction being actualized into opposition, and opposition positing its own ground. "In opposition, the determinate reflection, difference, finds its completion. It is the unity of identity and difference; its moments are different in one identity and thus are opposites" (GL 424). The opposition, however, that posits the one over and against the other, one term and *its* other, that unhinges the moment of similarity from that of dissimilarity, each posited by the other, the positive and the negative, must make the complete unity of these terms appear, a complete unity that preserves an appearance of independence:

> Difference in itself is essential difference, the positive and the negative such that the positive is the identical self-relation in such a way as not to be the negative, and the negative is the different by itself so as not to be the positive. Thus either has an existence of its own in proportion as it is not the other. The one is made visible in the other, and is only in so far as that other is. Essential difference is therefore opposition; according to which the different is not confronted by *any* other but by *its* other. That is, either of these two (positive and negative) is stamped with a characteristic of its own only in relation to the other: the one is only reflected into itself as it is reflected into the other. And so with the other. Either in this way is the other's own other. (EL §119)

Now empirical thought, which was seeing only positive existents, is completely reversed. Each thing is opposed to all the others, but this opposition concretizes itself into the opposition of one and of other. The one, the positive, is what it is only because it excludes its other, the negative, and yet subsists only through it; the other, the negative, excludes the positive, and likewise subsists only through it. The positive, however, appears as the reflection of opposition into similarity, while the negative appears as its reflection into dissimilarity. Each term shows in itself its own opposite. The positive is negative in itself, "it is contradiction in itself"; the negative is positive just as much as the positive is negative, but opposition as opposition is reflected into it. "The negative is, therefore, the whole opposition based, as opposition, on itself, absolute difference that is not related to an other; as opposition, it excludes identity from itself—but in doing so excludes itself; for as self-relation it is determined as the very identity it excludes" (GL 433).

The positive, therefore, is recognized as opposition only in the negative; one has to start from the negative in order to comprehend the positive. Every determination is negation, and, starting from the reverse side of empirical thought, one has to grasp determination as negation, but negation here is the posited difference of the self to itself. It is the contradiction of the determinate existent that is not identical to itself, but different from itself. This difference of the self to itself is the hidden driving force of all the real oppositions, those which are more or less capable of prefiguring the ontological opposition. The external relations of one thing to *its* other are also relations of the self to itself, of the self to its own alienation (thus the slave differs from the master and posits itself as master), but there is no separated interiority. In its external relation, the self posits itself; in the for-the-others alone, it is for itself. The dialectic of the real therefore makes diversity develop into opposition, opposition into contradiction, since each of the terms, the positive or the negative, is the opposite of itself; and contradiction resolves itself into the ground. Determinate things collapse by positing their ground. The Absolute is, because the determinate finite is not, but this "is not" is essential. It is only across this negation that the Absolute posits itself. Contradiction is already in empirical representation which does not comprehend (*n'en prend conscience pas*) that as such,

> representation everywhere has contradiction for its content, it does not become aware of it, but remains an external reflection which passes from similarity to dissimilarity, or from negative relation to the reflection-into-self, of the distinct sides. It holds these two determinations over against one another and has in mind only them, but not their transition, which is the essential point and which contains their contradiction. . . . Thinking reason, however, sharpens, so to speak, the blunt difference of the diverse, the simple variety of representation, into essential difference, into opposition. Only when the diverse has been pushed to the point of contradiction do they become active and and lively towards one another, receiving in contradiction the negativity which is the immanent pulsation of spontaneous and living movement. . . . More precisely, when the difference of reality is pushed a little farther, it develops from difference into opposition, and from this into contradiction, so that in the end the sum total of all realities simply becomes absolute contradiction within itself (the Absolute contradicts itself). Representation—not speculative thought—which abhors contradiction, as nature abhors a vacuum, rejects this conclusion; for in considering contradiction, it stops short at the one-sided resolution of it into nothingness, and fails to recognize the positive side of contradiction where it becomes absolute activity and absolute ground. (GL 441–42)

Through the contradiction of the self to itself, ontological thought develops itself; it grasps the determinations of the Absolute, or the categories, as negative moments, as differences of the Absolute, but the Absolute is itself only in this negativity or in this negation of the negation. It posits itself, and it is this self-position in opposition which constitutes infinite Mediation.

We thus see how negation, the negative in general, is for speculative thought the characteristic of determinations. But what are we to make of the negation of judgment? What is the negative judgment for empirical thought and for speculative thought? How does this difference, which is negation itself, get translated into the judgment? Empirical thought wants to know only the positivity of things; it does not grasp them in their determinations as differences of identity. It is therefore clear that empirical thought recognizes only the affirmative judgment as the expression of truth. This judgment alone can receive empirical content. It says of a thing what constitutes it, what exhibits its predicates. For empirical thought, however, the negative judgment says nothing; it posits no determinate content. If, from this viewpoint, we analyze negation as Bergson, for example, does in the fourth chapter of *Creative Evolution*, we rediscover the attitude of empirical thought or of dogmatic thought which dispels the reflection of being in order to drive it back into subjectivity: "We fail to see," Bergson says, "that while affirmation is an act of pure intelligence, there enters into negation an extra-intellectual element, and it is precisely to the intrusion of an alien element that negation owes its specific character" (CE 287) Kant already noted: "From the viewpoint of the content of our knowledge in general . . . negative propositions have for their proper function simply to forbid error. Negation is an attitude of the mind vis-à-vis an eventual affirmation. . . . It is a judgment about a possible judgment. It is not directly a judgment about the real" (A709/B737).[12] Such a perspective on negation refers to the empirical postulate that the real is given, that it is external content; and yet the real is for Bergson, as for Hegel, creation. How would creation be possible if negation were not inherent to the whole process, if, as still-deficient matter, it were not resistant to the creative impetus, for which it would be simultaneously determination and insufficiency? Bergson, however, does not conceive creation as sense; he does not like Hegel therefore attempt a logic that is the generating movement of being; this logic would have led him to rediscover the weight and the seriousness of negation, instead of seeing there a human critique, connected to human conditions, which degenerates too often into a vain dialectic, into a sophistry that Hegel indeed denounces many times.

Empirical thought cannot give a positive significance to the negation of judgment, because its postulate does not grant it the right to give a negative signification to the affirmative judgment. Since the real is always positive, the negative judgment can say nothing about the real; it

---

12. Translation from Immanuel Kant, *The Critique of Pure Reason*, tr. Norman Kemp Smith (New York: St. Martin's Press, 1965), 574.

is therefore subjective reflection. To say that the table is not white is not to say what it is, but merely to warn us against what we might think it is or to regret what it has been or could be. Negative judgment implies a delay in relation to the real, an evasion towards the possible or towards the hypothetical. Pedagogy begins with it, a useful discussion in the human, social environment, but this degenerates very quickly into wandering and inconsistent idle talk, which no longer knows where it is, which is cut off from the thing itself. The empirical attitude governs this critique of negative judgment. In order to give another sense to the negative judgment, one would have already to conceive negation within being. "Negation," Bergson says, "is but half of an intellectual act, whose other half we leave indeterminate. If I pronounce the negative proposition, 'This table is not white' I mean that you ought to substitute for your judgment, 'the table is white,' another judgment. I give you an admonition and the admonition refers to the necessity of a substitution" (CE 289). This substitution, however, is not contained in the negative judgment which refers only to new experiences. To say that this shape is not conical is to leave the indefiniteness of shapes open. In order that negation has a sense, it would have to be the case that the not-A of A be exactly its other. This would imply that A would be itself the negation of this other, its opposite. But then the position of A would already be a negation. Simultaneously, it would contain and exclude its other. So we return to our earlier analysis of negation within being.

The empirical does not present this opposition in its pure state as speculative thought does. This is why the thought of the empirical misunderstands the scope of negation. "In vain do we attribute to negation a power to create ideas *sui generis*, symmetrical to those that affirmation created and directed in an opposite direction. No idea will emerge from negation, because it has no other content than that of the affirmative judgment which it negates" (CE 290). Bergson can therefore conclude: "Let knowledge have its exclusively scientific or philosophic character. Assume, in other words, that reality comes to inscribe itself on a mind that is concerned only with things and is not interested in persons. We will only affirm that such and such a thing is; we will never affirm that a thing is not" (CE 291). Why, however, is there this stubbornness against putting affirmative judgment, the form of truth, and negative judgment, which denounces simple possible error, on the same level? Bergson gives us the reason for it with such profundity that it turns against him, by exhibiting the peculiar character of empirical judgment, its ambiguity, and undoubtedly the negation that is dissimulated in it.

> Why is it that affirmation and negation are so persistently put on the same level and endowed with an equal objectivity?

How comes it that we have so much difficulty in recognizing that negation is subjective, artificially cut short, relative to the human mind and still more to social life? The reason is undoubtedly that negation and affirmation are both expressed by propositions, and that any proposition, being constructed out of words which symbolize concepts, is something relative to social life and to the human intellect. Whether I say "the ground is damp" or "the ground is not damp," in both cases the terms, "ground" and "damp," are concepts more or less artificially created by the human mind, that is, extracted from the continuity of experience by means of its free initiative." (CE 291)

But, in Bergson, there are indeed also distinctions that are not artificial. Every judgment assumes that the continuity of experience does not exist without allowing these distinctions. The affirmative, empirical judgment is therefore heterological, synthetic in Kant's language; it says *A is B*. For Kant, tautology is empty formalism. Experience learns something, the content is enriched; the affirmative, empirical judgment allows us to go from A to B without repeating ourselves and without contradicting ourselves. The connection between A and B, however, can in effect be artificial, human, contingent; consequently, error exists, the negative, empirical judgment arises and is opposed to the positive judgment: "A is not B." This opposition forces empirical thought to return to experience, because it would be contradictory to say that A is simultaneously B and is not B; this contradiction is the sign of error, of absolute falsity. By means of contradiction, Leibniz defines the false and the true, passing through the detour of the false in order to define the True. He does not say that *Verum index sui et falsi*, but that the true is the opposite of or what contradicts the false. "Our reason is based upon two great principles, first, that of contradiction, by means of which we judge that to be false which involves contradiction and that to be true which contradicts or is opposed to the false."[13] Contradiction therefore destroys itself and leads us back to the affirmative, empirical judgment, to the heterological judgment. But isn't this judgment itself contradictory? To say that "A is B" is either to say nothing from the viewpoint of being which would be identical to itself or to say that A is not-A, that it is other than itself, that it differs from itself. Experience's synthetic judgment decomposes into an analytic judgment that tells us nothing and into a judgment that contradicts itself. Empirical thought, however, runs away from this dilemma.

---

13. Leibniz, *Monadology*, tr. George R. Montgomery, in Leibniz (LaSalle, Ill.: Open Court, 1973), §31, p. 238.

From this point on, the empirical, negative judgment acquires its speculative meaning; it negates the synthetic predication; it refers to the tautological reflection of the terms. To say that "A is not B" means that A is A and B is B; abstract tautology reappears in reflection, but this tautology is opposed to the heterology of experience. In his analysis of affirmative judgment, Hegel demonstrates the inherent contradiction of this form. This form says that the *singular is universal.* That the body is heavy means not only that this singular body possesses a property common to all the bodies in a field of gravity, but also that it is determined by the universal conditions of nature, the *a priori* laws that make a field of gravity possible. Now this body is this body insofar as it is for itself a singular existent. The affirmative judgment therefore becomes the negative judgment: the *singular is not the universal*; but this judgment has two tautological meanings: the *singular is the singular,* the *universal is the universal.* However, since what is at issue here is speculative moments, moments of the concept, these tautologies are the full and concrete identity; each is itself. The singular is itself only by being the non-singular, that is, the universal; the universal is itself only by being the non-universal, that is, the singular. Each is itself and its other, each becomes its other. In this way the affirmative judgment, the *singular is the universal,* is reconstituted, but this happens because each term, by being reflected into itself, sublates itself in its self-negation; the heterology of experience has become a tautology by transforming itself into a unity of opposite terms, by grasping difference as self-difference. Its progress really is synthetic, like that of empirical thought, but it is at the same time analytic. It is the unity of itself in the other, the tautology which is no longer formal identity. By means of the negative judgment, empirical thought negates merely itself; it negates the objectivity of its connections. It leads to the empirical subjectivity of experience, such as Hume brought to light. There are connections, but they lack significance; they are subjective, contingent, and always susceptible to being negated. But this negation of empirical thought is reflected merely into empty tautology: A is A, B is B. This thought, which is given the content, cannot engender it, cannot think mediation, which is the genesis of being as the self. Empirical thought *observes,* it does not comprehend *passage*; it indicates merely, in this oscillation between affirmative and negative judgment, what is required of speculative thought, the reconciliation of the empirical connection, which is rich with content but without reflection (affirmative judgment), and of the tautology, which is indeed reflection but reflection without content (negative judgment). The speculative judgment presents itself in such a way that

> the general nature of the judgment or proposition, which involves the difference of subject and predicate, is destroyed

by the speculative proposition, and the proposition of identity which the former becomes contains the counter-thrust against the subject-predicate relationship. This conflict between the general form of a proposition and the unity of the concept which destroys it is similar to the conflict that occurs in rhythm between meter and accent. Rhythm results from the floating center and the unification of the two. So, too, in the philosophical proposition the identification of subject and predicate is not meant to destroy the difference between them, which the form of the proposition expresses; their unity, rather, is meant to emerge as a harmony. The form of the proposition is the appearance of the determinate sense, or the accent that distinguishes its fulfilment; but that the predicate expresses the substance, and that subject itself falls into the universal, this is the unity in which the accent dies away. (PH §61)

The Absolute is subject, identical to itself or concept, but it is the self of being which posits itself in its determinations and is identified with itself in its negation. *The Logos is nature.* We will now have to consider this structure of the speculative proposition and its relations with the empirical proposition in order to discover the categories as moments of the Absolute, of this absolute genesis which is the Absolute itself.

PART **III**

THE
CATEGORIES
OF THE
ABSOLUTE

CHAPTER 1

EMPIRICAL PROPOSITION AND SPECULATIVE PROPOSITION

Hegel would not be able to maintain the distinction that Kant makes between thought and knowledge. There is no empty thought; every thought of self is at the same time a thought of being, just as every thought of being is a thought of self. No matter what, thought cannot escape from being. The thought of nothingness is also a thought of being; it finds being again in nothingness just as it finds itself again in every being that it thinks. Thought therefore has no need of an alien investment that, as content, would be added to the form. This distinction is valid only when we remain at the level of the phenomenon, that is, at the level of being's appearance, of its division for consciousness. As such, consciousness expresses this division, which is ontological; it corresponds to the diremption, if it is true that "self-division and appearance are identical."

Kant did not know how to overcome this moment of consciousness as such. His philosophy is a Phenomenology. He had not been able
to surmount the division of intuition and concept, particular and universal. The theme of his correspondence with Beck is the possibility of
beginning the critique with the transcendental deduction and not with
the aesthetic. What is at issue, however, is not only a question of method;
the opposition between sensible intuition and concept is what is central
in critical philosophy. Kantian philosophy is essentially a philosophy of
judgment. "To think is to judge," but the judgment is not a more or less
abstract connection of representations. On the contrary, it presents the
primordial division of what is originally one. On the level of judgment
(*Urteil*), singular intuition and conceptual determination distinguish
themselves. Kant thought he was able to discover, in Aristotle's formal
logic, the empty form that states the structure of judging. After abstracting from all the content of judgment, the quantity, the quality, the relation, and the modality of judgments remain. This table, however, is not
yet the table of the categories. It is only the guiding thread which allows
us to discover the categories, for the category states not the analytic but
synthetic unity of a diversity. It is already knowledge by means of its
objective orientation.

In his Logic, which is the discourse of being, Hegel reverses this
Kantian perspective. The forms of judgment, like the forms of the concept and of reason, are not empty. Thought is always at the same time
intuitive and discursive. Therefore these forms are significant by themselves. They say being as much as they say thought; they say the content
of the absolute form, which, as absolute, is all content. By therefore comprehending the judgment as such, which does not mean comprehending
the examples of the judgment—the rose is red or man is mortal—
thought will reflect on itself; it will be both the thought of the self and the
thought of being: "since they are laws of pure thought, and pure thought
is in itself universal, and therefore a knowledge which immediately contains being, and therein all reality, these laws are absolute concepts, and
are inseparably the essential principles of form and of things" (PH §299).

When Hegel, in his Logic, after having spoken of immediate
being and of essence, speaks of the concept and of the judgment, he
reverses the Kantian order that leads from the forms to the categories,
then to the schematism. He will discover sense as sense in the form of
thought. The universal is not the abstract medium of thought within
which the sensible determines itself conceptually. It is the primordially
synthetic unity, the not yet developed originary identity, but this means
the identity of being and thought. Hegel insists on the distinction
between this originary unity and the abstract ego. In Kantian philosophy,
Hegel catches sight of this originary unity in the form of the imagination:

conceived not as the middle term that gets inserted between an existing absolute subject and an absolute existing world. The productive imagination must rather be recognized as what is primary and original, as that out of which subjective Ego and objective world first sunder themselves into the necessary bipartite appearance and product, and as the sole in-itself. This power of the imagination is the original two-sided identity. The identity becomes subject in general on one side, and object on the other; but originally it is both. And the imagination is nothing but reason . . . as it appears in the sphere of empirical consciousness. (FK 73)

This appearance of reason in the empirical sphere is precisely the judgment which states the originary division. Just as the concept in general, as the concept of the concept, the universal of thought and being, expresses the originary unity, the judgment expresses division or determination, which is present in various ways, as the division of intuition (the sensible "this") and conceptual determination, of substrate and properties, of the existent and the category as universal predicate. This is why one has to seek the sense of this form of judgment without specifying in advance what the subject will be and what the predicate will be. It is necessary to abandon oneself to the intrinsic movement of thought. The judgment is the position of the moments of the concept. It is necessary to construct a dialectical history, not an empirical history of the judgment. In his *Logic*, Hegel treats judgment neither by reducing it to symbolic formulas which would be an abstraction from empirical content, nor by taking into consideration this empirical content (concrete examples of judgment). The absence of this content, of this other, is the driving force of this dialectic, because the form contains the content as something that has been hollowed out; it moves in order to sublate and surmount its own insufficiency. But it is the form immanent to all content. Its sense is the movement of thought in general which is at the same time the movement of being. What is at issue therefore is not static formal laws—a logic reduced to a natural history, to an observation of thought's mechanisms which erases sense—but the autonomous development of the absolute form of thought which is always more than form, since it bears in itself the content as *its* other. This diremption, which appears precisely in the judgment, turns abstract identity into a concrete identity as well—and therefore turns this concrete originary analysis into a synthesis as well.

The judgment is the ambiguous place where truth appears, but not yet where it is grounded. It is ambiguous because it is a judgment of things as well as the judgment of a consciousness. Empirical consciousness sublates itself by judging, by stating propositions and by affirming them. But its judgment claims to be valid simultaneously as an objective, universal judgment and as a psychological process. The consciousness that judges says being, the essence of things, but it knows as well that it is beginning to reflect on itself. And the determinations that this consciousness attributes to the things appear ambivalent to it: they are properties of things and intellectual instruments of their apprehension. They are being itself and the representation of being. If the judgment is ambiguous, insofar as it appears to be situated at the heart of an empirical consciousness whose intellectual event it is, it is ambiguous in still another way. It states the relative identity of moments of the concept: singular (or individual), particular, universal. These two ambiguities (subjectivity-objectivity, singular-universal) coincide in the critical question: "How are synthetic *a priori* judgments possible? They are possible through the original, absolute identity of the heterogeneous. This identity, as the unconditioned, sunders itself, and appears as separated into the form of a judgment, as subject and predicate, or particular and universal" (FK 72). To say what the things are is to judge; and what they are, even when the issue is that of empirical predicates like "the air is heavy," they are by referring to universal predicates, to what conditions all of nature. The judgment says immediately the logicity of being. What happens to Kant, however, according to Hegel, is that for which he himself reproached Hume. He did not see the full scope of his question; he remained at the subjective and external significance of the problem, as if the response could be only found in the relative, ambiguous identity of a self-consciousness and of an experience whose source would remain always in the dark.

Empirical consciousness is the place where judgment, the phenomenon of diremption and of relative identity, appears. Originally identical, thought and being are smashed in two. Judgment seems to be the judgment of one consciousness. We can still say, according to the other aspect, the aspect of determinations, that the universal presents itself in the singular and the particular. It *appears* immediately in them. This body is heavy. The singular is stated in conceptual universality and the universal is determined; in this determination, it negates itself and sublates itself. The universal is not the abstract (in the psychological sense), inert universal that we juxtapose, from the outside, to an opaque existent given in an unknown way; the universal is the movement of its own determination. The dialectical history of judgment consists in replacing an observation that congeals and that does not apprehend passage itself with this genesis of sense. Kant *finds* the forms of judgment, but the issue is not that of constructing them artificially, from the outside, in order to reconnect what is so found. The necessity of these forms is their internal dialectic: "However, this unity of universality and the activity does not exist for this observing consciousness, because that unity is essentially the inner movement of the organism and can only be grasped as concept; but observation seeks the moments in the form of being, of enduring being" (PH §261). Now, the discovery of the categories, of the species of the pure category, is the discovery of the difference at the heart of self-consciousness's originary unity:

> since the difference originates in the pure ego, in the pure understanding itself, it is thereby made explicit that the immediacy, the making of assertions and finding of differences, is here given, and we begin to conceive. But to pick up the plurality of categories again in some way or other as a welcome find, taking them, e.g., from the various judgments, and complacently accepting them so, is in fact to be regarded as an outrage on science. Where else should the understanding be able to demonstrate a necessity, if it is unable to do so in its own self, which is pure necessity? (PH §235)

Judgment is the difference that appears and the presupposed identity; to itself it is not its own ground. Judgment says simultaneously the unity and the opposition of terms, but it says this immediately and it is this immediacy that makes it be ambiguous. It does not yet appear as mediation. Judgment does not posit originary unity as something maintained in the duality of terms. It does not posit the Absolute of thought and being as mediation, which reason alone can do. (Recalling Aristotle, Hegel calls it the syllogism; he does this because dialectical reason, introducing the opposition of terms in order to comprehend mediation, replaces the Aristotelian syllogism whose ontological scope resembles dialectical reason but which congeals being instead of engendering it.) Judgment is therefore this precarious place where the understanding resides (*cette demeure précaire*), this precarious place that oscillates between the subjective and the objective, the empirical and the transcendental, perceptual judgment and experiential judgment. It fixes determinations without authentically conceiving their movement. Truth haunts judgment but judgment alone cannot ground it. Some would say that the deaf activity of thought seems to come out of the judgment completely formed, as if from the head of Jupiter. Judgment's immediacy appears in the non-developed copula; judgment appears simultaneously as being and as relation of thought (the two complementary aspects of the ambiguity, subjectivity-objectivity, universal-particular). Kant, however, responds to his question:

"How are synthetic *a priori* judgments possible?" They are possible through the original, absolute identity of the heterogeneous. This identity, as the unconditioned, sunders itself, and appears as separated into the form of a judgment, as subject and predicate, or particular and universal. Still, the rational or, as Kant calls its, the *a priori* nature of this judgment, the absolute identity as this mediating concept manifests itself, not in the judgment, but in the inference. In the judgment the absolute identity is merely the copula "is," without consciousness. It is the difference whose appearance prevails in the judgment itself. Here, the rational is, for cognition, just as much immersed in the antithesis as the identity is immersed in intuition for consciousness in general. The copula is not something thought, something cognized; on the contrary it expresses precisely our non-cognizance of the rational. What comes to the fore and enters consciousness is only the product, i.e., the subject and predicate as terms of the antithesis. Only these terms are posited as objects of thought in the form of judgment, and not their being one. (FK 72)

Their unity is not yet judgment's theme. Hegel again says in the *Logic*:

In the subjective judgment we want to see one and the same object double, first in its individual actuality, and then in its essential identity or in its concept: the individual raised into its universality, or, what is the same thing, the universal individualized into its actuality. In this way the judgment is truth: for it is the agreement of the concept and reality. But this is not the nature of the judgment at first; for at first it is immediate, since as yet no reflection and movement of the determinations has appeared in it. (GL 630–31)

In this function of mediation which appears between the universal and the real, the judgment is not only the process of thought; it is also the process of the things themselves which emerge from the universal and disappear into it, which determine the universal and allow it to be its own result. Judgment is indeed the *appearance* of truth in what we call reality as well as in consciousness.

In his *Logic*, Hegel follows judgment's progress from the qualitative judgment that states the immediate relation of the universal and the singular—this rose is red—to the modal judgment that finally makes the meaning of the copula explicit. The assertoric judgment is the pure and simple statement that turns out to be, when considered as such, only problematic. What is real is possible, what is possible is real: such is contingency. In the apodictic judgment, however, existence and necessity are joined together and empirical consciousness sublates itself since essence and existence coincide. The copula presents itself in its existential function as well as in its function of necessary relation. Then judgment is transcended, and reason makes mediation itself appear as the object. *Mediation is the object and the object is only mediation.* By studying qualitative judgment, Hegel already shows the meaning of negative judgment. If the singular appears immediately as the universal in the least significant sensible apprehension, then this relation turns out immediately to be contradictory by means of the negative judgment, and leads to the rejection of all predication in the infinite judgment which exhibits the absolute incompatibility of the terms: "Spirit is a bone—the *Logos* is nature." It is really the negative that makes this opposition emerge and transforms the immediate judgment into the judgment of reflection, then into the judgment of necessity, these two moments constituting the antithesis in the dialectic of the judgment. The judgment of reflection is the judgment according to quantity: the singular (or individual), particular, and universal. It reconnects by means of a relation which is measurement. Already, however, the particular judgment is negative, since it excludes as well as it posits; it states that some men are wise but others are not. Finally, the judgment of necessity (categorical, hypothetical, disjunctive) leads to the division of the genus, of the universal, in the "either . . . or"; it leads to the totality which expresses itself completely in the opposing duplication of the one and *its* other. In his account, Hegel takes up Kant's reflection on the forms of judgment, but he makes explicit their simultaneous subjective and objective sense. What Hegel studies is the form as sense. We have already noted that Hegel begins with the objective categories in order to ascend towards these forms which are its truth, its sense, and not the reverse. Causality, reciprocal action, are more immediate than the hypothetical judgment or the disjunctive judgment. These judgments, however, say the dialectical sense of the relations, the comprehension or the conceivability of being which conceives itself. It is really the reverse of the "Kantian guiding thread." Hegel wants to follow the dialectical progress of the judgment up to the emergence of the mediation that was merely there immediately in the copula. The truth of immediate truth is the movement of truth or mediation; the object which is there immediately, congealed by empirical observation, is not a substrate but is itself mediation. The same mediation that appears in thought as reason, appears in the object as its dialectical movement or its becoming. Aristotle tried to reproduce the immobile structure of being in the syllogism, and had already said that the middle term was reason. Hegel takes up Aristotle's attempt, but mediation becomes animated, it inhabits the terms, it engenders them. Absolute genesis replaces immobile contemplation. What we call substance, absolute truth, is undoubtedly translucent and simple rest as well as bacchanalian revel. This very duality is constitutive of the dialectic. For this movement, rest is the other just as movement is the other of rest; they are, however, identical and this comprehended identity is the absolute idea: "Here we see pure consciousness posited in a twofold manner: once as the restless movement to and fro through all its moments, aware in them of an otherness which is sublated in the act of grasping it: and again, rather as the restful unity certain of its truth. For this unity that movement is the other, while for this movement that restful unity is the other; and consciousness and object alternate within these reciprocal determinations. Thus on the one hand consciousness finds itself moving about searching here and there, its object being the pure in-itself and essence; on the other, it knows itself to be the simple category, and the object is the movement of the different moments" (PH §237).

The judgment—which is stated in propositions—is itself either the empirical judgment or the speculative judgment. How are the empirical proposition and the speculative proposition distinguished in their structure? This question amounts to asking how substrate and mediation are related to one another. The *Phenomenology*'s preface, the last pages of *The Science of Logic*, and the introduction to the *Encyclopaedia*'s Logic describe for us the specific characteristics of the speculative proposition in contrast to the empirical proposition. The *Phenomenology*'s preface, however, provides the most significant and the most plastic exposition.

What is the speculative—absolute knowledge—and how is it distinguished from empirical knowledge? The *Phenomenology* is only an introduction to absolute knowledge. It adopts the viewpoint of the consciousness that distinguishes its subjective certainty from truth, the consciousness for which truth emanates from an alien source. This viewpoint of consciousness is the viewpoint of experience. It rests on the formal distinction between subjective and objective. Consciousness discovers progressively in experience the very content of spirit, but it discovers it as the in-itself distinct from the for-itself. All that experience presents, as from the outside, to immediate consciousness, philosophy will rediscover but without this formal distinction of the subjective and the objective, of the for-itself and the in-itself, of certainty and truth. Speculative thought does not construct the Absolute by opposing itself to experience. It merely puts to the test the logicity of being; it performs what today some would call a *reduction*. It suspends the hypothesis of a source alien to knowledge, of an object distinct from thought, beyond it; it also suspends the hypothesis of an empirical human subject who knows according to his own particular opinions and his own viewpoint.

It ascends to a thought that is simultaneously subjective thought and thought of the thing itself. This thought is no longer opposed to being, but lives this being as sense; it reduces being to universal sense and in this universal sense it sees precisely all being constituting itself as the determination of thought; it illuminates all particularity in the universality of this sense, which is absolute thought, or better still, which is the Absolute itself as *Logos*. The viewpoint of experience is the viewpoint of observation which receives and immobilizes; absolute knowledge is absolute genesis: "For consciousness, what is brought forth exists merely as object (*Gegenstand*); for us, it exists at the same time as movement and as becoming (*Entstehen*)" (PH §87).

This Logos is the Absolute which intuits itself and says itself by passing through human consciousness. It exists as such only in absolute knowledge which is not opposed to immediacy, because it is the unity of mediation and immediacy. This knowledge is subjectivity, sense; this does not mean that it is the particular knowledge of some such individuality that adheres to its particular opinions. Thought is freed, as such, from this particularity. It is subjectivity, however, because it is sense, comprehension, and the movement of comprehension: "Thinking immediately involves *freedom*, because it is the activity of the universal, a self-relating that is therefore abstract, a being-with-itself that is undetermined in respect of subjectivity, and which in respect of its *content* is, at the same time, only in the *matter* [itself] and in its determinations" (EL §23). Hegel adds that philosophy is humility or modesty since it is the forgetfulness of all particularity, since it is the life of the universal as such. It would be impossible therefore to accuse this philosophy of pride, "since thinking is only genuine with respect to its content insofar as it is immersed in the *matter*, and with respect to its form insofar so it is not a *particular* being or doing of the subject, but consists precisely in this, that consciousness conducts itself as an abstract ego, as *freed* from *all particularity* of features, states, etc., and does only what is universal, in which it is identical with all individuals" (EL §23). To ascend to universal self-consciousness, which is pure speculative life, the universal which reflects itself in all the determinations of thought (and therefore in all the determinations of being), is to ascend to absolute knowledge. Empiricism, however, is only a false viewpoint, when it claims to be unsurpassable; it is justified in its opposition to a dogmatic philosophy of the understanding which congeals all the determinations of thought and attributes them to things, the soul, the world, or God; it is correct when it asserts the basic principle that "what is true must be in reality and exist for perception." The *Phenomenology* shows that what appears, what we call experience, is not alien to thought; but there is not a being in itself which appears or which is hidden. The Absolute appears and is entirely in this appearing. The illusion of the empirical viewpoint is its viewpoint, its way of thinking which presupposes the radical distinction of being and sense, of what appears and the appearance. Speculative philosophy does not go in the opposite direction of experience; it is another way of taking all of experience back into the light of sense, of comprehending itself and of comprehending the illusion of being as substrate. Thus absolute knowledge is nothing mysterious or proud. It is a reduction of being or of the (presupposed) substrate of sense. It is an identification of absolute being with the movement of comprehension. This self-comprehension is philosophy, the life of truth. Thought (not the representation that assumes that the substrate and the ego are both substantial) is objective thought. Its thoughts are the thoughts of the thing itself: "Thoughts can be called *objective* thought. . . . Thus *logic* coincides with *metaphysics*, with the science of *things* grasped in *thoughts* that used to be taken to express the *essentialities* of the *things*" (EL §24). This is why expression (objective thoughts) designates the truth which must be the absolute object and not only the end of philosophy; these thoughts, however, are determinate and their finitude (no longer merely the opposition of certainty and truth) lies in being determinate. One has to apprehend therefore the thoughts as moments, as nodes of the complete form or of the thinking movement. "In my view, which can be justified only by the exposition of the system itself, everything turns on grasping and expressing the true, not only as substance, but equally as subject" (PH §17). Substantiality, immediacy, however, is not only the substantiality of being in opposition to thought, it is also the substantiality of thought when it remains at its abstract universality, when it rejects difference. The Absolute is neither the Spinozistic substance beyond its expressions and its reflection, nor the pure knowledge of every determination, immobile and indeterminate thought: "It is the mediation between its own becoming-other and itself." This mediation, this reflection, is the concrete universal, the universal not opposed to its determinations but penetrating them, the universal expressing itself through them and sublating them. The absolute form is formless not because it abstracts itself from particular forms (that is, from its content) but because, like Proteus, it embraces them and sublates them. Its absoluteness lies in this complete determination, which is the internal sublation of all the determinations. "Only this self-restoring sameness, or this reflection in otherness within itself—not an original or immediate unity as such—is the true, and not an originary unity as such or an immediate unity as such. The true is the process of its own becoming, the circle that presupposes its end as its goal, having its end also as its beginning; and only by being worked out to its end is it actual" (PH §18). The true is not an immediate, originary Absolute that thought would rediscover; it is not an Absolute from which thought would be distinct. The true exists only in its own becoming-other, in its determination, and what it is it is as a result which is presupposed at the beginning and is posited at the end. This life of a truth which becomes and justifies itself progressively is speculative life. This life could not however be stated in empirical propositions because the empirical proposition assumes two complementary hypotheses: the *empirical self* that reconnects all the represented determinations and the *substrate*, the being that would be the inert support of these representations. To say that the Absolute is *subject* is to sublate this conception of knowledge that is expressed in the empirical proposition. The empirical proposition assumes that predication has a fixed base, a pre-existing being, and a subject which reconnects all the predicates more or less arbitrarily to this base. By analyzing the empirical proposition's structure, we can understand why it constitutes an obstacle to the speculative proposition. The proposition is already the statement of a mediation: "Whatever is more than such a word, even the transition to a mere proposition, contains a becoming-other that has to be taken back, or is a mediation. But it is just this that is rejected with horror, as if absolute cognition were being surrendered when more is made of mediation than in simply saying that it is nothing absolute, and is completely absent in the Absolute" (PH §20). Hegel rejects this mystical or aesthetic intuition of the Absolute as well as empirical reflection. Mediation is not external: "But this abhorrence in fact stems from ignorance of the nature of mediation, and of absolute cognition itself. For mediation is nothing beyond self-moving selfsameness. . . . The ego, or becoming in general, this mediation, on account of its simple nature, is just immediacy in the process of becoming and is the immediate itself. . . . [Reflection is therefore] a positive moment of the Absolute" (PH §21).

Empirical consciousness judges, and it attributes predicates to a subject; but this term, the subject, is ambiguity itself. It has three senses which are important to distinguish:

1. The subject is first the thing of which one speaks, that upon which the judgment bears. In that case it is the judgment's base, a base which already presents itself at the level of simple perception prior to the judgment of experience. It is the *hypokeimenon* or the *subjectum*. This base seems to precede knowledge; the thing is there before we have any knowledge of it. We are in a relation with it before we even judge it (and this thesis will be justified for Hegel if the thing is the *forgetfulness* of its own mediation). In the *Phenomenology*'s chapter on perception, Hegel shows how the first intuitive knowledge is already constituted as a knowledge of things. This salt crystal is white, tasty, is shaped in a cube, with a determinate weight, but it is a "this" solidified into a thing. The movement of the knowing subject which apprehends it, which points to

it, which considers it under its different aspects, is distinguished from this thing posited prior to its concrete apprehension. "One of them, the object, defined as the simple, is the essence regardless of whether it is perceived or not; but the act of perceiving, as a movement, is the unessential moment, the unstable factor which can as well be as not be" (PH §111). Yet perception apprehends the thing's diverse properties, its relations with the knowing ego as much as with other things. Concrete perception leads us from properties to properties. It discovers similarities and constant successions, but it does not ascend to the universal and genuine necessity: "Empiricism no doubt offers many, perhaps innumerable, cases of similar perceptions: but, after all, no multitude, however great, can be the same thing as universality. Similarly, empiricism affords perceptions of alterations succeeding each other and of objects in juxtaposition; but it presents no necessary connection. If perception, therefore, is to maintain its claim to be the foundation of what must count as truth, universality and necessity appear unjustified, like a subjective contingency, a mere habit whose content can be constituted the way it is or in some other way" (EL §39). Hegel, moreover, notes that Hume's skepticism, which is founded on sensible perception, is really different from ancient skepticism, which showed, in contrast, the dissolution, the evanescence of the sensible. In fact, perception is already guided (but it is unaware of it) by determinations of thought, by a structure which originates from this fixed base. This base is only the name to which the predicates alone confer a sense, but the empirical proposition always refers to this substrate and posits it at the foundation. It is the thing, or in a more general way, that of which one speaks, and that, moreover, each can understand in his own way: "What is familarly known is not known" (PH §31). This substrate is the presupposition of every empirical proposition and all empirical knowledge.

2. In the second place, the subject is the empirical ego, that refers to this substrate, the thinking thing as opposed to the extended thing. In immediate certainty, as in perception, Hegel moves constantly from the thing of which one speaks to the "I" who speaks, from what would be truth to certainty. The subject's self is opposed to the object's self, but the philosopher sees them as constituted in the same way: "the one being the movement of pointing or the act of perceiving, the other being the same movement as a simple event or the object perceived. In essence the object is the same as the movement" (PH §111). It is clear why Hegel speaks of the object's *self*. The object is mediation; it is the being of sense; but empirical perception and the understanding do not ascend to this identity of being and sense. They remain at the presupposition of this substrate and at the presupposition of this empirical subject that speaks about the substrate. Experience (in the most vague sense of the term, in

the sense where I speak of my experience) is then attributed sometimes to the objective substrate, sometimes to the subjective substrate. It is the empirical ego which reconnects the predicates to the thing, establishes the relations among the diverse predicates, compares them and distinguishes them. This process is empirical knowledge itself, the one that ascends from blind and instantaneous intuition to general determinations. The air is heavy, transparent, composed of many gases. Having delimited a certain base (which can be already more or less general, the air, for example), empirical knowledge seeks to attach the diverse predicates back to this base. The empirical proposition states these relations, but it is the work of the knowing subject which concretely constitutes its object. In the *Phenomenology*, Hegel shows how this knowledge ascends from classifications to laws, to relations, but the substrate always returns. The empirical subject does not recognize itself in this constituted object; it nevertheless reflects and then attributes all or part of this experience to itself. It is true that we can consider the predicates to be truly universal, predicates that are no longer *sensibilia* but actual determinations of thought. These predicates are the categories, and the subject of the proposition, the base, is then everything, or the Whole. The question, however, of the relation between the subject of the proposition (that of which one speaks) and these truly universal predicates is posed differently. The proposition becomes speculative; its base is no longer a more or less artificially isolated representation. The empirical subject which knows is what we usually understand by subjectivity; it is intimately mixed with the empirical object. With some difficulty at first, it can detach itself from the arbitrary course of its representations. Hegel insists on the negative and positive conception that this subject can have of its knowledge. Negatively, when this subject can reflect on itself outside of the content, raise itself up over its representations, as representations of the thing, it ends up by being able to produce nothing but idle talk about the thing. It knows how to refute, how to find what is missing everywhere, but it does not know how to conceive, to transvalue its negation into position. This thought says what the thing is not:

> it knows how to refute and destroy [the content that it apprehends]. That something is not the case, is a merely negative insight, a dead end which does not lead to a new content beyond itself. In order to have a content once again, something new must be taken over from elsewhere. Argumentation is reflection into the empty ego, the vanity of its own knowning. This vanity, however, expresses not only the vanity of this content, but also the fluidity of this insight itself; for this insight is the negative that fails to see the positive within itself. (PH §59)

Hegel insists on this merely negative power of the self which raises itself above all determinate content. "Because this reflection does not trans-value its own negativity into its content, it is never at the heart of the matter, but always beyond it. For this reason it imagines that by establishing the void it is always ahead of any insight rich in content" (PH §59). Pure culture ends up by being nothing but conversation which raises the ego over everything, but it does this in order to take from everything the satisfaction of its own vanity. This ego "understands very well how to pass judgment [on the substantial], but has lost the ability to comprehend it. This vanity at the same time needs the vanity of all things in order to get from them self-consciousness; it therefore creates this vanity itself and is the soul that supports it" (PH §526). In regard to the content, the empirical subject also behaves in a positive way: "For whereas, in its negative behavior, which we have just discussed, ratiocinative thinking is itself the self into which the content returns, in its positive cognition, on the other hand, the self is a subject to which the content is related as accident and predicate. This subject constitutes the basis to which the content is attached, and upon which the movement runs back and forth" (PH §60). The presupposition of this substrate is the main obstacle to the speculative proposition, because this substrate is the non-reflected. When the issue is that of attributing empirical predicates, this presupposition is inevitable, but in the speculative proposition, the subject, that is, the Absolute, can no longer be understood in the same way.

3. We can finally understand by subject the subject of the speculative proposition, the Absolute that is precisely the Whole. This subject is neither the base of the empirical proposition nor the empirical ego, but the universal subject-object, which is never conceived as a fixed substrate but as becoming and mediation. In this last case, the speculative proposition no longer has the same structure as the empirical proposition. If we say, "The Absolute is being, nothingness, essence, etc.," we form speculative propositions that are very different from empirical propositions such as "the air is heavy or man is a vertebrate." When a determination of thought is attributed to the Absolute, that is, when it is an authentically universal predicate, the behavior of the knowing subject can no longer be the same as in the case of an empirical proposition.

In the empirical proposition, we have seen that the subject was a base, assumed to be fixed and prior to knowledge; the base is that to which knowledge refers. This base is at the foundation of a representation badly delimited in the field of experience. The predicates must be connected to it and their connection is synthetic. In empirical induction, as in mathematical deduction, the base remains fixed. The predicates are conferred upon it only through an external process, a process of the knowing subject. This base is not demonstrated in the proof; the proof remains alien to it. The entire process is a process of knowledge. It is not the same in philosophical demonstration which is dialectical: "The proposition should express what the true is; but essentially the true is subject. As such it is merely the dialectical movement, this course that generates itself, going forth from, and returning to, itself. In non-speculative cognition proof constitutes this side of expressed interiority. But once dialectic has been separated from proof, the notion of philosophical demonstration has been lost" (PH §65). This is why the true is not expressed in a proposition but in the mediation. Mediation is the sole subject and not a substrate. "The dogmatic way of thinking is nothing other than opinion according to which the true consists in a proposition which is a fixed result or yet in a proposition which is immediately known." Hegel shows then how the empirical proposition and the passage which goes from the object's self to the knowing self are constituted. "Usually, the subject is first made the basis, the objective, fixed self; thence the necessary movement to the multiplicity of determinations or predicates proceeds . Here, that subject is replaced by the knowing ego itself, which links the predicates to the subject holding them" (PH §60). The presupposition of the fixed base entails this necessary consequence, that the connection of predicates to the subject, and their mutual connection, depends on the subject which knows. It replaces this inert base; it becomes the agent of knowledge. The knowing subject continues to affirm that in principle *praedicatum inest subjecto*, but in fact it alone is the movement that is underway. The empirical subject (or even in a more profound perspective the transcendental subject) says what the thing is, white, tasty, heavy, but this attribution is *its* work. This is why, as we have said, this subject's reflection leads to skepticism or to vanity. The connection of predicates depends on the imagination; it is a connection lacking in necessity. When empirical reflection is now transformed into transcendental reflection, the substrate becomes unknowable. It is inaccessible, and the unity of predicates attributed to the transcendental ego is present instead. Since the object cannot be given as such, the experience, which must however relate to it, alone possesses this unity which adheres to what its predicates relate to one identical object. Kant says,

> Now we find that our thought of the relation of all knowledge
> to its object carries with it an element of necessity; the object is
> viewed as that which prevents our modes of knowledge from
> being haphazard or arbitrary, and which determines them *a
> priori* in some definite fashion. For in so far as they are to
> relate to an object, they must necessarily agree with one
> another, that is, must possess that unity which constitutes the

concept of an object. But it is clear that, since we have to deal
only with the manifold of our representations, and since that
x (the object) which corresponds to them is nothing in us—
being, as it is, something that has to be distinct from all our
representations—the unity which the object makes necessary
can be nothing else than the formal unity of consciousness in
the synthesis of the manifold of representations. It is only
when we have thus produced a synthetic unity in the manifold of intuition that we are in a position to say that we know
the object. (A104–5)[1]

The knowing self always substitutes its spontaneity for the object's self.
Empiricism stays at the level of an inconsistent connection; critical
thought ascends to the necessary unity of experience. But in both cases,
the notion of the substrate makes the identification of the subjective self
and the objective self which would allow us to apprehend the Absolute
itself as subject impossible. In every representation, this substrate constitutes the unsurpassable limit. Even Leibniz's monad, which is nevertheless reflection, closes this absolute limit back into itself, this in-itself
which is for-itself only in a theological representation which is an alienation of reflection.

   Speculative thought, however, must stop being the moving and
arbitrary principle of the content, it must "sink this freedom in the content, letting it move spontaneously of its own nature, by the self as its
own self, and then to contemplate this movement" (PH §58). Philosophical dialectic is no longer a process of the philosopher; in the
philosopher, it is the movement of the thing itself, its "monstration." In
regard to the philosopher (who in this way becomes the universal self),
he must refuse "to intrude into the immanent rhythm of the concept,
either arbitrarily or with wisdom obtained from elsewhere; [this refusal]
constitutes a restraint which is itself an essential moment of the concept"
(PH §58).

   To say that the Absolute is subject is to say that the unity of the
proposition is not the unity of a human subject, or the empty unity of a
substrate. Rather it is the unity of sense which appears across the
proposition.

   The need to represent the Absolute as subject has found
   expression in the propositions: God is the eternal, the moral
   world-order, love, and so on. In such propositions the true is

---

   1. Translation based on Immanuel Kant, *The Critique of Pure Reason*, tr.
Norman Kemp Smith (New York: St. Martin's Press, 1965), 134–35.

only posited immediately as subject, but is not presented as
the movement of reflecting itself into itself. In a proposition
of this kind one begins with the word "God." This by itself is
a senseless sound, a mere name; it is only the predicate that
says what God is, gives Him content and sense. Only in the
end of the proposition does the empty beginning become
actual knowledge. This being so, it is not clear why one does
not speak merely of the eternal, of the moral world-order,
and so on, or, as the ancients did, of pure notions like
"being," "the one," and so on, in short, of that which gives
the sense without adding the senseless sound as well. But it is
just this word that indicates that what is posited is not a
being, or essence, or a universal in general, but rather something reflected into itself, a subject. (PH §23)

Of course, this subject is neither the empirical subject nor even the transcendental subject, but being's universal self. "But at the same time,"
Hegel adds, "this is only anticipated. The subject is assumed as a fixed
point to which, as their support, the predicates are affixed by a movement belonging to the knower of this subject, and which is not regarded
as belonging to the fixed point itself; yet it is only through this movement that the content could be presented as subject" (PH §23).
Constituted as it is here, this movement cannot belong to the subject; the
speculative proposition is falsified if it is interpreted through the empirical proposition.

The speculative proposition, however, is shown to be speculative by means of the resistance that it exerts against the empirical subject's reflection. The speculative proposition, in effect, is a proposition in
which the predicate is no longer a classification, a sensible generality, but
a category, a universal determination. Then the predicate is the substance, the essence of that of which one speaks. The empirical subject can
no longer return from the predicate to the proposition's subject; the
weight of the essential determination restrains it entirely. The essential
determination becomes the subject.

Since the concept is the object's own self, which presents
itself as the coming-to-be of the object, it is not a passive subject inertly supporting the accidents; it is, on the contrary, the
self-moving concept which takes its determinations back into
itself. In this movement the passive subject itself perishes; it
enters into the differences and the content, and constitutes
the determinateness, i.e. the differentiated content and its
movement, instead of remaining inertly over against it. The

> solid ground which argumentation has in the passive subject
> is therefore shaken, and only this movement itself becomes
> the object. The subject that fills its content ceases to go
> beyond it, and cannot have any further predicates or acci-
> dents. (PH §60)

In an empirical proposition such as "the air is heavy," the air is not only heavy but *also* transparent, *also* fluid. The proposition's subject, therefore, overflows any one particular predicate. The speculative proposition, however, does not work the same way: the subject loses itself in its determination, it becomes this determination which, in turn, becomes deeper and moves. "Conversely, the dispersion of the content is thereby bound together under the self; it is not the universal which, free from the subject, could belong to several others" (PH §60). In the empirical proposition, the predicates are general determinations which are proper to this subject, but also to others; fluidity is not merely a predicate of air. In the speculative proposition, the determination is the subject's determination; the determination does not sublate the subject any more than the subject sublates the determination.

> Thus the content is no longer in fact the predicate of the sub-
> ject, but is the substance, the essence and the concept of that
> of which one speaks. This is why empirical thought is
> brought to a halt by the speculative proposition. With the
> speculative proposition, it cannot behave in the same way,
> outstripping the accidents and the predicates: it puts the
> brakes on when what has the form of a predicate in the
> proposition is the substance itself. Trying to imagine this,
> empirical thought suffers a counter-thrust. It starts from the
> subject as if this were a permanent foundation; but then,
> since the predicate is the substance, it discovers that the sub-
> ject has passed over into the predicate and is therefore sub-
> lated. Because of this, what appears to be the predicate has
> become the whole and independent mass. Thought then no
> longer wanders here and there; rather it is held back by this
> weight. (PH §60)

The speculative proposition's subject is posited completely in its determination or its difference; in turn, this determination, which constitutes it, has become subject. It shows itself not as an abstract universal but as a self. Then the knowing ego can no longer be reflected into itself, can no longer function and demonstrate from the outside, can no longer decide more or less arbitrarily concerning the suitability of this or that predicate for the primary subject. "Rather it deals with the self of the content; it must not be for itself but be one with the content itself."

Such a speculative proposition, which expresses what Hegel calls the concept, has the originary unity, the Absolute, for its starting point. This is why its predicate would not be able to be appropriate for anything else. On the other hand, this attribution is a conceptual determination, not a representation. It is the Absolute itself identical to its determination; this is why the determination fulfils the subject. It expresses the subject better than the attribute, in Spinoza, expresses the substance, because the entire substance posits itself in its attribute. Nevertheless, the substance has not disappeared; it is the movement of this attribute which then is no longer one expression among others but a moment that must sublate itself since it is actually the subject. In his *Logic*'s last chapter, on the absolute Idea, Hegel shows the importance of this determination considered as the subject itself.

Let us consider one speculative proposition, like the one Kant discusses, *the world is finite*. This proposition is speculative because the subject, the world, is already in itself the Whole. Kant, however, opposed another proposition to this one, *the world is infinite*. This proposition has the same base, the world, but an opposed predicate. Kant then speaks of an antinomy. In effect, the subject of the proposition is fixed, immobile, it is that of which one speaks, the world. But the predicates, finite or infinite, are left alone in their immediacy. The conflict, therefore, is merely the one that results from their attribution to a one identical base, to one identical substrate which must itself be free of contradiction. Dogmatic thought is here the one which claims to chose between the determinations while letting them subsist as they are. Is the world finite or infinite? Is the soul simple or complex? Critical thought also lets the determinations subsist as they are, but it does not attribute them to the substrate in order to keep it from contradiction; it merely puts the contradiction therefore in the thinking subject. What the speculative proposition must show, in contrast, is the movement of the determination itself become subject. The world is neither finite nor infinite, nor is it both finite and infinite. But the contradiction shows itself in each of the determinations. The finite contradicts itself as much as it contradicts the abstract infinite, and this is how the world appears as subject. It does not pre-exist, fixed to its own position in its determination. The base posited identically to itself, immobile, makes the dialectical movement impossible. The dialectical movement then is nothing but the expression of a subjectivity which takes the contradiction upon itself in order to separate it from its object. "On this assumption, the subject matter or the knowledge is represented as a subject into which the determinations in the form of predicates, properties, self-subsistent universals, are introduced in such a manner that, fixed and correct as they are by themselves, they are brought into dialectical relationships and contradiction only by external and contingent connection in and by a third thing" (GL 833). But it is the determination itself which must show itself to be dialectical—and reflect itself—and, thus, it is subject. The limit of reflection, the substrate, must disappear into it.

The speculative proposition presents itself as an empirical proposition; it first evokes this mode of synthetic knowledge that adds predicates to the subject from the outside, but it turns out to be one identical proposition. The subject has become its predicate; it is the determinate universal. But, in turn, the predicate has become the subject. It is the subject of the content and no longer the subject of knowledge, or yet, it is the identity of these two subjects by means of the disappearance of the base and of the empirical self which was useful only for an external reflection. The difficulty of understanding the philosophical proposition, for Hegel, results from this situation: we would like to understand it as if it were an empirical proposition. In fact, non-speculative thought is also justified, since the sublation of the non-speculative form—the return to identity—must not be produced immediately by referring to intuition. The return of the concept into itself must be presented. Mediation must appear. This movement of identification is not that of a proof, but that of a dialectic. It is necessary that the predicate show itself as subject, and it can do this only through its dialectical development. This is why it would not be possible for any single proposition to state the speculative explicitly. One can then object that the dialectical movement refers from proposition to proposition and that the difficulty always returns: "This is like what happens in ordinary proof, where the reasons given are themselves in need of further reasons, and so on *ad infinitum*" (PH §66). Philosophy, however, does not start from a base, from a presupposition; it starts from the concept, that is, from the content which is in itself perfectly subject, which does not refer to a substrate. "Apart from the self that is sensuously intuited or represented, it is above all the name as name that designates the pure subject, the empty unit without thought-content. For this reason it may be expedient, e.g., to avoid the name 'God,' since this word is not immediately also a concept, but rather the proper name, the fixed point of rest of the underlying subject" (PH §66). Thus the dialectical Logic will be the presentation of a universal subject, a universal subject which reflects itself but which is not external to its reflection, which is only the very movement of this reflection, and this movement is circular. Its progression is its own ground. Being, essence, concept are the categories of the Absolute, or rather are the Absolute itself in its self-reflection.

CHAPTER 2

THE CATEGORIES
AS THE
CATEGORIES OF
THE ABSOLUTE

The analysis of the speculative proposition has introduced us to Hegelian Logic. The elimination of the presupposed substrate has led us to a subject which is from one end to the other reflection, which reflects only itself, but this "itself" is still reflection. Immediacy and reflection are no longer opposed. There is no longer any in-itself which is not susceptible to becoming for-itself, and, consequently, there is no for-itself which would always remain alien to the in-itself. Being's reflection does not run into an unsurpassable limit. It is open and if it turns back upon itself, if it is circular, this is so that it will not fall into a false infinite which would reintroduce the limit. This openness appears at the beginning of the Logic in the identity of being and nothingness, in the mediation. One has to think the Absolute as mediation, but this mediation is also immediate.

149

Mediation is not a means of thinking the Absolute; the Absolute itself is mediation. Its being is its sense, and its sense is its being. The Spinozistic substance still lacked this principle of self-reflection. It was in itself pure activity, self-causing, but its activity did not exhibit itself as mediation, as self-becoming. "The Absolute cannot be a first, an immediate, for it is essentially it own result" (GL 537). The Spinozistic substance represents the positive and therefore immediate unity, the unity of all content, "but this diverse and varied content does not discover itself as such in the very substance, but in exterior reflection" (GL 537). We could think that the Leibnizian conception of substance eliminates this non-reflected positivity, this presupposed immediacy, because the monad is the negative unity of the world's content, or the reflected unity; the monad is therefore truly subject. But in fact, it has nothing to do with this, for "the monad is thereby also determinate, distinguished from others. . . . This limitation of the monad necessarily falls, not in the self-positing or representing monad, but in its in-itself; or it is the absolute limit, a predestination which is posited by another being than itself. Further, since limited entities exist only as related to other limited entities, the harmony of these limitations, that is, the relation of the monads to one another, falls outside them and is likewise pre-established by another being or in-itself" (GL 539). Leibniz's theological representation is an alienation of reflection. It stops the Absolute from actually being subject; it consecrates the separation of the in-itself and the for-itself. What is absolutely reflected is in-itself, beyond actual reflection; it is only a representation of reflection. What is actually reflected is a viewpoint, a limited self. After having elaborated a conception of substance which in principle eliminates all substrate, Leibniz reintroduces this immediacy as a predestination, as a closure. Despite the technical progress that it represents over that of Spinoza, Leibniz's metaphysics is definitely less open than that of Spinoza. The theological representation leads back to "flowing representations," which have not undergone a philosophical development and have not been raised to the height of speculative principles. The Leibnizian Theodicy is the result of this representation which is not the concept and which cannot become it. It was not useless to cite Hegel's appreciation of Leibniz in order to mark out his conception of the absolute subject, the unique monad (and not the Monadology) which is the theme of the *Logos*. Speculative reflection goes across the empirical self, man, but it knows no pre-established limit. Absolute being reflects itself and thinks itself. Representation, which is characteristic of empirical consciousness as such, is replaced by the concept. There is no longer any substrate.

The speculative proposition then has determinations of thought—categories—for predicates, categories which are themselves the subject.

These categories become dialectically and express the Absolute's self-consciousness, and no longer express a human consciousness's viewpoint on an always alien reality which is nevertheless supposedly capable of truth. In the *Logic*, Hegel returns to this critique of the substrate:

> But the concept, or at least the essence and the universal in general, is first given by the predicate, and it is this that is asked for in the sense of the judgment. Consequently, God, spirit, nature, or whatever it may be, is as the subject of a judgment at first only the name; what such a subject is as regards its concept is first enunciated in the predicate. When enquiry is made as to the kind of predicate belonging to such subject, the act of judgment must already have a concept for its base. But this concept is first enunciated by the predicate itself. Properly speaking, therefore, it is the mere representation that constitutes the presupposed sense of the subject and that leads to the naming of it; and in doing this it is contingent and a historical fact, what is, or is not, to be understood by a name. So many disputes about whether a predicate does or does not belong to a certain subject are therefore nothing more than verbal disputes, because they start from the form above mentioned; what lies at the base (*subjectum, hypokeimenon*) is so far nothing more than the name. (GL 624–25)

If the *Logic*, however, reveals itself as the philosophic discourse *par excellence*, if it is the self-development of the categories, categories which are the very determinations of the Absolute, it is important to grasp what new sense Hegel gives to these categories, what the category means for him, as a category of the Absolute.

That the category is a predicate is already stated in the Greek term, *category. Kategorein*, in Aristotle, has the sense of attribution. A category is an attribute for Aristotle, or at least it is a universal notion that can be an attribute. This definition fits all the categories except primary substance which is defined precisely by not being able to be attributed of anything. The categories in Aristotle are the supreme genera, but genera which are not arranged under one common genus. These are not the specifications of being but the most general viewpoints on being, genera of being which moreover do not communicate among themselves. There is in Aristotle something like a disparity of these viewpoints on being, of these general and real determinations of every existent. These are the first attributes of things, which belong to them, but which do not communicate among themselves. Although we can grasp quantity in being, or quality, we cannot pass from one to another. Being as being is known

through the categories which are its real aspects. This absolute distinction of the categories, this pluralism of genera of being in Aristotle is
what opposes it to Parmenides and to Plato; and if Hegel owes a lot to
the Aristotelian system as a whole, as a logician he owes a lot more to the
Platonic dialectic of the *Parmenides* and the *Sophist*: "The genera of
being," Aristotle says, "are irreducible to one another and cannot be
related back to one alone" (*Metaphysics* IV.2).

Nevertheless, Aristotle clarifies for us already one characteristic
of the categories; they are universal predicates which fit all existents as
such (even substance fits every existent, since to be a subject is a general
modality of being). Thereby, they are ontologically different from other
predicates, from predicates which are still *sensibilia*.

Hegel, who has chosen the concept as the element of his Logic
and who vigorously opposes the thesis according to which the concept is
by itself empty and in need of a sensible material for which it would be
merely the sign, nevertheless distinguishes the concept of the concept,
the originary unity, ground of all recognition, from empirical concepts.
These pseudo-concepts (which only need the medium of the universal)
are the product of a sensible abstraction: "In this view, to abstract means
to select from the concrete object for our subjective purposes this or that
mark without thereby detracting from the worth and status of the many
other properties and features left out of account" (GL 587). The authentic
concept is not dependent on a prior sensible reality, but on its dialectic.
The sensible itself is negated and grounded: "Conceptual thought, therefore, is not to be regarded as a mere setting aside of the sensuous material, the reality of which is not thereby impaired; rather it is the sublating
and reduction of that material as mere phenomenal appearance to the
essential, which is manifested only in the concept" (GL 588). The categories, which are the moments of thought and of being, are not therefore
classes or genera that are still sensible. They are not the categories which
empirical knowledge attains.

When I want to classify sensible things, I subsume them under
universals which are still sensible, under determinations which participate simultaneously in the indeterminate universality and in the purely
sensible sensible. Speaking of observation's attempt to classify things,
Hegel writes in the *Phenomenology*:

> Observation, which kept them properly apart and believed
> that in them it had something firm and settled, sees princi-
> ples overlapping one another [monsters, chance in Aristotle],
> transitions and confusions developing; what it at first took to
> be absolutely separate, it sees combined with something else,
> and what it reckoned to be in combination, it sees apart and

> separate. So it is that observation clings to passive, unbroken
> selfsameness of being, inevitably sees itself tormented just in
> its most general determination—e.g., of what are the *differen-*
> *tiae* of an animal or a plant—by instances which rob it of
> every determination, invalidate the universality to which it
> had risen, and reduce it to an observation and description
> which is devoid of thought. (PH §247)

This consciousness that observes nature indeed moves away from classifications, proper to ancient science, to the relations or the laws proper to
modern science, but it always refers to this sensible exteriority. This is
why it isolates general determinations or juxtaposes them. It cannot succeed in grasping their movement, their passage from one to the other.
This attitude is the one that *finds* and not the one which comprehends.
This is how Aristotle treated the Logic, like a sort of natural science; he
found the forms, the laws of thought, and Kant, despite using an entirely
different principle, has taken over this way of finding the categories
without grasping their movement:

> But the way in which this form or content presents itself to
> observation *qua* observation gives it the character of some-
> thing found, something that is given, i.e. a content that
> merely is. It becomes a quiescent being of relations, a multi-
> tude of detached necessities which, as in and for themselves a
> fixed content, are supposed to have truth in their determi-
> nateness, and thus are, in fact, withdrawn from the form.
> This absolute truth of fixed determinatenesses, or of a num-
> ber of different laws, contradicts, however, the unity of self-
> consciousness, or of thought and form in general." (PH §300)

However, we have sublated the sensible concepts that are suitable only
for particular regions, only for classes of singular objects, and that maintain relations among them as indifferent as those among the sensible
individualities themselves. The diversity of these sensible concepts, the
more or less general predicates (certain of which state relations rather
than characteristics), have nothing to do with the categories. At best,
according to the Logic, they will become valuable determinations of a
philosophy of nature or of finite spirit.

The categories differ first from these sensible predicates in how
they are suitable to every existent; they are predicates which are said of all
being. Substance, causality, and reciprocal action are universal determinations in a sense wholly different from sensible generalities. Although
attributed to sensible things, these predicates no longer characterize them

as sensibles but as intelligibles. This is a thought and no longer a sensible image (quality or quantity in general for example in opposition to green or the length of three meters). The categories (and Aristotle already noted this) are therefore absolutely universal predicates, and are not vague and badly defined, that is, are not limited to particular regions. This universality uproots the categories from the sensible. The categories so understood have nothing sensible about them, but their intelligibility does not imply another world which could be only another sensible world (in the imagination). Their intelligibility means the taking into consideration of the totality. The sensible is merely the partial, the apparent indifference to the *rest*, the diverse as such. The intelligible is the immanence of the totality to each sensible and therefore the support of the sensible. These categories constitute therefore the universal structure of the sensible as such, its armature. Representation and the empirical understanding do not know that these universal determinations condition the sensible itself and ground its objectivity: "But it is, in fact, these essentialities within which perceptual understanding runs to and fro through every kind of material and content; they are the cohesive power and mastery over that content and they alone are what the sensuous is as essence for consciousness, they are what determines the relations of the sensuous to it, and it is in them that the process of perception and of its truth runs its course" (PH §131).

These universal predicates are not classes, but they allows us to classify and organize phenomena according to *proper functions*. Kant had grasped the categories precisely as such functions and no longer as *genera* of being, and this is true not only of these types of relations in which substance and cause consist but also of quality and quantity, the very determinations of the immediate existent. These are the instruments of the mathematization of the universe. Thought, such as Hegel conceives it, here going beyond Kant, is not complete in the sensible but rediscovers the sensible in its essence (a primary part of the Logic is the logic of immediate being and Hegel can say that this immediacy is preserved in the Logic itself: "Philosophy, however, provides a conceptual idea of what, strictly speaking, the reality of sensible being represents"). Hegel is going to unify these two aspects of the category, genus of being and function of thought.

By defining the category as a function of thought, transcendental idealism replaced the being of logic with the logicity of being, the divine understanding with the transcendental understanding. It created a new ontology. The category is an attitude of spirit which comprehends and unifies. It is a way of comprehending as well as a characteristic of what is comprehended; this identity of the category in the existent and in thought is the theme of Kant's deduction that Hegel takes up: "The category, which formerly had the sense of being the essentiality of the existent—and it was undetermined whether of the existent as such, or of the existent contrasted with consciousness—is now the essentiality or simple unity of the existent only as a reality that thinks; in other words, the category means this, that self-consciousness and being are the same essence, the same, not through comparison, but in and for themselves" (PH §235).

However, for Hegel, Kant did not remain faithful to this definition of the category as absolute sense; he "lets this unity again come on the scene as consciousness, on one side, confronted by an in-itself, on the other" (PH §235). In the *Logic*'s chapter on the concept, Hegel has indeed shown the importance of this Kantian turn, which turns a genus of being into a moment of the universal ego. But this ego is not the human ego: "It is one of the profoundest and truest insights to be found in the *Critique of Pure Reason* that the unity which constitutes the concept's essence is recognized as the original synthetic unity of apperception, as unity of the *I think*, or of self-consciousness" (GL 584). As synthetic, this unity is objectivity itself as it is the ego.

> According to this exposition, the unity of the concept is that whereby something is not a mere mode of feeling, an intuition, or even a mere representation, but is an object, and this objective unity is the unity of the ego with itself. In point of fact, the comprehension of the object consists in nothing else than that the ego makes it its own, pervades it and brings it into its own form, that is, into the universality that is immediately a determinateness, or a determinateness that is immediately universality. As intuited or even in a simple representation, the object is still something external and alien. When it is comprehended, the being in-itself-and-for-itself which it possesses in intuition and representation is transformed into a positedness; the ego in thinking it pervades it. But it is only as it is in thought that the object is truly in and for itself; in intuition or representation it is only phenomenon. (GL 584–85)

However, this ego of which the categories are moments, or the category of which the determinations are species, that is, the concept, is not the human ego or the substantial soul of the dogmatist: "If we cling to the mere representation of the ego as it floats before our ordinary consciousness, then the ego is only the simple thing, also called soul, in which the concept inheres as a possession or property. This representation which makes no attempt to comprehend either the ego or the concept cannot serve to facilitate or bring nearer the comprehension of the concept" (GL 585). For Kant, the categories characterize a subjective understanding as

much as a structure of what is understood (but in Kant what is understood is always possible experience). They are determining and reflecting
simultaneously (although the category of modality is only reflecting).
Hegel is going to go beyond Kant by grasping at the same time the intuitive and discursive character of the understanding, by seeing in absolute
thought the thought which is determinate while remaining absolute
thought. This movement of thought (and with thought, the movement of
all being) will be the philosophic Logos. But another characteristic is
already revealed in the Kantian category. The category is a function of the
understanding insofar as it is universal, non-sensible, and always takes
into consideration the *Whole* in relation to the part; hence also its necessity, or its function of necessity. This idea of totality, or of a quasi-totality
(the set of phenomena as possible experience in Kant), is fundamental. To
think according to the categories—that is, to think—is always more or
less to ascend to the totality. Perhaps every consciousness envelops this
totality in the slightest perception. The categories are universals not only
because they are suitable to every singular, to every "this," but also
because they are the predicates of the Whole, because that of which one
always speaks with them is the Whole, and because the categories are
functions which allow us to think the Whole in relation to the part, the
understanding in the sensible. The sensible is the singular intuition; the
immanence of the understanding is the horizon of Totality. The categories
envelop the Whole within the singular experience. They are therefore universals because they are necessary. Thought always has the world for its
object; its non-thematic object is the universe as a Whole.

The ambiguity of Kantianism appears once more here. If experience *is*, this experience as *being* does not resemble a particular experience.
Thought cannot be cut off from being, but then being is no longer for it
the singular being, but the being of the Whole, the being which the
absolute concept signifies and which thinks itself and determines itself in
the diverse categories which are its species. It must be the case that the
ego which is at work in the most humble experience be as universal as its
object. Otherwise, we are still in a monadism, in a plurality of experiences
which do not constitute all experience as one sole and unique context.

Hegel apprehends the categories as determinations of this
Whole which is being in thought. Henceforth, they are moments which
are structured dialectically; each reflects the others, states a viewpoint on
the Whole which demands its sublation.

> Now, because, in this way, the pure essentiality of things, like
> their difference, belongs to reason, we can, strictly speaking,
> no longer talk of things at all, i.e. of something which would
> be for consciousness merely the negative of itself. For to say

that the many categories are species of the pure category means that this latter is still their genus or essence, and is not opposed to them. But ambiguity already attaches to them, since in their plurality they possess otherness in contrast to the pure category. In fact, they contradict the pure category by such plurality, and the pure unity must sublate them in itself, thereby constituting itself a negative unity of the differences. (PH §236)

The category appears therefore as the category of the Whole, of being as much as of the universal self. Each of them, we were saying, is a viewpoint like the Leibnizian monad. But while this monad is a limited individuality, limited externally, this viewpoint contains in itself the driving force of its sublation, of its passage to another viewpoint. The category is not a substantial individuality like the monad; it is an expression of the Absolute, a for-itself which resolves itself into the for-itself of all the for-itselves. The Absolute, however, does not exist outside of these expressions. It is the universal category which is what it is in its result and not in the first presupposition, the being which is only nothingness.

The categories of Hegel's Logic are not therefore only genera of being, as in Aristotle, or functions of the ego which are used to think the quasi-Whole of possible experience, as in Kant, but expressions of the Absolute itself. This is why these categories not only are the categories of phenomena, the support of the sensible or of the empirical sciences, but also are moments of a *Logic of Philosophy*. Each of them has had its presentation in a philosopher who stopped with that one, in a philosopher who thought the Absolute across it. Although this remark is external to the dialectic of the Logic, it allows us to establish some correspondences between Logic and the history of philosophy; the Logic, however, is not a history in the strict sense. What it develops is the structuring of the categories, an absolute genesis of being. Aristotle's ontic logic became Kant's transcendental logic, then speculative logic, Hegel's onto-logic (ontological and ontic simultaneously).

The categories are therefore definitions of the Absolute and not only of the world and of the subject thinking the world *hic et nunc*. They indeed express the movement of knowledge—Being, Essence, Concept—but they must be grasped independently of this movement, as pure *Logos*:

> When this movement is represented as the path of knowing, then this beginning with pure being, and the development that sublates it, reaching essence as a mediated result, appears to be an activity of knowing external to being and

irrelevant to being's own nature. But this path is the movement of being itself. It was seen that being interiorizes itself
through its own nature, and through this movement into
itself becomes essence. If, therefore, the absolute was at first
defined as being, now it is defined as essence. (GL 389)

With this *Logic of Philosophy*, Hegel undertakes the supreme task
of philosophy. Not only does he want to conceive the fundamental determinations of experience, those which allow him to think experience in its
generality and in its coherence, but also he sees in each of these determinations a moment which, by itself, reflects the Whole. Parmenides comprehended the Absolute as being, and this comprehension is one
moment of the Absolute. It is necessary to penetrate this moment as
such, to know how to remain there without bringing it into confrontation with another moment from the outside. Absolute reason presents
itself as immediate being by opposing itself to nothingness. This presentation is also constitutive of sensible experience; it is the first thought of
the sensible. This thought, however, is not alongside another thought, for
example, that of being as quantity—the indifference of determinations
belongs only to nature—it is a node in a dialectical chain and this node is
reconnected to another, by itself becomes this other. The difficulty of the
task lies in the fact that this logic of philosophy—if it more or less reproduces history—is not the history of philosophy, where the absolute idea
gets dispersed into time. It is not a recollection of successive worldviews,
because these worldviews are still presented as being subjective. This
logic of philosophy is the eternal history of being which, at first immediate, reflects itself as essence and grasps itself as its own concept, as sense.
But the originality of this reduction lies in turning the Logos into the
absolute element of sense and of every sense. It lies in eliminating the
hypothesis of the substrate and of the empirical ego in order to open the
ontological dimension of the comprehension that is not opposed to
being, so that every signifying comprehension must discover its place in
this infinite and circular discourse, in this Logos. Sense and non-sense
are put face to face in it. This Logos is the absolute form that implies the
inadequation of every particular form which is then a specific content. It
is Everything (*Tout*); it includes (*compris*) there the anti-Logos, non-sense,
and it is the comprehension (*compréhension*) of non-sense as such, as the
very alienation of the Logos. Kant was unaware of nature and was
reflecting only on the truth of nature in a specific science. His philosophy
was able to be extended into a critical epistemology, leaving nature as
such always outside of it. But the Hegelian Logos also comprehends this
nature; knowledge also knows its own negation. If finally Hegel rediscovers the historical systems of the past in this logic of philosophy, he

penetrates them not as personal worldviews, with the curiosity of historical contingencies, but as moments which are in themselves an organization, which have unveiled the Absolute under a certain aspect. This does not indicate any disdain for these systems, a way of treating them merely as means. On the contrary, it is to take these philosophies seriously, to seek what of absolute being is reflected in them. The refutation of these moments could not come from the outside; it does not consist in a comparison, but in a deepening. The dialectic of the systems must more or less reproduce the dialectic of being, if the dialectic is to be more than mere idle talk and vanity.

CHAPTER 3

THE ORGANIZATION OF THE LOGIC: BEING, ESSENCE, CONCEPT

Hegelian Logic is the absolute genesis of sense, a sense which, to itself, is its own sense, which is not opposed to the being whose sense it is, but which is sense and being simultaneously. This genesis resembles an organic growth, a perpetual reproduction and self-amplification. There is no external purposiveness, but an immanent purposiveness whose image in nature is organic life. The contradiction of this growth is its immanent intentionality; how can it grow? Does not its beginning already contain implicitly all of what its end will be? Isn't the immediate being at the beginning already the absolute Idea of the end? An artist constantly reproduces the same faces. Across his paintings, we can follow something like an intention which becomes explicit and precise, and which nevertheless was unaware of itself in the first works. He does not, however, repeat himself. This reproduction is creation; it is simultaneously intuitive and discursive. The totality is always immanent, the beginning indicates the end, only the end allows us to comprehend retrospectively the beginning. There is no other way to conceive Hegelian Logic. It is always the Whole that develops itself, that reproduces itself in a more profound and more explicit form. The circle of Essence takes up that of Being, and the circle of the Concept that of Essence. "The Whole possesses nothing astonishing" (PH §32); what is astonishing is that it divides itself, that it expounds itself, but as totality it is never excluded from any one of its positions. Or rather, in the medium of the Logos, no one word would be able to imply this disappearance of the Whole. The Whole is there insofar as it is excluded, sublated; it is there because it is lacking; it is there as negation in the position and as internal negativity. The Whole that we would like to put outside is in fact inside, like the exterior which is only an interior; these words of representation, *inside* and *outside*, fit a nature that realizes the absolute Idea in spatial indifference, but they are nothing but dialectical terms in the the absolute form or in the element of the Logos. We happened to cite Bergson while speaking of Hegel. It is certainly difficult to imagine philosophical temperaments as different as theirs. The same creative idea is, however, present in the Hegelian Logic and in the Bergsonian dynamic schema. The idea, however, in Hegel, is truly an idea, sense, while, in Bergson, it is this side of or beyond sense. In the Hegelian Logos, genesis is comprehensive genesis; being comprehends itself and comprehends itself as far as the ontic limits of all comprehension. One has to see in Hegelian Logic this absolute medium of all comprehension, of all meaning, which is creation at the same time as it is comprehension, because it does not refer to anything other than itself (it contains this other), because it is not therefore the comprehension of something, but self-comprehension, and, by being self-comprehension, comprehension of everything, being and sense. What the Hegelian Logos alone excludes is a monadism which would limit reflection; a monadism is the existence of unsurpassable, individual structures. The Whole is indeed Singularity, but the authentic Singularity is only the Whole in the opening of its own development—the concrete universal—the understanding which is at the same time intuitive and discursive. If we do not enter into this absolute genesis, it is easy to refute it, as, for example, Léon Brunschvicg does in *Modalité du Jugement*: "Far from being the product of the dialectic, absolute spirit is on the contrary its condition and principle. Dialectical evolution owes its movement not to the point from which it starts, but to the end towards which it tends—and it is external at the same time as being parallel to being—it is a dualism.""[1] Hegel's originality, however, lies in the rejection of this calling forth by the end. Dialectical evolution is attraction and instinct; it starts from immediate being and returns to immediate being. It is truth only as engendered truth. On the other hand, it is indeed *also* dualistic, but this dualism is not, as in Spinoza, the parallelism of Logos and Nature which never encounter one another. It is the dualism of mediation. Nature and Logos are simultaneously opposite and identical. This is why the Logos can think itself and the other, contradict itself in itself, and why Nature, which is the anti-Logos, can appear as Logos.

The Logos is the absolute truth as self-genesis. However, how can we speak of a truth of the form? The logic, as the science of the absolute form, is the truth for itself, and by means of being opposed to the other philosophical sciences, those of nature and spirit, it is *pure* truth: "For this reason, this form is of quite another nature than logical form is ordinarily taken to be. It is already on its own account truth, since this content is adequate to its form, or the reality to its concept; and it is the pure truth because the determinations of the content do not yet have the form of an absolute otherness or of absolute immediacy" (GL 592–93). Truth is, as Kant said, the agreement of knowledge with its object, and this definition has the greatest, or rather the highest value. But in this case, what are we to think of Kantianism, according to which the knowledge of reason is incapable of grasping things in themselves, and actuality is alien to the concept?

> If we remember this definition in connection with the fundamental assertion of transcendental idealism, that reason as knowing is incapable of apprehending things-in-themselves, that reality lies absolutely outside the concept, then it is at once evident that a reason such as this which is unable to put itself in agreement with its object, the things-in-themselves, and things-in-themselves that are not in agreement with the concept of reason, the concept that is not in agreement with reality, and a reality that does not agree with the concept, are untrue conceptions. If Kant had considered the idea of an intuitive understanding in the light of the above definition of truth, he would have treated that idea which expresses the required agreement, not as a figment of thought but rather as the truth. (GL 593)

---

1. Léon Brunschvicg, *La modalité du jugement* (1897), 73: "The system of the reasons of understanding only reproduce a rational system of being." [Translated from Hyppolite's French.—Tʀ.]

In effect, the absolute form is not contentless. Its content is itself. It has its being within itself because it is the universal. It is intuitive thought. Kant, however, stated this principle of *a priori* synthesis (in which duality could be known in unity). Therefore he would have been able to see that his critique, in regard to formalism, was genuinely lacking in scope—the critique of a criterion which would be valuable for all knowledge. "It is alleged that it would be absurd to ask for the criterion of the truth of the content of knowledge; but according to the definition it is not the content that constitutes the truth, but the agreement of the content with the concept" (GL 593). To separate in this way the content as an alien being and seek the *truth* of such a content, while forgetting that truth is *agreement*, is to turn this content into an inconceivable content, into a soulless content, a senseless content. Now, if, on the basis of this separation, we consider the logic itself as contentless, thought as purely abstract and empty, in the usual sense of formalism, then it is just as vain to speak of agreement (since in order for there to be agreement there must be two), and therefore to speak of truth. The question of truth was really posed in a much more penetrating way by Kant with his notion of an *a priori* synthetic thought, that is, with his notion of a thought capable of being its content for itself: "Logic being the science of the absolute form, this formal science, in order to be true, must possess in its own self a content adequate to its form; and all the more, since the formal element of logic is the pure form, and therefore the truth of logic must be the pure truth itself" (GL 594). What characterizes the logical element is precisely this adequation between actuality and concept which is the complete development of the form. Logic is not concrete truth, that of the Idea in nature or in spirit, but the pure truth, the development of the concept in its actuality and of actuality in its concept, the life of the concept. When we consider the forms of logic, we note that, in their isolation, they are without truth, because, insofar as they are *some* forms, they have a content inadequate to the whole thinking movement, to conception itself. For example, the affirmative Judgment is considered in its form as true, since it is referred exclusively to the content. But this Judgment is dialectical in its form. It states that the singular is universal, that being is concept. It contradicts itself in itself. It lacks what the definition of truth requires, the agreement of the concept and the object. The absolute concept (the unique form), therefore, must rediscover itself in all of its moments, in the forms which, insofar as they are manifold, present themselves as content. Then each determination of the form is nothing but a magnitude vanishing into the totality of this truth which is an absolute life, an absolute self-consciousness: "The true is thus the Bacchanalian revel in which no member is not drunk; yet because each member collapses as soon as he drops out, the revel is just as much transparent and simple respose" (PH §47).[2] The science of logic therefore is the pure truth. Hegel's difficulty lies in explaining "absolute being-other or absolute immediacy," nature and spirit, insofar as they are also, in philosophy, concrete sciences, a philosophy of nature and a philosophy of spirit, what Hegel called at Jena *Realphilosophie*. These sciences are not the empirical sciences considered in the *Phenomenology*:

> These concrete sciences do, of course, present themselves in a more real form of the idea than logic does; but this is not by turning back again to the reality abandoned by the consciousness which has risen above its mode as phenomenon to the level of science, nor by reverting to the use of forms such as the categories and concepts of reflection, whose finitude and untruth have been demonstrated in the logic. On the contrary, logic exhibits the elevation of the idea to that level from which its becomes the creator of nature and passes over to the form of a concrete immediacy whose concept, however, breaks up this shape again in order to realize itself as concrete spirit. (GL 592)

a spirit which, in the highest degree, is precisely the Logos, philosophy. The logical element shows itself therefore indeed as the supreme mediation. It is there immediately as nature and as finite spirit, but as spirit it completes itself, it returns to itself.

The Logic is the genesis of the absolute Idea. This absolute Idea, which in the element of universality contains the whole life of thought, for Hegel, "alone is being, imperishable life, self-knowing truth, and is all truth" (GL 824). It is the sole object and the sole form of philosophy: "Since it contains all determinateness within it, and its essential nature is to return to itself through its self-determination or particularization, it has various shapes, and the business of philosophy is to recognize it in these" (GL 824). Thus nature and spirit are distinct modes through which the Absolute Idea presents its Dasein—spatial indifference and temporal dispersion—just as art and religion are distinct modes through which it apprehends itself and endows the image of the self with that of a being. Philosophy, however, is the highest—the only authentic—mode of grasping the absolute Idea, because its modality is the highest, the concept, the only one in which truth exists as truth.

---

2. Rest is not the end—as some would speak of an end of history—but the other of the movement, and movement the other of rest, and the Truth is their dialectic.

Philosophy comprehends, therefore, the figures of real finitude, nature, and the figures of ideal finitude, spirit. Philosophy conceives them as it conceives religion and art, but it conceives itself. This self-conception is "above everything else the Logic." The qualification, *above everything else*, means that the Logic can indeed be considered as a particular mode, "but whereas mode signifies a particular kind, a determinateness of form, the logical aspect, on the contrary, is the universal mode in which all particular modes are sublated and enfolded" (GL 825). To comprehend nature and spirit in this way, for philosophy, is to see the creative source itself in the Logos; it is to see across the Logos. Language is the house (*la demeure*) of being as sense. The Logos is the primordial, originary voice (*le verbe originaire, primordial*) which is indeed an exteriorization, but an exteriorization which, as such, disappears as soon as it appears. Hegel says that the only determination is then for this sense to hear itself, to comprehend itself. It is the pure thought in which difference (the one that will be set free in external nature and in finite spirit) is the alterity that leads thought to sublate itself.[3]

There are two opposite critiques made of Hegel concerning the relation of Logic to nature and spirit. Marx, for example, has accused him of always rediscovering the logical element in the philosophy of nature and history, instead of seeing in this element a reflection of concrete being, a fleshless shadow. Hegel's concrete philosophy would be impoverished and hardened by the idea which is always rediscovered and taken up instead of real content. Some indeed, however, have also said that the immense richness of Hegel's Logic comes from what he borrows from all the experiences of the concrete sciences, and that his Logic conceals a thoroughgoing empiricism. In fact, these two charges destroy one another. They can be justified in this or that particular case. Yet, on the whole, they misunderstand Hegel's concepts of the Logos and of experience, of the *a priori* and of the *a posteriori*. The Logic is opposed to experience as ontology is opposed to anthropology. Hegel does not want to do without experience but to *reduce* (in the modern sense of the term) anthropology and to show, at the very heart of the onto-logic, that "philosophy must alienate itself." Thus philosophy alone is the element of truth and of all truth.

If the Logos is the complete and organic development of intellectual intuition, the *method* of the Logic appears as the universal self-consciousness that accompanies the whole movement: "the method is nothing but the structure set forth in its pure essentiality" (PH §48). The

---

3. We still have to repeat that the concept is, for Hegel, sense which is at the same time its own sense, and that philosophy is not one project replacing others, but the element, the medium in which *everything* is clarified as sense.

ordinary sense of the word *method*, however, is no longer at work here and one has to dispel a false interpretation. The method, which is the universal of the Logic, does not separate the objective from the subjective. As absolute method, it is the opposite of instrumental knowledge or of external reflection, which would be merely subjective. Method is conceived through the Logic's notion of the beginning, which must be presuppositionless. The beginning can be only an immediacy. Thus the Logic's three instincts, Being, Essence, Concept, are immediacies, but the genuine beginning of the Logic is the first immediacy, Being. This is not sensible immediacy, but the immediacy of pure thought "that we can, if you like, just as well call super-sensible or inner intuition." In finite knowledge, we do not stop repeating that one has to refer thought to being, that is, that it is necessary *to show*, to delimit the being which is there, but this indication and this delimitation are already a mediation. When we require a demonstration of being, we mean thereby that we want to determine being, to make it emerge from the abstraction of pure thought, from the mere self-relation. To demonstrate being is therefore to realize the concept, to determine it. In the *Science of Logic*, from the start we rediscover this very experience of knowledge which is the realization or the determination of the concept. Being, considered as irreducible to pure thought, is the absolute self-relation which is also pure thought. Thought does not lack being; it lacks determination. And being, this mere self-relation, also lacks determination. In the form of being and nothingness, of being and the question of being, their opposition is reciprocal. What is required is the sublation of this pure self-relation.

For the method, the beginning is the universal, which is indeterminate. But this very simplicity of the beginning is its determination. Insofar as it is the consciousness of this indeterminate universality, the method knows that it is only a moment and that the concept is still not determined in itself and for itself. If the method, however, remains at the level of this subjective consciousness, it takes this beginning merely as the abstract from which something is *lacking*. It understands abstraction as the psychological process which, having at first put aside that from which it is abstracted, claims to be made complete through that from which it is abstracted. The method seeks, therefore, what one has to *add* to this beginning, as if thought, which is thought and being, was not to itself its own content, as if its progression were not immanent.

The immediacy of the beginning, because it is the beginning, is in itself its own negation and the instinct to sublate itself as beginning. The universal is not only the abstract, it is also the objectively universal, the concrete totality in itself but not for itself. Therefore, the being in itself that is not yet for itself, the Whole as immediacy and not yet as mediation is there. The beginning is therefore really the Absolute; it is the Absolute in itself and progress is the presentation of the Absolute, its becoming for-itself. Because, however, the Absolute is still in itself, it is not the Absolute, nor the posited concept, nor the Idea. The progressive presentation is not a surplus, not an *excess*, the Absolute already being there before its presentation. "Progression consists rather in the universal's self-determination, the universal's becoming for-itself, that is, the Subject" (GL 829). Truth is truth only in its genesis. By positing immediacy as objective totality, we oppose the immediate to mediation. The beginning is immediacy, but its determination, its negation is there; its self-relation is not yet the unity that has become, the posited relation. The immediacy, that has not become, is *nothing*, but this nothing is already its mediation, its first position. By means of this nothing, it expounds itself and becomes. What is essential is that the absolute method finds and recognizes the determination of the universal within itself. Finite knowledge takes up what it had left out by means of the process of abstraction, but the absolute method, not being external to its object, finds in it the determination which is immanent to it. Absolute method follows the object's movement and does not work from the outside. This is why the method is *analytic*: "It adheres to the absolute objectivity of the concept of which the method is the concept's certainty. The issue is not to stray and to think the thing itself from something else than that which thinks the thing. As Plato demanded of knowledge, the issue is to think the things themselves in themselves and for themselves, to consider them just as they are" (GL 830). The method, however, is *synthetic* as well, since its object, determined in an immediate way as simple universal, shows itself as an other because of the determination of the immediacy that it possesses. This analytic (immanent) and synthetic (passage to the other) process is the dialectic. This is why the philosophic method is the *dialectic*.

We usually conceive the dialectic as ending up at a merely negative result and this result is understood in many senses. The dialectic would exhibit the non-existence of the object; thus the Eleatics deny change and movement through the dialectic. It would exhibit the emptiness of a knowledge, the emptiness or vanity of the dialectic itself. Thus Diogenes silently walks back and forth in order to oppose the dialectic that denies movement. Thereby he disdainfully claims to show the inanity of this language that proves too much, and opposes a silent response to it. Dialectic responds to dialectic; Socrates indulges in an ironic dialectic in order to oppose the unstable dialectic of the Sophists. He himself becomes the victim of this dialectic, of the anger raised against it; he is accused of disturbing the stable positions of ethics. Finally, dialectic would show the inanity of pure knowledge as a whole; hence the transcendental dialectic of the *Critique of Pure Reason*. Hegel notes, however, that, since it carries on an attack against the object or against types of knowledge, we do not see clearly enough that it attacks determinations as well. We see in Kant's transcendental dialectic especially the opposition of "either . . . or . . . ," which leaves each of the determinate hypotheses intact. These, however, are the determinations that are truly prey to the dialectic, and there is no stable object below them. The thing itself is dialectical in its determinations, or, if you like, the dialectical movement of the determinations constitutes the thing itself. Then we understand the positivity of the dialectic, "for every negative is the negative of that of which it is the result" (GL 834).

The first term is always the universal as immediate, but then it is determined, and this determination is the negation which it has in itself. This is why the first term passes into the second which is the negative; it is *its* other. Being is not itself; it is nothingness. This second term is the pivot of the dialectical movement; it is *doubly negative*. It is at first the other, the negation of the first; but, taken by itself, it re-establishes the first. Nothingness is always the nothingness of being; as other, it constantly re-establishes the other of which it is the other. In itself, it is the other of the other; this is why the dialectical point gets sharpened in it. It is infinite negation, the second negative, the negation of the negation or negativity. Then the first positivity reappears as the third term, as the emergence of the whole movement. But this positivity is one that has become, and, as such, it is a second positivity which is given as a new immediacy. The justification of the beginning is its new advancement, because a new immediacy and the beginning of a new cycle is there. Thus the conflict of being and nothingness exhausts itself in the instability of becoming, but what has become, the being there (*l'être là*), is a new immediateness. Somehow, the process gets congealed. In the total movement, essence is the instability of the second dialectical moment. In essence, being is negated—no longer in the immediate form of being, as nothingness—but in itself. Being appears; it is being and non-being, as essence and appearance. It appears in itself and is only this reflection. This negation of immediate being, however, negates itself. The concept which completes itself with the absolute Idea re-establishes the immediate being of the beginning. The absolute Idea is identical to nature. "The retrospective justification of the beginning and the progression towards new determinations are, essentially, only one movement" (GL 839).

Being, Essence, Concept constitute the three instincts of the Logos, the three circles which reproduce at different levels the same fundamental theme. The seed, the initial cell is being, nothingness, becoming. Being is determined only by nothingness. It is itself the nothingness of itself, as that will appear at the level of essence, because essence is the internal negation of the whole sphere of being. Nothingness was negation in the shape of being. Nothingness is an immediate just as being is; the transition from being to nothingness, likewise from nothingness to being, is only a passage, becoming, a foreshadowing of what will be genuine passage, mediation. The sphere of essence, which is the first negation of being—then the negation of itself—is the field of reflection, of diremption. Being opposes itself to itself; it negates itself as being and it posits itself as essence. But essence is appearance. Essence is posited in appearance, that is, in negated being, and there alone. The doubling of essence and appearance is completely appearance, so that essence is itself an ontological appearance. Reflection negates itself; being as conception of being, essence of being, is not distinct from being itself, the ontological possibility of actuality. This is why the third sphere, that of the concept, takes up the same theme in the element of mediation, in the element of self-comprehension. Immediate being passes away and becomes; its conception falls outside of itself. Essence is the reflection of being, its appearance and its intelligibility. But this intelligibility, this conception, is simultaneously separated and inseparable from appearance. As reflection opposed to immediacy, essence is the non-resolved contradiction. This is why reflection reestablishes the first immediacy of being, just as this immediacy had been reflected into essence. Immediacy itself is conceived. Real actuality not only is there as in the immediacy of being, nor comprehended only by means of its essence, as in essence and reflection, but is also itself its sense, and this Sense is its being. Being is reflected in itself, and, in this reflection, it is as sense. The subjective logic, or the logic of the concept, is the logic of sense, but this sense is not a subject opposed to the object. It is the being which is its self-consciousness, its sense, and this self-consciousness, in turn, is being itself, the absolute Idea scattered into nature and into history. In the Logos, being is thought. It does not ground its intelligibility behind itself, but in itself; *it thinks itself just as much as it finds itself.* The Logos's three moments are contained in this German word: *Selbstbewußtsein*—being, appearance, the self.

The logic of being corresponds to the *transcendental aesthetic.* It is the logic of the sensible insofar as the sensible is preserved in the Logos. "Philosophy provides the conceived intellection of what the actuality of sensible being is," and it can do this because sense is sensible, is there in speech "in order not to be as soon as it is there." The Logic of essence corresponds to the *transcendental analytic;* it is the understanding of being. But the logic of essence is not only the logic of the science of the phenomenal world. It is still the logic of this metaphysics which makes essence be the condition of existence. In fact, the categories are as much the categories of experience as of the Absolute. Finally, the logic of the concept corresponds to the *transcendental dialectic,* the Idea that Kant had considered only as regulative, wanting to recognize as metaphysics only the old dogmatism, the metaphysics of the intelligible world, and not explicitly comprehending that transcendental logic was in itself already speculative logic, that the logicity of being was replacing the being of logic. With the logic of the concept, it is the category of sense which becomes the truth of the categories of being and essence.

The logic of being is the logic of immediacy. It says this appearance and this disappearance of the sensible, which the *Phenomenology's* first chapter describes. The being of the sensible is its annihilation; it passes away. However it returns in its annihiliation. Being gets continued into nothingness and nothingness into being. Becoming is permanent. Immediacy does not conceive itself. Mediation is indeed there too, but there immediately as becoming. Being negates itself and preserves itself in its negation, but at the level of immediacy contradiction and identity are not there as contradiction and identity. Being becomes another being. This collapse of the sensible is the condition of its intelligibility, of its own recollection. We can say that the becoming of the sensible is in itself its essentialization, but essentialization is not there as such. This is why the determinations in this sphere of immediacy exclude themselves or identify themselves immediately. Being is there; it is no longer there; it becomes, and becoming is the unstable exchange of being and of nothingness. Being does not pass into itself. It does not relate to itself in its other; it does not reflect itself. Contradiction and identity are there immediately just as they exist in nature with movement.[4]

The opposition of being and nothingness, and then the first concrete synthesis, becoming, constitute the base of the whole logic. But the three terms are inseparable. We can still say that being divides itself into being and nothingness and shows itself then as becoming. Hegelian logic does not start from two alien terms that it would combine, but from mediation. Explicitly, the logic of being knows only the opposition of being and nothingness; implicitly, as what follows will reveal, this opposition is just as much that of being and the thought of being, of being and the question of being. Being is its own question to itself. But in its immediate form, for example, in nature, it is pure becoming which is the existing mediation. Because being passes away, it interiorizes itself and comprehends itself. Forgetfulness and memory have an ontological signification. However, the sphere of being will have to be completely negated as the sphere of immediacy so that essence appears.

Unstable becoming re-establishes a positivity. Dasein is the being that has become. Mixture of being and nothingness, it is essentially finite,

---

4. "External, sensible movement itself is the immediate Dasein of contradiction" (GL 440).

but its finitude presupposes infinity. Infinity is also there immediately; it is the bad infinite, the indefinite series of a something and its other. Quality and quantity are the two fundamental categories of this Dasein, and the logic of being is a descriptive logic and a logic of pure quantity. Quality is the immediate determination which is unified with being, while quantity marks a return to the first indetermination. Their synthesis, measure, is the transition from being to essence. It is the beginning of the self-relation in immediacy. Quantitative change, the indefinite of the *quantum*, "toujours à soi pareil qu'il s'accroisse ou se nie,"[5] is self-exteriority. Self-exteriority always leads back to intrinsic and qualitative determination. It is never anything but an oscillation around a measure. "Everything has its measure." This, Hegel says, is one of Greek philosophy's highest thoughts. In this logic of immediacy, which is the darkness or the truth of the sensible depending on how one considers it, the infinite presents itself in its immediate opposition to the finite. Indefinite progression, however, what is without end, is the immediate difference which is not reflected as identity, as self-relation. Measure is already essence in immediacy. It is the immediate return to self in exteriority.

To say that the Absolute is being is to say that it is in itself. It is the well-rounded sphere about which Parmenides speaks. But for whom is this in itself, determined as being, in itself? Being is in itself; it is solely self-relation. These judgments already sublate this immediate being. The very essence of the self-relation is a sublation of being. Being is not yet in-itself for itself. The first philosophies of nature are a naive expression of this thought of being, and Parmenides says this thought of being.

Essence is being which becomes in itself for itself. This being was in itself identical to itself in its opposite, nothingness. It was passing away but always was finding itself again, being in imperishable becoming. This return to self, however, is not accomplished at the level of immediate being. Being was not reflecting itself. We were not able to say that it was finding itself again, because this *itself* assumes a reflection as reflection, an absolute *self* of being.

The logic of essence presents this reflection. Being no longer passes indefinitely outside of itself; it passes into itself, it reflects itself. The logic of essence corresponds to knowledge, to the elaboration of the sensible. What is there, however, is merely a correspondence. Reflection

---

5. This is a line from Mallarmé's "Plusieurs Sonnets I" in *Oeuvres complètes* (Paris: Bibliothèque de la Pléiade, Gallimard, 1945), 67. Roughly, the line could be translated in the following way: "always the same as itself whether it increases or decreases." See also Jean Hyppolite, "La 'Phénoménologie' de Hegel et la Pensée Française Contemporaine," in *Figure de la pensée philosophique* (Paris: Presses Universitaires de France, 1971), 1:233.—TR.

is not the external reflection of being in a knowing subject; it is being's own internal reflection. The Logos, on the contrary, is what allows the knowledge and the ontological moment of consciousness to be comprehended. Being interiorizes itself while essentializing itself. It interiorizes itself just as, in knowledge, memory interiorizes sensible intuition. The past is essence.

Essence is the negation—the first—of being, and of being in its totality such as it is presented in the prior sphere. The determinations of being will be reproduced at this level, but as reflected determinations. Immediate being, negated in its totality, becoming its own nothingness, is *essence*. It is the intelligibility of being, its in-itself for itself, but still in the element of the in-itself. It is *appearance* as well, for what is appearance other than negated-being? To speak of appearance, where we were speaking of being, is still to speak of being, because appearance really is in a certain sense. But it is also to negate the being in it, because one must say that appearance is not since it is merely appearance. These two aspects of the logic of essence—namely, immediate being negates itself and therefore posits itself behind itself fundamentally as *essence*, and immediate being, negating itself, has become *appearance*—are one and the same movement. And such is the contradiction of essence or of reflection: it is essence and appearance simultaneously. It is negation of being as immediate and, in this negation, position of being as essence. The whole logic of essence is the logic of appearance; being has entirely become *appearance* and we can just as well say "this is only appearance," and "everything is in appearance."

The distinction between the essential and the inessential is, at the level of essence, only a reminiscence of immediacy, because there are not two beings. Moreover, this distinction is arbitrary. It depends on a third term, and is relative to an external reflection. Essence, however, is the internal reflection of being which appears in itself: "Appearance is the same thing as reflection." This reflection as such is identity, difference, contradiction. These essentialities are constitutive of reflection. Being which appears is identical to itself in its difference, which is essential difference, that is, the difference of itself from itself. It is different from itself in its identity; it contradicts itself. Essence, moreover, is the non-resolved contradiction, since it is simultaneously negation of being and negation of this negation, but still abstract negativity, reduced to pure dialectical conflict. The movement of the logic of essence is a double movement in one alone. It is the movement by which being negates itself, turns itself into appearance, and the movement by which, while negating itself, it posits itself, makes itself essence in appearance.

Essence is the recoil of being into its nothingness, the *ground*, and the emergence of the ground in *appearance*. This is why its three moments are: *Reflection*, which results in the ground; *Phenomenon*, which is being negated and grounded; *Actuality*, which is the unity of ground and phenomenon, of essence and appearance. Essence is the division of being in itself, the secret of being and the initiation into this secret, but this secret is its intelligibility, its conceivability. The secret of being is the very possibility of being, but this possibility, separated from being, is an ontological mirage which leads one to believe in a metaphysics, in a substance distinct from its accidents, in a cause distinct from its effects, in an ontological possibility distinct from ontic actuality. In order to be comprehended, in order to be posited, being alienates itself. Essence is the dialectical moment of this alienation of being. We could say that this is ontology's *unhappy consciousness*.

Immediate being plunges into essence as into its conditions of intelligibility, but these conditions are unified with the manifestation itself. Manifestation in its Totality is essence. Intelligibility exists entirely in the development of manifestation in the category of Actuality. In actuality, there is no absolute content (substance) whose form would be manifestation (*mysterium magnum revelans se ipsum*); it is the *relevans si ipsum* which is everything, and which is the *mysterium magnum* itself: "As this movement of exposition, a movement which carries itself along with it, as a way and manner which is its absolute identity-with-self, the absolute is manifestation not of an inner, nor of something other, but it is only as the absolute manifestation [*Manifestieren*] of itself for itself. As such it is actuality" (GL 536).[6] The *Phenomenology*'s preface says: "Appearance [*Erscheinung*] is the arising and passing away that does not itself arise and pass away, but is in itself and constitutes the actuality and the movement of the life of truth" (PH §47).[7]

Actuality is conceived necessity, and the analysis that Hegel provides of the relations of the possible, of the real and the necessary, is perhaps the most illuminating of all the dialectics of essence. Actuality does not have its ground in a possibility that would be beyond it. It is itself its own possibility. Certainly being is grounded, but it is grounded upon itself; it is because it is possible, but it is possible because it is. This transcendental chance, which Kant spoke of in *The Critique of Judgment* and which was the encounter of contingency and conditional necessity, is for Hegel absolute necessity, because actuality refers to nothing else, and yet

---

6. In this discussion, Hyppolite use the French *manifestation* to render Hegel's *Manifestieren*. In most other cases, it seems that Hyppolite is rendering Hegel's *Darstellung* with *manifestation*. So, in those other cases, we have used "presentation."—Tr.

7. Here Hyppolite uses *manifestation* to render Hegel's *Erscheinung*. See also note 6.—Tr.

it is grounded, it is conceived. The Logos is not the possibility of the existent, outside of the existent; it is the conception of the existent, and the existent as other is included in its own conception. The possible, which is only possible, is impossible; it contradicts itself. This is why it is possible because it is, just as it is because it is possible. Actuality as Totality is truly the dialectical synthesis of possibility and actuality. This is why it is comprehended necessity.

Comprehended necessity, however, is not necessity comprehending itself. It is known but does not recognize *itself*. Essence is indeed being-in-itself-and-for-itself, but it is still in itself. Its comprehension is not its own comprehension. Essence has reintroduced the immediacy of being; this is why it is no longer essence, but concept.

In essence, being-in-itself appears, but this appearance is its appearance, its position. It is not being which appears; it is itself which appears and therefore recognizes itself. The movement of its self-position is what Hegel calls the *concept*, which we could translate by *sense*. The logic of the concept takes all the determinations of being and essence up to its level, but it takes them up in order to show how they *constitute themselves*, how they posit and engender themselves. This genesis of sense was implicit in the prior spheres; this genesis is the Logic, because the Logic is the constitution of being as sense, comprehension, not as reference to a thing comprehended distinct from the movement of comprehension, but this movement itself as intelligible genesis of the thing (and the thing itself is only this movement). The Logic is the absolute form which is its object for itself, like a poem whose object would be poetry and which would contain thereby intrinsically the particularity of every poem. This "to contain," however, has nothing spatial about it. Universal sense contains intrinsically every particular sense. This sense, however, was not yet for itself in the Logic's other parts. It was there immediately in the becoming of being; it was the ground behind the appearance as essence. It now knows itself as the sense of all the senses. Hegel calls this logic of concept or sense subjective logic, but what is at issue is the subject or self which is immanent to every object and not a subjectivity distinct from being. Its proof is the dialectic of being and sense that leads this end of Logic back to its beginning. Being is shown across essence as sense, but sense is being as well; or rather being already was referring to sense. Being is a *lost sense*; it is a *forgotten sense*, since sense is the interiority of memory taken back into being. In the field of knowledge, forgetfulness and memory correspond to this dialectical distinction of being and sense, insofar as one does not make memory congeal into an in-itself (this would be essence); one has to see in memory the movement of recollection, the comprehensive genesis that constitutes the past. Reminiscence does not refer to the first essence; rather, the essence is constituted through the originary act of reminiscence. Sense is the essence that comprehends itself by positing itself as essence. In relation to sense, essence is what being was in relation to essence. Being was essence in itself; essence is sense in itself. It is like a second being behind the first, but when we no longer abstract from its position, when we comprehend it as self-positing, as self-constituting, then it is no longer essence but sense.[8]

The concept is at first the medium of sense in general, the medium of every comprehensive genesis. The concept is the universal sense that always remains universal in every particular sense, sublating itself, as in the word, and this sublation is there. Its self-determination is the judgment that reproduces at the level of the concept the diremption of essence, the appearance of the particular in the universal, and of the universal in the particular. The determination received into the universal is sense, but the immediate relation is developed only through mediation, only through reason which makes the relations of the particular and the universal explicit. Henceforth, sense is developed as such, and this is why it is; its being of sense is object and objectivity. *Mediation is the object itself* and *the object is mediation.* This unity is what Hegel calls the absolute Idea, the sense which is, and the being which is sense. Sense is not only its own object, it is also the sublated object. The absolute Idea is, as sense, the Logos, as well as, as lost sense, immediacy, nature.

The logic of the concept corresponds to the major turn that transcendental logic represents in the history of philosophy. In a letter, Kant calls it his ontology and what is at issue indeed is in effect a new ontology since it replaces a world of essence, the being of Logic, with the logicity of being. By pushing the reduction of anthropology initiated by the transcendental to its limit, Hegel's speculative Logic is the deepening of this dimension of sense. Being is its own self-comprehension, its own sense, and the Logos is being positing itself as sense. It is, however, being which posits itself as sense, and this means that sense is not alien to being, is not outside of or beyond it. This is why sense also comprehends non-sense, the anti-Logos; it is in itself just as much as it is for itself, but its in-itself is for itself, and its for-itself is in itself. The dimension of sense is not only sense, it is also the absolute genesis of sense in general, and it is self-sufficient. Immanence is complete.

---

8. By passing through reflection, the circle, Being-Sense, Sense-Being, is not the closure *of* senses, but the openness. On the contrary, it is the indefinite separation of being and sense that would be the *limit*.

LOGIC AND
EXISTENCE

We can extend Hegel's philosophy in two different directions. One direction leads to the deification of Humanity; the other, the one that we have followed in this work, leads to the Absolute's self-knowledge across man. In each of these cases, the term Existence, applied to human reality, has a different sense. Perhaps it would not be useless to outline briefly these senses.

Hegel, it is said, *engendered (genuit) Feuerbach, who engendered (genuit) Marx,* and this historical relationship is significant. Hegel is the author of the *Phenomenology* just as much as he is the author of the *Science of Logic,* the author of the *Philosophy of History* just as much as he is the author of the conclusion of the *Encyclopaedia.* Consequently, the absolute Idea, which actualizes itself in history, this sense of human

177

history, can appear not as the revelation of an absolute spirit, but as the realization of Humanity. Christian religion is revealed or manifest religion. What is revealed in it "is that the divine nature is the same as human nature" (PH §759). Religion, however, is still *representation*; it presents this identity as not being our work, but the work of a mediator. Reconciliation, the transfiguration of the world, is not actual in religion. The religious spirit is still alienated from itself. Only philosophy, as concept, sublates all transcendence. Self-consciousness surmounts all alienation; and, without retreating into a vain subjectivity, it thinks itself in all content, in all objectivity. Nature and history are the presentation of the Absolute in space and time, but this Absolute thinks itself as the *Logos*; it knows itself. This *Logos* is not a divine understanding which would exist somewhere else in another world. It is the light of Being in human reality.

The religious spirit therefore is still affected with a diremption. Its self-consciousness is not reconciled with its consciousness.

> Its reconciliation, therefore, is in its heart, but its consciousness is still divided against itself and its actual world is disrupted. What enters its consciousness as the in-itself, or the side of pure mediation, is a reconciliation that lies in the beyond: but what enters it as present, as the side of immediacy and Dasein, is the world which has still to await its transfiguration. The world is indeed in itself reconciled with essence, and regarding essence it is known, of course, that it recognizes the object as no longer alienated from it but as identical with it in its love. But for self-consciousness, this immediate presence still has not the shape of spirit. (PH §787)

Religion presents what is already there as a "beyond." It does not conceive itself; it experiences the identity but does not think it. However, the *Phenomenology of Spirit* constantly criticizes the illusion of another world, and this critique takes the form of the critique of *alienation*. This concept appears as the key concept of the *Phenomenology of Spirit*. Alienation is indeed the concept to which Feuerbach and Marx will fasten themselves. Not only will they extend the Hegelian critique, in the form of a critique of religion, but also they will try to show that speculative philosophy, Hegel's absolute knowledge, is itself also a form of alienation, a substitute for religion. Man believes in another world in order to escape from the hostility of the one in which he lives; he projects into the "beyond" his own essence because his essence is not realized in this world. History is, however, the realization of the universal "divine man." It is Hegel himself who has turned history into a genesis of man. Why speak then of absolute spirit? "Absolute spirit," Feuerbach says, "is man." Marx pushes the critique of religion and of absolute knowledge found in Feuerbach farther. In his *1844 Manuscripts*, which are written in the margins of the *Phenomenology of Spirit* and the works of economists, he proposes to replace the term "self-consciousness" with the term "man," and thereby to demystify Hegelianism.

This replacement, however, transforms all of Hegel's philosophy. What the *Phenomenology* unveils to us across "conceived history" is the existence of an universal self-consciousness which is "the ether of the life of spirit." This self-consciousness is not human self-consciousness, but Being's self-consciousness across human reality. Absolute knowledge is not an anthropology (one need only read Hegel's *Logic* in order to realize this); it is the knowledge which has sublated the opposition of self and being, but this absolute knowledge is what appears in history. Consequently, why not turn this revelation into a genuine end of history? Why not make this end of history coincide with the realization of the human essence? In order to bring about this coincidence, one need only unveil the deception which consists in explaining nature by the Logos and not the Logos by nature. More penetrating than that of Feuerbach, the whole Marxist critique amounts to showing, by interpreting every objectification as an alienation and every alienation as an objectification, the confusion which victimizes Hegel.

In order to show this, one has to place the Hegelian system back on its feet. This system defines the Absolute as mediation, as the mutual relation of the Logos and nature, but nature is first and the Logos only an abstraction. Marx moreover does not wonder how this abstraction is possible and how nature can reveal itself as sense, abstract itself from itself, and think itself. He takes up Feuerbach's argumentation which opposes the sensible world to the abstraction of being. What the Logic reveals in fact is that what is at issue is only an abstraction, and that it is necessary to emerge from it in order to rediscover finally intuition and carnal nature.

> The abstract idea which becomes direct intuition is absolutely nothing other than the abstract thought which renounces itself and decides to become intuition. This entire transition from the Logic to the Philosophy of nature is nothing other than the transition—so difficult to establish for the abstract thinker and for that very reason described by him in a way just as strange—from abstraction to intuition. The mystical feeling, what pushes the philosophers from abstract thought to intuition, is boredom, the living desire of a content. Man alienated from himself is also the thinker alienated from his being, that is, from natural and human being. (MM 190)

It is necessary therefore to start from the natural and human being, from man produced by nature and objectifying himself in nature through work. By substituting the term "man" for the term "self-consciousness" one discovers a valuable description of the human condition in the *Phenomenology*. One discovers there this fundamental idea: "to consider the proper production of man as a process . . . to conceive therefore the essence of work, and to see in objective man, in true man because real, the result of his own work" (MM 177). Man reproduces and produces himself by increasing himself. He engenders his own history, and Hegel has laid the foundations of this philosophy of history, which is a philosophy of man grappling with nature and with his own species being. Universal self-consciousness is the realization, through the intermediary of the struggle for recognition, of human species being, what we used to call the essence of man. It is clear that Marx replaces the Hegelian absolute Idea with this species being, this essence of man. History is therefore the realization of Humanity. The Hegelian universal is immanent to each human individual, as ideal totality, "as the subjective existence of society thought and felt for itself." The individual dies because he is inadequate to this universal. "Death appears as a hard victory of the species over the individual and seems to contradict the unity of the species, but the determined individual is only a determined species being, and as such he is mortal" (MM 138). This humanity emerges from nature and transforms it in order to give it a human face:

> Just as society itself produces man as man, society is produced by him. As for their content, activity and spirit, according to their mode of existence, are equally social, social activity and social spirit. The human being of nature exists only for the social man, for it is only there that nature exists for him as a connection with man, as existence for others and as existence of others for him. It is only there that his natural existence became for him his human existence and that nature became for him human. Society is therefore the achieved consubstantiality of man with nature, the true resurrection of nature, the realization of the naturalism of man and of the humanism of nature. (MM 137)

The Hegelian idea therefore becomes the idea of concrete and social man, and history is this monumental genesis of man; from Hegel, Marx retains this genetic conception of history, not according to the model of a natural history which would not be our history, but according to the model of a comprehensive creation of the self by the self. This production is not a fact of nature like others; it is—despite certain of Marx's overly objective expressions—the Absolute which is subject, the divine universal man, the God who makes himself instead of the God contemplated in heaven:

> Man appropriates his universal being in a universal manner, that is, as total man. Each of his human relations to the world—seeing, hearing, smelling, tasting, thinking, observing, experiencing, wanting, acting, loving—in short, all the organs of his individual being, like those organs which are directly social in their form, are in their objective orientation or in their orientation to the object, the appropriation of that object, the appropriation of human reality. The way in which the organs behave in relation to the object is the manifestation of human reality. This manifestation is as varied as the determinations and human activities, human activity and human suffering, for suffering taken in the human sense is a proper joy of man. (MM 139)

Hegel, however, has confused *objectification* and *alienation*. In objectification, he has seen an alienation of the Logos. Nature is in this way the Other of the Logos; Hegel has transposed a particular process of history into speculative philosophy and just by that he is condemned, condemned to misunderstand nature and falsify history. He has misunderstood nature because, instead of starting from it, he has seen there a relative, non-originary term. Hegel has falsified history, because to overcome alienation became for him identical to overcoming objectification. And, since he could not make the sublation of nature the issue without mystification, the sublation of alienation is reduced for him to speculative philosophy, to self-consciousness rediscovering itself in its alienation. In fact, the alienation specific to history is not thereby sublated. The worker continues to see the products of his work, and even his own work as being alien to himself. The capitalist continues to be prey to a mechanism which he believes himself to direct. Alienation is not objectification. Objectification is natural. It is not a way for consciousness to make itself alien to itself, but a way to express itself naturally:

> An objective being acts objectively and he would not act objectively if the objective were not to be found in the determination of its being. He creates and posits objects only because he is posited by objects, because, from the beginning, he is nature. In the act of positing, he does not therefore emerge from his pure activity in order to create the object, but his objective product presents simply his objective activity,

his activity as the activity of a natural objective being. We see here that consistent naturalism or humanism differs from idealism as well as from materialism, and is at the same time the truth which unites them both. We see at the same time that naturalism alone is capable of understanding universal history. (MM 180–81)

This history, however, indeed became an alienation insofar as it has engendered—as a necessary moment—capital, the development of value out of value. Thereby, the objectification of man became—moreover for his greatest future good—an alienation. "Alienation appears as well in this sense, that my means of subsistence is that of another, that the object of my desire is the inaccessible good of another, that everything is itself something belonging to another, and finally that (and this holds equally for the capitalist) overall an inhuman power dominates" (MM 115). The alienation of man in history is capitalism, and not the objectification of man which is the extension of his nature. This is why the history that comprehends the genesis of this alienation, on the basis of social work and the mutual relation of men, discovers also the means of their liberation, communism, which "as fully developed naturalism, equals humanism, and as fully developed humanism equals naturalism; it is the true solution of the antagonism between man and man, the true solution of the strife between origin and being, between objectification and subjectification, between freedom and necessity, between the individual and the species. Communism is the riddle of history solved and it knows itself to be this solution" (MM 135).

Marx praises Feuerbach: "(1) For having provided the proof that philosophy is nothing else but religion rendered into thought and expounded by thought, hence equally to be condemned as another form and manner of existence of the alienation of the being of man; (2) For having established true materialism and real science since Feuerbach also makes the social relationship of 'man to man' the basic principle of the theory; (3) For having opposed to the negation of the negation, which claims to be the absolute positive, the self-supporting positive, positively based on itself" (MM 172). Undoubtedly the whole debate is concentrated on this last point. For the negation of the negation, it is necessary to substitute the first positivity of nature; it is necessary to understand man objectifying himself on the basis of this positivity. Let us not discuss this principle which is self-supporting, because the position of nature is really more than nature; all of us would be harmonized by means of this self-foundation. There is however a negation in history, an alienation; but it holds only for history and it is up to history to resolve this problem that it poses. Marx adds this historical dimension to

Feuerbach. He rediscovers then, more or less, Hegelian dialectic in the concrete conflicts of history, but he refuses to reduce the positive to the negation of the negation. The distinction is important. The Absolute, for Hegel, will never be an immobile synthesis. His position will always contain negation, the tension of opposition; but Marx, like empiricism, starts from the positive, from the immediacy which is not in itself a negation, from nature. Human objectification is not for him an alienation, because the determined object is not a negation; it is first. History then has created the conflicts and will put an end to them. We could already wonder about the source of this negation in history; why we do not remain just in nature? Undoubtedly, the response would be to speak of human nature, which did not stay put within pure nature, but which overcame itself, which created itself and continues to create itself. When we read *Capital*, we have the impression of a will to power which has built up a world, which increases value from value itself. Without, however, insisting on this ambiguous term of the will to power (there is in Hegel a struggle for pure prestige as the condition of history), one has to speak of a negativity in human self-consciousness, an existence which does not let itself be engulfed in objectivity, an existence which therefore is discovered alienated in every determination, in every manner of being in the world. We rediscover on this new level the problem of the origin of negation which we have already encountered in considering empirical reflection and critical reflection.

One is quickly tempted to grant to Marx that nature is first there in its positivity, that one has to begin with it, that the Logos is only an abstraction (but what does this abstraction mean?), that man objectifies himself by means of nature and that alienation is a secondary process, essential in order to explain our history up to the present, but, in the final account, destined to disappear. Human nature will then present itself after the resolution of historical conflicts. Positivity is first, positivity will be last, and this positivity must have no fissures in it, nothing negative. Despite being a philosophy of history, Hegelianism preserves in its immanence the negation at the heart of every position; in actual history, there is a real negation, but the Logos comprehends this negation since negation is ontological. The Logos is the thought of itself and of all actuality.

For Marx however, what is the source of this real negativity, this prodigious historical growth, an edification whose *utility* in the strict sense could not be explained? What is human existence such that it engenders this history? One has to admit that Hegel went a lot farther than Marx on this point. While remaining in anthropology, he opened perspectives that Marx neglected, and these perspectives bear precisely on the fact that for him every determinate objectification is an alienation. He discovered this dimension of pure subjectivity *which is nothingness*.

The ground of self-consciousness is what, in nature, presents itself as dis-appearance and death. Negation is indeed in nature, in particular in life, but it is there as the concept for the spirit who discovers it; animals die but know nothing of it; negation is external because it is internal. Therefore, by comprehending death, man attains this supreme freedom or rather suspects it in himself, because it always sustains his determina-tions: "Man is the being who is not what he is and is what he is not," an always future hollow. Death is the revelation of absolute negativity, because man, as pure self-consciousness, exists this nothingness (*existe ce néant*). By apprehending death, man becomes the supreme abstraction which was nature's interiority, its nothingness, its detachment from every Dasein, from every determination:

> For this consciousness has precisely felt this anxiety, not of this or that particular thing or just at odd moments, but its whole being has been seized with anxiety; for it has experi-enced the fear of death, the absolute master. In this anxiety, it has been intimately dissolved, has trembled in every fiber of its being, and everything solid and stable has been shaken to its foundations. But this pure universal movement, the abso-lute melting away of everything stable, is the simple, essential nature of self-consciousness, absolute negativity, pure being for itself, which consequently is implicit in this consciousness. (PH §194)

This melting away of everything stable is the negation of the negation, because everything stable is for man a negation, a self-limitation. In Marx, the proletariat is the comprehension of human alienation and this comprehension is its existence. By discovering self-consciousness' alien-ation, Hegel extends this term to every objectification. However, being-for-itself cannot not objectify itself; it is always there in the world and "the individual is what his world is." He is there for others and this for-others is the limit over which his subjectivity cannot go. "Each individ-ual is first for the other in the manner of any object whatsoever." Each refuses to be only his work, to coincide with this appearance for the other which he cannot realize completely. Each is beyond his expression and this "beyond" is only immanent negativity. At the heart of this inevitable objectification, consciousness sublates itself. If objectification were not an alienation, history would stop, being-for-itself as such would disappear. Hegel described the alienation of consciousness in nat-ural life as well as in the Wealth and Dominion which constitute social powers:

> Dominion and Wealth are the supreme ends of its [the self's]
> exertions, it knows that through renunciation and sacrifice it
> forms itself into the universal, attains to the possession of it,
> and in this possession is universally recognized and
> accepted: dominion and wealth are the real and acknowl-
> edged powers. However this recognition and acceptance is
> itself vain; and just by taking possession of dominion and
> wealth, it knows that them to be without a self of their own,
> knows rather that it is the power over them, while they are
> vain things. (PH §526)

In the dialectical beginning of history, there is unlimited desire for recognition, the desire of the desire of the other, a groundless power (groundless because it lacks a first positivity). Hegel has shown the specific
character of the alienation of self-consciousness in Wealth, and the sundered world that results from it:

> Its object is a being-for-self, i.e., its own being-for-self; but,
> because it has an object, it is at the same time *ipso facto* an
> alien reality which has its own being-for-self, which has a
> will of its own; i.e., it sees itself in the power of an alien will
> on which it is dependent for possession of its own self. . . .
> The self sees its self-certainty as such to be completely devoid
> of essence, sees that its pure personality is absolutely not a
> personality. The spirit of its gratitude is, therefore, the feeling
> of the most profound dejection as well as of extreme rebel-
> lion. When the pure "I" beholds itself outside of itself and
> rent asunder and is destroyed, then everything that has conti-
> nuity and universality, everything that is called law, good,
> and right, is at the same time rent asunder and destroyed. All
> similarity dissolves away, for the utmost disparity now occu-
> pies the scene; what is absolutely essential is now absolutely
> unessential, being-for-self is now external to itself: the pure
> ego itself is absolutely disrupted. (PH §516, §517)

Existence appears therefore as freedom, which sub-tends all the
particular shapes of self-consciousness. Self-consciousness always sublates the shapes, never stays at the place at which we would like to attain
it or fix it. Nevertheless, this sublation has a sense; when we replace "the
aspect of free Dasein, presenting itself in the form of contingency, history," with "the aspect of the conceptual organization of these shapes or
the *Phenomenology*" (PH §808), we see them engender one another in a
conceived history which, in temporal dispersion, incarnates this supreme

sublation that is the absolute Idea. In fact, self-consciousness cannot retreat into this complete freedom—the mere form of subjectivity—without dissolving itself. This freedom is the supreme abstraction; when self-consciousness retreats from every determination, it stops acting, stops making itself, it stops being-in-the-world or being-there (être-là, Dasein). Its being is its nothingness; it vanishes, "its light dies away little by little within it and it vanishes like a shapeless vapor that dissolves into thin air" (PH §658). Nothingness is there only as the nothingness of a particular determination of which nothingness is the soul and the sublation. Nothingness presents itself as negativity. Hegelian dialectic is not the dissolution of all the determinations, like skepticism, but their mediation. Being-for-itself must consent to mediation, to the history which thinks itself as common work, the work of all and each. This work thinks itself by making itself; this work is the history of finite, *objective* spirit, and there is a philosophy of history because it is impossible to conceive history, at least retrospectively, without determining it as sense. It is here that Hegelianism presents almost insurmountable difficulties. What is the relation between absolute knowledge, the Logos, and this philosophy of history? For Hegel, is the common work Humanity? We can respond to the second question quite clearly. Humanity as such is not the supreme end for Hegel. When man is reduced to himself, he is lost; this is how he is in Greek comedy and in the *Aufklärung*. He makes use of his freedom in order to retreat into abstract self-certainty, but this certainty is contentless and gives itself an empirical, a finite project. Man is an intersection; he is not a natural Dasein which would have a primordial positivity. To connect abstract self-certainty to this natural Dasein is to be condemned "to know only what is finite, and, moreover, knowing it as truth, and thinking that this knowledge of the finite as true is the highest knowledge attainable" (PH §562). Man then is defined by this last platitude: "Just as everything is useful to man, so man is useful too, and his vocation is to make himself a member of the group, of use for the common good and serviceable to all. The extent to which he looks after his own interests must also be matched by the extent to which he serves others, so far is he taking care of himself: one hand washes the other. But wherever he finds himself, there he is in the right place; he makes use of others and is himself made use of" (PH §560). Here Hegel anticipates Nietzsche. Humanistic reflection is the fall into the "the human, all-too-human." Perhaps even one can say that this reflection, which turns the human project into the Absolute, results at the reverse of what it claims to attain. Hegel indeed speaks of history having a sense, the absolute Idea, but this idea is not man. It is not the rational project of the individual. On the contrary, the individual learns to recognize a certain necessity in the destiny of history:

The individual self must discover himself in all of what he
plans and does: even the pious individual wishes to be saved
and happy. This pole of the antithesis, existing for itself, is—
in contrast with absolute essence, the universal—a particular
which knows and wills particularity. In short, it plays its part
in the region of mere phenomena. This is the sphere of particular purposes in effecting which individuals exert themselves
on behalf of their individuality—give it full play and objective realization. This is the sphere of happiness and its opposite. Happy is he who has made his existence conform to his
character, to his will and to his fancy, and so enjoys himself in
his existence. World history is not the theatre of happiness.
Periods of happiness are blank pages in it. (HI 26)

Existence, however, as mere sublation, as the impossible adven-
ture of man, is also an impasse. It defines man by the freedom of being-
for-itself which is simultaneously always opposed to being-in-itself and
always related to it. Man does not possess the freedom that allows him
to wander from one determination to another or to be dissolved in
abstract nothingness; rather, freedom possesses man. Nothingness is not
then between the for-itself and the in-itself; it is the very nothingness of
being or the being of nothingness. It opens to man, not the mere real negativity that makes history objective, but the dimension of the universal at
the heart of which all sense is determined and engendered. Through this
freedom, which Hegel says is immanent to all history, which Hegel says
is the absolute Idea of history (and of course, equivocity is evident in the
relation of the philosophy of history to the Logos in Hegel, and in this
very term "freedom"), man does not conquer himself as man, but
becomes the house (*la demeure*) of the Universal, of the Logos of Being,
and becomes capable of Truth. In this opening which allows the existents
of Nature, and history itself, to be clarified, to be conceived, Being comprehends itself as this eternal self-engendering; it is Logic in Hegel's
sense, absolute knowledge. Man then *exists* as the natural Dasein in
which being's universal self-consciousness appears. Man is the trace of
this self-consciousness, but an indispensable trace without which self-
consciousness would not be. Logic and Existence are here joined, if
Existence is this human freedom which is the universal, the light of
sense. In this Logos, everything has a sense, and the very sense of sense.
We then have to return to our first question: what is the relation between
absolute knowledge, the Logos, and the philosophy of history? Hegel's
own response is ambiguous, perhaps different in the *Phenomenology* and
in the *Encyclopaedia*. This ambiguity explains the radical differences
among his disciples. One has to note, however, that, like nature, history

is a presentation of the complete alienation of the Logos, a presentation that the Logos also expounds in itself: "The self-knowing spirit knows not only itself but also the negative of itself . . . spirit displays the process of its becoming spirit in the form of free contingent happening, intuiting its pure self as time outside of it, and equally its Being as space" (PH §807). But space is the indifference of determinations. Time is negativity, the pure restlessness of difference. In time, alienation alienates itself: "The negative is the negative of itself" (PH §808). Thus history is the objectivity of spirit's becoming, its temporal incarnation (*its sense, without being yet the sense of sense*).

However, absolute knowledge is the ground of the knowledge that appears in history, and history opens this dimension; history is the place of passage from temporal objective spirit to absolute spirit and to the Logos. History is the appearance of freedom, that is, the appearance of the concept through which man has access to the eternal sense. This sense, however, is not another world behind history. The Logos is there; it comprehends itself and comprehends also this nature and this history. This self-comprehension is not a plan similar to a human plan. Hegelian logic sublates every human and *moral view* of the world. Being is grounded in itself. It is because it is possible; but it is possible because it is. History's real negativity is there, and comprehends itself as the negativity of being in the Logos. The issue is not one of justifying being, because every justification is a justification of sense, and the question of Sense and Being is the Logos itself. History does not produce the Logos, the self-knowledge of the Absolute, as we produce an effect according to a plan conceived in advance. Philosophy is not a conscious end, but man *exists* because he is a philosopher.

This passage from history to absolute knowledge, the passage from the temporal to the eternal, is Hegelianism's most obscure dialectical synthesis; history is self-creating, like the Logos, but this creation is there temporal, here eternal. The Logos is not an essence. It is the element in which being and sense reflect one another, where being appears as sense and sense as being. The Logos is absolute genesis, and time is the image of this mediation, not the reverse. Time is the concept, but the concept in its immediate Dasein because time is the exstasis of difference, which in the Logos presents itself as the internal movement of determinations, temporality as eternal. The Hegelian eternity is not an eternity before time, but the mediating thought which presupposes itself absolutely in time. This is why history's objective spirit becomes absolute spirit; this is a becoming which seems to us difficult to conceive as an epoch of world history: "But the spirit which thinks world history, stripping off at the same time those limitations of the several national spirits and its own temporal restrictions, lays hold of its concrete universality, and rises to apprehend absolute spirit, as the eternally actual truth in which the contemplative reason enjoys freedom, while the necessity of nature and the necessity of history are only ministrant to its revelation and the vessels of its honor" (ES §552). The leading difficulty of Hegelianism is the relation of the *Phenomenology* and the *Logic*. Today we would speak of anthropology and ontology. The one studies the properly human reflection, the other the absolute reflection that passes through man. In the *Phenomenology*, Hegel believed himself able to comprehend human reflection in the light of absolute knowledge (the work's "for us"), and it seems to us that the principle of this comprehension is contained in the meaning of the Hegelian ontology. He, however, believed himself able to exhibit human consciousness's becoming-absolute-knowledge, as if this becoming were a history. History is indeed the place of this passage, but this passage is not itself a *historical fact*. And then there is forgetfulness and memory. Existence, the relation of man to the Logos, indeed puts the Logos back where it was at the beginning:

"Mais rendre la lumière suppose d'ombre une morne moitié."[1]

---

1. This quote comes from Paul Valéry, "La Cimitière Marin," in *Oeuvres de Paul Valéry*, 1:148. English translation by David Paul in *Paul Valery: An Anthology*: "But to reflect the light / Bespeaks another half of mournful shade" (p. 271).—TR.

APPENDIX

GILLES DELEUZE

REVIEW OF JEAN HYPPOLITE, *LOGIQUE ET EXISTENCE*

Genesis and Structure of Hegel's Phenomenology of Spirit preserved all of Hegel and was its commentary. The intention of this new book is very different. Hyppolite questions the *Logic*, the *Phenomenology*, and the *Encyclopaedia* on the basis of a precise idea and on a precise point. *Philosophy must be ontology, it cannot be anything else; but there is no ontology of essence, there is only an ontology of sense.* That, it seems, is the theme of this essential book, whose very style is extremely powerful. That philosophy must be ontology means first of all that it is not anthropology.

Gilles Deleuze's review of *Logique et existence* was originally published in *Revue philosophique de la France et l'étranger* (1954): 144, 457–60. ©1954 by Presses Universitaires de France, Paris.

Anthropology wants to be a discourse *on* man. It assumes, as such, the empirical discourse *of* man, in which the one who speaks and that of which one speaks are separated. Reflection is on one side and being on the other. Knowledge understood in this way is a movement which is not a movement of the thing. It remains outside the object. Knowledge is then a power of abstraction, and reflection is an external and formal reflection. Thus empiricism refers to a formalism, just as formalism refers to an empiricism. Empirical consciousness is a "consciousness which directs itself towards pre-existing being and relegates reflection to its subjectivity" (p. 76 above). Subjectivity will therefore be treated as a fact, and anthropology will be constituted as the science of this fact. That with Kant subjectivity becomes a principle changes nothing essentially. Critical consciousness is a consciousness which "reflects the self of knowledge by relegating being to the thing in itself" (p. 76 above). Kant indeed raises himself up to the synthetic identity of subject and object, but the object is merely an object relative to the subject: this very identity is the synthesis of imagination; it is not posited in being. Kant goes beyond the psychological and the empirical, but remains within the anthropological. As long as the determination is only subjective, we have not left anthropology. Is it necessary to leave it, and how? The two questions are the same: the means of leaving it are also the necessity for leaving it. Kant really did see that thought posits itself as presupposed: it posits itself because it thinks itself and reflects itself; and it posits itself as presupposed because the totality of objects assumes it as what makes knowledge possible. Thus in Kant, thought and the thing are identical, but what is identical to thought is only a relative thing, not the thing as being, in itself. Hegel is thus concerned to raise himself up to the genuine identity of the position and the presupposed, that is, up to the Absolute. In the *Phenomenology*, we are shown that the general difference of being and reflection, of the in-itself and the for-itself, of truth and certainty, is developed in the concrete moments of a dialectic whose very movement is to sublate this difference or to preserve it merely as a necessary appearance. In this sense, the *Phenomenology* starts from human reflection in order to show that human reflection and what follows from it lead to the absolute knowledge that they presuppose. The issue is really, as Hyppolite says, one of "reducing" anthropology, of "eliminating the hypothesis" of a knowledge whose source is alien (p. 158 above). Absolute knowledge, however, *exists* not only at the end as well at the beginning. It was already in all the moments: a shape of consciousness is in another view a moment of the concept. The external difference between reflection and being is in another view the internal difference of Being itself, in other words, Being identical to difference, identical to mediation. "Since consciousness's difference has returned into the self, these moments then present themselves as determinate concepts and as their organic self-grounded movement" (p. 88 above).

Some will say that there is "pride" in taking oneself for God, in ascribing absolute knowledge to oneself. One has to understand, however, what being is in relation to the datum. Being, according to Hyppolite, is not *essence*, but *sense*. To say that this world is sufficient is not only to say that it is sufficient *for us*, but that it is sufficient unto itself, and that it refers to being not as the essence beyond the appearance, not as a second world which would be the intelligible world, but as the sense of this world. Undoubtedly, one finds already in Plato the substitution of sense for essence, when he shows us that the second world itself is the subject of a dialectic which turns it into the sense of this world; it is no longer an other world. Kant, however, is still the one most responsible for the substitution, because the critique replaces formal possibility with transcendental possibility, the being of the possible with the possibility of being, logical identity with the synthetic identity of recognition, the being of logic with the logicity of being—in short, essence with sense. Thus, that there is no second world is, according to Hyppolite, the major proposition of Hegel's Logic, because it is at the same time the reason for transforming metaphysics into logic, and for the transformation of logic into the logic of sense. That there is no "beyond" means that there is no "beyond" of the world (because Being is only sense), and that in the world there is no "beyond" of thought (because being thinks itself in thought). Finally, it means that in thought itself there is nothing beyond language. Hyppolite's book is a reflection on the conditions of an absolute discourse; the chapters on the ineffable and on poetry are essential in this regard. People who engage in idle talk are the same ones who believe in the ineffable. Because Being is sense, true knowledge is not the knowledge of an Other, nor of something else. In a certain way, absolute knowledge is the closest, the simplest, it *is there*. "There is nothing to see behind the curtain" (p. 60 above), or, as Hyppolite says, "the secret is that there is no secret" (p. 90 above).

We see then what the difficulty is, a difficulty that Hyppolite emphasizes forcefully: if ontology is an ontology of sense and not of essence, if there is no second world, how can absolute knowledge still be distinguished from empirical knowledge? Do we not fall back into the simple anthropology that we had criticized? Absolute knowledge must simultaneously comprehend all empirical knowledge and comprehend nothing else, since there is nothing else to comprehend, and yet comprehend its radical difference from empirical knowledge. Hyppolite's idea is the following: despite appearances, essentialism was not what safeguarded us from empiricism and permitted us to overcome it. In the vision of essence, reflection is no less external than in empiricism or in pure critique. Empiricism posited determination as purely subjective; essentialism only goes as far as the ground of this limitation by opposing determinations among themselves and by opposing determinations to the Absolute. One is on the same side as the other. In contrast, the ontology of sense is the total Thought knowing itself only in its determinations, which are the moments of form. In the empirical and in the absolute, it is the same being and the same thought; but the external, empirical difference of thought and being has given way to the difference identical with Being, to the difference internal to the Being which thinks itself. Thereby, absolute knowledge actually distinguishes itself from empirical knowledge, but it distinguishes itself only by also negating the knowledge of indifferent essence. In the Logic, there is no longer, therefore, as in the empirical, what I say on the one side and on the other side the sense of what I say—the pursuit of one by the other which is the dialectic of the *Phenomenology*. On the contrary, my discourse is logical or properly philosophical when I say the sense of what I say, and when in this manner Being says itself. Such a discourse, the specific style of philosophy, can be otherwise only circular. In this regard, one should take note of Hyppolite's discussion of the problem of the beginning in philosophy, a problem which is not only logical, but also pedagogical (see part III, chapter 3).

Hyppolite positions himself therefore against all anthropological or humanistic interpretations of Hegel. Absolute knowledge is not a human reflection, but a reflection of the Absolute in man. The Absolute is not a second world, and yet, absolute knowledge is actually distinguished from empirical knowledge just as philosophy is distinguished from all anthropology. Nevertheless, in this regard, if one has to consider the distinction that Hyppolite makes between the Logic and the Phenomenology decisive, does not the philosophy of history have a more ambiguous relation to the Logic? Hyppolite says: the Absolute as sense is becoming. Undoubtedly, this becoming is not a historical becoming; but what is the relation of the becoming of the Logic to history, the historical here designating everything other than the simple character of a fact? The relation between ontology and empirical man is perfectly determined, but not the relation between ontology and historical man. And if Hyppolite suggests that it is necessary to reintroduce finitude itself into the Absolute, are we not going to risk a return of anthropologism in a new form? Hyppolite's conclusion remains open; it creates the path of an ontology. But we would like to indicate that the source of the difficulty was perhaps already in the Logic itself. Following Hyppolite, we recognize that philosophy, if it has a meaning, can only be an ontology and an ontology of sense. The same being and the same thought are in the empirical and in the absolute. But the difference between thought and being is sublated in the absolute by the positing of the Being identical to difference which, as such, thinks itself and reflects itself in man. This absolute identity of being and difference is called sense. But there is a point in all this where Hyppolite shows himself to be altogether Hegelian: Being can be identical to difference only insofar as difference is carried up to the absolute, that is, up to contradiction. Speculative difference is the Being which contradicts itself. The thing contradicts itself because, in being distinguished from *all* it is not, it finds its being in this difference itself; it reflects itself only by reflecting itself into the other, since the other is *its* other. This is the theme that Hyppolite develops by analyzing the three moments of the Logic, being, essence, and concept. Hegel will reproach Plato as well as Leibniz for not having gone *up to* contradiction, the one remaining with simple alterity, the other with pure difference. This assumes, at the least, not only that the moments of the Phenomenology and the moments of the Logic are not moments in the same sense, but also that there are two ways of self-contradiction, phenomenological and logical. The richness of Hyppolite's book could then let us wonder this: can we not construct an ontology of difference which would not have to go up to contradiction, because contradiction would be less than difference and not more? Is not contradiction itself only the phenomenal and anthropological aspect of difference? Hyppolite says that an ontology of pure difference would return us to a purely external and formal reflection, and would prove in the final analysis to be an ontology of essence. However, the same question could be posed otherwise: is it the same thing to say that Being expresses itself and that it contradicts itself? If it is true that the second and third parts of Hyppolite's book ground a theory of contradiction in Being, where contradiction itself is the absolute of difference, in contrast, in the first part (theory of language) and the allusions throughout the book (to forgetting, to remembering, to lost sense), does not Hyppolite ground a theory of expression where difference is expression itself, and contradiction its merely phenomenal aspect?

INDEX